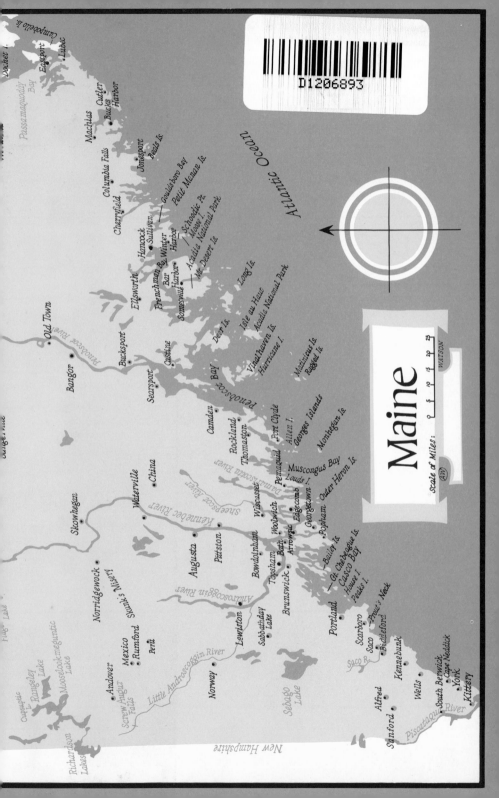

STATE O' MAINE

Books by Louise Dickinson Rich

STATE O' MAINE

THE NATURAL WORLD OF LOUISE DICKINSON RICH

THE PENINSULA

THE COAST OF MAINE

INNOCENCE UNDER THE ELMS

MY NECK OF THE WOODS

WE TOOK TO THE WOODS

REGIONS OF AMERICA

*A series of books that depict our natural regions,
their history, development and character*

Edited by Carl Carmer

STATE O' MAINE
by Louise Dickinson Rich

Already Published

PENNSYLVANIA: *Seed of a Nation*
by Paul A. W. Wallace

THE HEARTLAND: *Ohio, Indiana, Illinois*
by Walter Havighurst

LOVE SONG TO THE PLAINS
by Mari Sandoz

MASSACHUSETTS: *There She Is—Behold Her*
by Henry F. Howe

SOUTH CAROLINA: *Annals of Pride and Protest*
by William Francis Guess

YANKEE KINGDOM: *Vermont and New Hampshire*
by Ralph Nading Hill

VIRGINIA: *A New Look at the Old Dominion*
by Marshall W. Fishwick

A REGIONS OF AMERICA BOOK

HARPER & ROW, PUBLISHERS
NEW YORK, EVANSTON, AND LONDON

STATE O' MAINE

by Louise Dickinson Rich

ILLUSTRATIONS BY ALDREN A. WATSON

CONTENTS

The sons and daughters of Maine, whether by birth or adoption, are sometimes known as Mainiacs. This is a singularly apt term. Their feeling for the knobby fist of granite and pine thrust defiantly into the icy waters of the North Atlantic is irrational, far exceeding the love and loyalty normally entertained for one's native province. To Mainiacs, Maine is not merely a place. It is a spiritual home and shelter as perfectly fitting and comfortable and natural as its shell is to a snail; which, like snails, they carry with them wherever they may go. To them, Maine is a state of mind and a way of life inseparable from the geography and topography of the area and from their own bones and blood and thoughts and dreams. It is an element, as necessary to them as water is to fish. It is almost a religion.

Mainiacs away from Maine are truly displaced persons, only half alive, only half aware of their immediate surroundings. Their inner attention is always preoccupied and pre-empted by the tiny pinpoint on the face of the globe called Down East. They try to live not in such a manner that they will eventually be welcomed into Paradise, but only so that someday they can go home to Maine. Walls of amethyst and gates of pearl hold no appeal for those who have seen the great blue wall of Katahdin rising above the forest or entered the mountain country through the narrow, granite-faced gate of Grafton Notch. A street of pure gold seems a poor thing to those who have followed a thread of dusty road through fields of blowing daisies to the sea. The music of Heavenly harps and cymbals compares ill with the singing of the wind through tamarac trees and the trample of surf on an off-shore reef. Choirs of angels could not lift their hearts as does the faint bugling of a skein of wild geese arrowing northward against a cold Maine sky.

There are so many, many Maines that it would take lifetimes to learn them all by heart, as children say, which is more than knowing them with the mind and memory. There is the land itself: the hills rising ridge upon ridge in slow majesty to the west, and the loon-haunted lakes—Moosehead, the Rangeleys, Sebago, Cupsuptic—strewn like fragments of splintered crystal on the thick green carpet of the forest. There is the vast forest, the Maine woods, where in winter the snow sifts down, day after day, in a windless silence, and in summer the thrushes sing in the level light of late afternoon. Flowers carpet the forest aisles—shy twinflowers, tiny white violets, the ghostly Indian pipes; and the foxes, bears and beaver go about their business undisturbed by human interference. There are the rivers—the Kennebec, the Androscoggin, the Penobscot and the wild Allagash—tumbling from the hills, sweeping across the lowlands, hurrying to keep their appointments with the sea. They are not the longest rivers in the world, nor the oldest, nor the most important, but they may very well be the best loved. They're of a convenient size to be taken to the heart.

The coast of Maine with its granite ledges, twisted spruces, crying sea birds and pounding surfs has something tough and grand and knife-edged about it. Great storms sweep in from the sea—three-day nor'easters, drenching line storms, real old lamb-killers and goose-drownders—to be followed by spectacular clearings. The ocean turns in an instant from dull gray to deep blue, fountains of leaping spray shatter the sudden sunlight into all the colors of the prism, and tremendous rainbows, brilliant and perfect, arch from horizon to horizon. The air becomes so clear that each beach pebble stands out like burnished bronze and the line between sky and sea is a hard, dark ruler edge. Sometimes epic fogs move in from the Bay of Fundy in a mile-high wall to shroud the land for days on end. The world is reduced to a dim circle of low-bowed, moisture-beaded grass tops, dripping blueberry bushes and spectral, perimetrical trees. Everything is distorted. A fish shack looks small and huddled, while a cat looms as large as a bear. The neighbors' voices are muffled, the barking of a dog on a distant island sounds sharp and clear, and the tolling of a bell buoy drifts in from the wrong direction. Visitors find these fogs depressing, but to Down-easters they are restful, beautiful and right.

None of Maine's cities are very large. By heritage and choice State-of-Mainers are basically country people, and they prefer cities small enough to retain much of the village quality. There is Portland, sedate beneath its murmuring tent of trees, where the child Longfellow played under Deering's Oaks and the young commanders of the *Boxer* and the *Enterprise* sleep side by side on a quiet knoll; Bangor, with its famous salmon pool and its statue of Paul Bunyan and the jets roaring over from Dow Air Base; Rumford on an island in the Androscoggin, rolling out miles of paper from its mills; Brunswick, with the widest Main Street in New England and the church where Mrs. Stowe, inattentive to her husband's sermon, beheld a vision of the dying Uncle Tom; the border city of Houlton, trading potatoes in the shadow of a great glacial esker; Augusta, crowned with the golden dome of Bulfinch's gracious State House.

Over half the population lives in villages: Bethel, as peaceful as its name; Searsport, where the mansions of the clipper ship captains dream in old age; Mexico, China, Norway, Sweden, Peru—strange names to find Down East; Greenville, on the edge of the wilderness; Calais, with its twenty-eight-foot tides; Lubec, the most easterly village in the United States, where all the little houses face the sea; Bucks Harbor, near a shingle beach of pure jasper.

Then there's an entire Maine world of tiny hamlets of which nobody has ever heard, where men and women live out their whole lives contentedly and fully. In summer, the men and boys pitch horseshoes in the late-fading northern twilight, and the quiet air rings with the clean sound of metal on metal. During the long, black winter evenings, the women put their bread to rise and catch up with their mending, and the men sit around in the General Store. They talk about the depth of snow and deer yarding in the swamps, and whether it will be a good year for crops, and why the mackerel disappeared. Always there is a cribbage game going on, with dry Maine voices saying, ". . . and six for thutty gives me two for the pair and one for the last." The fire snaps and crackles in the pot-bellied stove, frost flowers form on the window panes, and the money-cat asleep on the counter yawns and stretches.

The people, too, are Maine; the close-mouthed, level-eyed men and women with their horse sense, their bitter humor, their Puritan consciences, and their good old Yankee names—Briggs, King, Spurling, Chase, Gerrish, Cowperthwaite, Gould. They are a strange and contradictory breed, misfit perhaps in the modern world, but completely at home in the simpler world of their own choosing or making. On the coast the men wear hip boots, oilskin frocks and long-billed caps against the sea's glare. When they bare their heads in church, their brows are white as milk above their faces of leather. They curse lustily,

drink on occasion and break the law once in a while. Yet they
come in from the sea with faces glowing and innocent in child-
like delight at having seen a school of porpoises at play, or a
baby seal tagging along after its mother; and nowhere are there
better, gentler and wiser fathers of small children.

In the woods, the lumberjacks wear plaid shirts, wool caps
and felt snow pacs on their feet. They eat four meals a day—
barrels of potatoes, mountains of bread, tons of beef and pork,
acres of pies, bushels of doughnuts, all washed down with quarts
of syrup-sweet tea—but they never get fat. The astronomical
daily count of calories, greater than that of any other group in
the world, is quickly burned up by Herculean labors in the
iron cold of Maine's winters. Their lives in the camps, far from
normal diversions, are dull and monotonous, so they learn to knit,
carve little wooden objects of great delicacy with their huge,
gnarled hands, patiently tame snowbirds, chickadees and Canada
jays, on which they lavish a touchingly tender care. When the
winter is past and the spring log drives over, and their pockets
are lined with accumulated wages, they hit the Front Streets
and Water Streets of the river towns with the impact of an
avalanche. They get drunk, become involved in fights, lose all
their money, laugh at the wrong people and land themselves in
jail. Yet if ever they become civilized, unionized and staid,
something that was essentially Maine will have vanished.

The Maine guides, with their soft, soleless moccasins and their
battered felt hats stuck full of trout flies, occupy an uneasy
position. They are technically in charge of the parties that they
take into the woods, their word when safety is concerned being
as final and indisputable as the word of the captain of a ship.
But they are also chief cooks and bottle washers, baby-sitters
of greenhorns and dancers-in-attendance. This being at beck

and call goes against the native grain. To prove to themselves that they are no man's lackeys, the guides warn their sports against side-hill badgers, imaginary beasts of tremendous ferocity whose legs through a lifetime of walking on the sides of hills are of vastly different lengths, and against giant dragonflies that will sew up the lips of the unwary. They say that the wind streaks on a lake are tracks left by sledges crossing the ice during the previous winters; and that quills can be thrown long distances by porcupines and will, once they hit their mark, inevitably work their way to the heart, with fatal consequence; and any other ridiculous thing that occurs to them. Thus they establish to their own satisfaction the independence of mind and spirit necessary to any Down-easter.

Maine businessmen, bankers and college professors dress more conventionally, conduct themselves more circumspectly and speak with more restraint than these others; but they look at you with the same cool eyes, address you in the same dry tones, and listen to you with the same skeptical air. They generally go about their affairs with controlled competence, but even they sometimes cut off their noses to spite their faces, simply to prove that they've the Yankee right to do so if they please.

The women of Maine know their place, which is one of equality with anybody on the face of the earth. They run their homes and families with a firm hand, taking no nonsense from anyone. They waste little time on beauty culture or fancy clothes, but they set great store by neatness and cleanliness. They are confirmed wearers of aprons, to save their good garments. Often they wear two, the older, faded one to be whipped off, should there come a knock on the door, to reveal a decent, freshly starched model to the caller's critical eye. They keep alive the old handicrafts, hooking and braiding rugs, piecing patchwork quilts in intricate designs, crocheting lace doilies, doing complicated embroidery. This is called fancywork, in contrast to the routine chores of mending, darning, knitting socks and mittens, and tying lobster trap heads and bait bags. Nobody goes visiting of an afternoon without her fancywork. They are genealogical experts, being able to trace on both sides of the blanket relationships of individuals through a snarl of ramifications back to the very first settlers.

Maine women keep their houses conscientiously, scrubbing floors bone-white, chasing dust rolls out from under beds, never leaving dishes in the sink, and considering an unironed sheet a sign of slackness. They are equally competent outside the house, able in the absence of their menfolk to milk the cow, shore up the underpinning of the porch, split the firewood, pump out the boat, get the hay under cover or put a coat of paint on the barn. More than the men, who have been seduced by internal com- bustion engines and electrical gadgets from the old ways, the women have retained the frontier skills and knowledges. They know how to break up a broody hen, how to kill the witch- grass on a grave, what leaves to use for poulticing an injury, in what phase of the moon to plant the corn. Their flower gardens are their passion. Undemonstrative in human relationships, philosophical about death and taxes, they pour out love and care on their plots of brilliant bloom and fight mealy bugs and cut- worms with fanatical zeal. It has always been that way. All over Maine, as memorials to long-forgotten pioneer women, great purple lilacs and tiny yellow Scotch roses still bloom by ancient cellar holes, ground phlox runs wild through the tall grass of overgrown clearings, and short-stemmed golden daffodils toss in the spring against tumbled-down stone walls.

To Mainiacs, the world is divided into Maine and elsewhere.

A native is said to hail from Machias or Dover-Foxcroft or Trap Corners or some other specific place. The nonnative simply comes from Out-of-State. That's all that needs to be known, since anywhere that isn't Maine is much of a muchness and a pretty poor excuse of a pea patch to boot. The rest of the world is in general agreement that those regions toward the top of the map will be referred to as *up*, and those toward the bottom as *down*. Maine Yankees go down east to Nova Scotia, and to reach Massachusetts—plainly down south from Maine—they go up west. This reckoning is a carry-over from the days of sail when ships went down the prevailing westerlies from Boston to the Maine coast, and up the wind again on return. The Out-of-Stater who finds himself using this orientation unconsciously and habitually has taken a first step toward becoming eligible for adoption. He still has a lot to learn, of course, but at least he has made a beginning.

Some of the things he should know are included in this book, but no book can do more than serve as a signpost to the many Maines. Really to know Maine, you must go there yourself, with all your senses alive. You must see for yourself the cloud shadows on sea and mountain and the cold fire of the Northern Lights streaming up from the horizon; must hear the cobblestones rattle on a windward beach and the yowling of bobcats at night. You must feel salt spray and the sting of sleet on your face, breathe air scented with pine and clam flats, taste goose-grass greens and sun-cured strip-fish and parsnip stew.

When you have done all this, there is one more lesson to learn. Never admit your feeling for Maine. Say of her, "Could be worse, I s'pose," or "She'll do to go on with till something better turns up." Only when you can thus mask your love and pride will you qualify as a true State-of-Mainer.

Part One

THE PROVINCE OF MAINE

I. IN THE BEGINNING

Long, long ago, in the aeons before the beginning of history, the topography of Maine was very different from what it is today. A wide plain lay between interior ranges of mountains and a comparatively short, even coastline. Streams that had their sources in the highlands slowed their tumbling, brawling pace long before reaching the sea, and wandered for miles as leisurely rivers. Seen from the ocean, had there been anyone to see them, the mountains were dim shapes on the far horizon, distance softening their fairly rugged contours. In that prehistoric time, Maine was probably a pleasant enough country, although in a rather conventional way.

Then came the Ice Age. The glacier that capped the North Pole expanded, creeping slowly and inexorably southward, scouring the land, plowing furrows in the terrain, honing the edges from crags, until it covered all of Maine and indeed all of New England. The thickness of the ice was inconceivable. Probably at its southernmost thin edge, near Nantucket and Martha's Vineyard, it rose sheer for a thousand feet. The weight of this tremendous burden finally became too much to be borne, and the crust of the earth cracked at a line near Long Island. All the land north of the fault tipped down, and the whole area sank beneath the ocean. There it remained for many centuries, cut off from the light of day, lost and drowned beneath fathoms of cold, green sea water.

Then, thousands of years before the birth of Christ, the ice-cap began a slow retreat. As it shrank to the north, rivers of melted ice water gushed from beneath it to carve new valleys in the land, and millions of tons of silt, gravel, rock and other rubble were released from the frozen grip of the glacier to form ridges called *terminal moraines*. Some of these served as dams for the newly formed streams, and a countryside thickly dotted with lakes and ponds came into being. Some of these dams eventually gave way under the increasing pressure of water building up behind them, but enough held and still hold to make Maine a land in which it's almost impossible ever to be very far from a beautiful fresh-water body, large or small.

The coast underwent an even greater change. When the ice had disappeared far to the north, the resilient crust of the earth responded as best it could to the lifting of the weight that had oppressed it for so long; but the damage was too great for complete recovery. The land never regained its original position. Beach gravels and clay containing marine fossils at the 225-foot level on Isle au Haut and Mount Desert Island show the relatively small extent of the repair. The sun never again shone on much of the submerged land. The old plain was now a wide, sunken shelf to the continent, and the nearer mountains had moved out to sea, fringing the mainland with over two thousand islands, and with dangerous shoals and reefs. The further mountains were now sea-facing, surf-washed capes and promontories, and the old mountain valleys and river courses were winding bays and estuaries. The former upland hollows and ravines had become safe coves and sheltered harbors, and the coast between Kittery and Eastport, which in preglacial days had probably not exceeded 250 miles in length, now measured 2,500 miles, so indented and broken was it. What had been a more or less featureless shoreline was now one of the most irregular and rugged in the world, what geologists label descriptively a *drowned coast*.

The effect of the glacier is of more than academic concern. Geography dictates history; and while man makes history, how and where he makes it depend on mountain ranges and river courses, on ocean currents and coast contours, on climate and weather and soil and natural resources, on all the complicated and interrelated factors that make up the geography of a land. Geography also determines to an extent the types of populations: certainly their occupations and ways of life, and almost certainly their outstanding physical traits, their beliefs and philosophies and superstitions, their strengths and weaknesses, their dispositions; in short, the bent of their minds, bodies and skills.

The drowned coastline with its hundreds of good harbors,

deep-water approaches and long, sheltered reaches made the building and sailing of ships so obvious an occupation as to be almost obligatory. The continental shelf with its banks and shoals was the perfect breeding ground for all manner of cold-water fish, a source of food and profit that could not be easily overlooked. The many streams and rivers of the interior made possible the lumbering operations that were to become so important to Maine, and those same clear streams supported the once thriving ice trade. The great crops of Maine—the blueberries and apples and potatoes—draw sustenance from the rich, ice-deposited silt. Even Maine's latter-day big business of catering to tourists and vacationists rests firmly on the fascination of the incredibly lovely and various land carved out by the glacier.

But all these things were far in the future from the day the ice disappeared. For a long, long time, the land was a barren waste, littered with glacial refuse and malodorous with the stench of the rotting seaweed that had clothed the ledges in the period of submersion. Gradually, however, simple forms of plant life—mosses and lichens, cotton grass, rushes and sedges—took root, and the nakedness of the rocks was covered by a thin blanket of vegetation until it resembled the tundras of the far north. Over the next four thousand years, conditions continued to improve. First came the birch forest, creeping up from the south where the glacier had not penetrated, to be followed by the evergreens—pines, spruces, firs—and then by the slower-growing oak, maple, ash and elm. With the forests came the animals, the wild ox and wolf and wildcat, the red deer and fox and caribou, the bear and the moose; and myriads of sea and land birds. Only man delayed his coming.

It is commonly accepted that the vikings were the first Europeans to visit Maine, and that the English were the first

European settlers. This is open to dispute, based chiefly on definition. Certainly the vikings came first within history, but original man in Maine was prehistoric, and he came from Europe by the long way of the west.

At the time of the final retreat of the glacier, which had covered northern Europe and Asia as well as North America, human life existed in central Europe and in Siberia. Although at that time all men were hunters, two distinct cultures existed. The Siberians, who may be identified with the Eskimos, lived largely from the sea, going out in boats of skin to fish and to kill the seal and walrus.

The Europeans were forest dwellers of France and Spain, Nordic types who knew the use of the bow and arrow, the trap and pitfall. Although they had not yet learned that wild seeds could be gathered and sowed and reaped, or that wild sheep and goats could be domesticated, they did have dogs very much like small huskies which they trained to retrieve game, guard their little villages and serve as pets and companions. They knew about fire, possibly from lightning-kindled forest fires, but more probably from spontaneous combustion in the beds of hay and leaves upon which they slept. This would be a less awesome experience and therefore one more likely to be turned to good and practical use. Here would be no leaping, roaring, terrible holocaust, but only a gradual and comforting warming of the pallet on which one lay, then a timid rising of smoke, and finally a small, useful, easily controlled flame.

It was the descendants of these people who first inhabited Maine. As the glacier withdrew, they followed. Gradually they spread to the north and east over Asia and at last, probably no later than 3000 B.C., arrived at and crossed over the Bering Straits. Their progress through the forest belt of North America to the Atlantic coast and Maine was fairly rapid, taking only eight or nine centuries—which is a short time, archaeologically speaking.

Whether these original settlers should be considered Europeans or not doesn't really make much difference. They came from Europe and they brought with them a culture very little changed by time or distance. An L-shaped skinning knife and the parts of a pottery bowl dug up in Maine are identical with the same objects found in Europe. On the other hand, it may be argued that eight or nine hundred years of life on this continent made them Americans. It's not important. The important thing is that they were there, the first human life in Maine.

Although there are large gaps in our knowledge of these Stone Age men, some things can be deduced from their artifacts, which are occasionally uncovered at Caratunk and other places. They had a sense of beauty, for one thing, that was strangely modern, with the same clean, uncluttered sparseness that we admire today. After all, they were of the same breed who did the marvelous cave paintings of Altamira and Lascaux, who carved the little Venus of Lespugue, a six-inch figure of a woman, fashioned from mammoth ivory, which would look entirely at home in any museum of modern art. No such impressive discoveries have been made in Maine, but less important objects made for everyday use of personal adornment have been found. They are as fine as any of the Stone Age, designed with taste, executed with painstaking care. The flint spear and arrowheads are sharp and delicate, and the skinning knives hollowground to the keenest possible edge.

Another of their weapons was a weighted rawhide, similar to the bola of South America, which was thrown to entangle the legs of deer and other game, and so bring it down for the kill with a knife. The stones used to weight the ends of the ropes are shaped into perfect size and proportion, as would be more or less expected. But rather unexpectedly, they are decorated with little three-petaled flowers of great elegance, which serve no practical purpose but must have been engraved with such care to satisfy some aesthetic or religious demand. Whether for luck or for vanity's sake, these people wore necklaces of bright, crescent-shaped pebbles, pierced near each end so that they could be threaded on a thong. The thongs are long gone to dust, but the new-moon beads remain to testify to a love of beauty.

No trace of the clothing or shelters of these people remains. Probably they wore garments of skin and lived in skin shelters or in lean-tos of brush. They had no agriculture. They lived on game and fish and wild fruit and berries, which they either ate raw or cooked with the fire they had brought with them from the other side of the world. In that long-ago time, the climate of Maine was much warmer and drier than it is now, so they did not suffer from cold as much as might be thought. Probably they spent most of their time in the open, in the shady forest or on the long sun-and-surf-drenched shore. For all its occa-· sional hardships, theirs must have been a rather idyllic life.

This lost race is sometimes called the Red Clay people, from their custom of placing in the graves of their dead clay stained red with iron oxide. This, too, was a practice brought from Europe, where similar red-lined graves have been found. Whether this was an attempt at the preservation of the bodies or a religious ritual is not known. The source of the red clay, however, has been determined by scientists: a pit on the side of Mount Katahdin, at a great distance from some of the graves in which it has been found. Probably the length and difficulty of the journey to dig it and carry it back accounts for the fact that often these Maine graves are not completely lined with the clay, as they are in most other places. Many contain only a few lumps placed about the area where the long-vanished bones once lay. Evidently there was some magic attached to the substance that made its inclusion a necessity to the dead and a duty to the living, but what that magic was, we don't know.

The prehistoric, Eskimo-like men of Siberia were, for some reason or other, about two thousand years behind the forest men of middle Europe in crossing the Bering Straits. When they finally got around to it, they worked their way across North America by a route far north of that taken by the original settlers, along the northern coast of Alaska and Canada to Greenland, Nova Scotia and eventually Maine. Here the two cultures met and borrowed so largely from each other that their identities blurred, and there emerged the so-called Oyster Shell people, the tribe that left as a monument to high living the enormous heaps of oyster shells along the entire coast, but especially on the tidal reaches of the Damariscotta River. Here the piles of shells rise more than twenty-five feet in some places, and one is almost two thousand feet square, containing an estimated fifty million cubic feet of empty oyster shells.

The Oyster Shell men did not live on oysters alone. Unquestionably they ate fish and game and wild fowl and berries and fruit as well; but dogs and foxes carry off the bones of bear and venison, and fishbones and apple cores are fragile refuse. Only oyster shells are inedible, nonuseful and durable enough to have survived down to the present day. Although of no special value in themselves, the shell heaps mark the locations of tribal gatherings, where artifacts and even bones are often found, and provide clues to the lives and natures of the people who feasted there.

Some of the bones suggest that these people were big, standing over six feet tall. There is no way of telling how they died, and as soon as the bones are exposed to air and before any detailed examination of them can be made, they crumble to dust. More interesting than these rather macabre relicts are the things that were broken or lost in the excitement of the oyster bake: crude copper spoons, bits of rough pottery decorated with comb markings, primitive axes and knives, arrow and spear heads, bone needles and combs. Evidently these excursions to the oyster beds consumed days or even weeks, and the people prepared accordingly. They took with them not only the necessary cooking utensils, but toilet articles, sewing kits and probably other emergency items as well.

Looking at the charred remains of an ancient cooking fire, surrounded by oyster shells and buried now under thick turf and tangled vines and bushes, it is possible to imagine the scene as it once was. The fire glowed red on the dark forest behind and the darkly rippling water before. All around it sat the Oyster Shell men and their families, eating their fill, tossing the empty shells onto the heaps behind them, reaching for more. Then, replete, they went about the camp chores—hushing the children, probably, feeding the dogs, mending torn clothes, restringing bows, chipping out new arrowheads, and all the while talking and laughing in holiday mood. The feeling of the affair couldn't have been too different from that of the modern clambake commonly arranged for the summer visitors.

These inhabitants were long gone from Maine by the time the first Europeans from the east—the vikings—arrived. In their place were two distinct types of Indians, the Micmacs and the Abenakis or Wabanakis. The Micmacs were in the minority and lived on the northeastern coast of Maine. Their economy was based almost entirely on fishing, and it is felt that in them were preserved and passed on the dominant characteristics of the old Siberian Eskimo types, somewhat modified and diluted, but evident all the same. Even today their descendants, the Passamaquoddies, who live largely on the Indian reservation at Pleasant Point, near Eastport, differ markedly in skills and appearance from the Abenakis of the Indian Island Reservation at Old Town. They are more squat and square, with flatter features, and they are still superb fishermen and skillful handlers of boats.

Most of Maine, however, was occupied by the Abenakis, who called themselves the Dawn People. Their nation was composed of a great many tribes, although we don't know exactly how many or what they were named. The early settlers were too busy with the practical details of establishing homes, making a living or simply keeping alive to take any very scholarly interest in the natives. The Indians were regarded as a necessary evil, to be used if possible, to be regarded as potential enemies for a while, and to be recognized eventually as actual and very dangerous enemies. This hostility that the English whites managed through stupidity to arouse accounts for the exaggerated estimate of the number of Abenakis living in the territory. If we were to believe the old accounts, the Indian population was enormous, and the war parties that in the end swooped down to wipe out settlements were vast armies.

In all probability, there were never at any time more than three thousand Indians in all of Maine, and the largest war party on record consisted of less than two hundred braves—large enough, admittedly, but not precisely a countless horde. The sparse, thickly forested, stony countryside could not support more than this comparatively small number of people. Much of the interior was totally uninhabited, except for small hunting parties that penetrated briefly and then returned to their villages near the coast or along the shores of rivers and the larger lakes. So each of the many Abenaki tribes must have been very small, hardly more than two or three blood-related and neighboring villages apiece.

The Abenakis had a common basic language and could make themselves understood to each other, although each tribe had a dialect of its own. A conversation between members of two different tribes was much like a conversation today between a native of Mississippi and a Down-easter. Each gets the gist of what the other is trying to say, although some of the fine points may be lost in a welter of elisions, regional pronunciations and unfamiliar local terms. Each tribe had its own well-defined hunting grounds, its own government, its particular social structure and special customs, and its own distinctive style of clothing, weapons, shelters and canoes. Each tribe minded its own business pretty well, although on provocation they sometimes fought each other. In times of general peril, though, they forgot their differences and banded together to fight the common foe. It was rather like the situation that is found in most large families, where brothers and sisters may squabble among themselves but quickly turn a united front against strangers.

Primarily, the Abenakis were farmers. As farmers do everywhere in the world, they hunted and fished and trapped, and they could be tough and resourceful warriors when necessary. But their real concern was their small fields of squash, corn, beans and pumpkins, which they cultivated with clamshell hoes, spades of wood or moose horn, and rakes made by shredding and binding with bark fiber the ends of saplings, so that they resembled the bamboo lawn rakes of today. They fertilized their crops by planting with them herring and shad, which they called menhaden, meaning "They manure." In some parts of Maine even today, these fish are still known as menhaden, although now they are canned in oil and sold as sardines. However, the waste of the process—the heads and rejected fish—is bought by commercial fertilizer factories to be used in their product. So the menhaden still manure.

The Indians had not learned to domesticate animals, so they hunted with bows and arrows and fished with hooks and lines, and with nets. Their surplus in good times they cured against a time of need, when the snow lay deep and the ice was frozen thick, or when the game was unaccountably scarce.

Although they lived in total ignorance of vitamins, mineral salts, protein content and all the other things we worry about so much, the Indian diet was complete and well balanced. During the summer, they picked and dried wild grapes and berries, and when fall came, they collected nuts and edible roots and stored them for the winter, to supplement the meat diet. As a further safeguard against scurvy—instinctively, since they could have known nothing of the cause of the disease—they brewed and drank quantities of spruce tea. In earliest spring, led by that same instinct, they restored possible vitamin deficiency by eating dandelion and goose-grass greens, and the tender, curled fern fronds called fiddleheads. They tapped the maple trees, too, and collected the newly rising sap, from which they made maple syrup and sugar. Although they were without some things that we consider almost necessary—coffee, dairy products, potatoes, for example—their fare was more than adequate. The earliest white settlers adopted many of these Indian practices and profited greatly thereby.

Prehistoric man was fairly free to roam around as his fancy or the movements of the game population dictated. The later Indians in Maine couldn't afford to indulge their wanderlust to any great extent. Their fields weren't much by modern standards, being full of rocks and stumps and having no great depth of tilled soil; but without good axes for felling the huge trees or decent digging tools, the Abenakis had to put a prodigious amount of back-breaking labor into even the little amount of clearing and improving that they accomplished. They were not going to abandon lightly this investment of time and energy. So their villages, in contrast to the makeshift tents and lean-tos of the Red Clay and Oyster Shell peoples, were permanent. The houses were built of timber and roofed with bark or thatch, and for added warmth in winter, the foundations were banked with sod, branches and leaves, a practice still common in rural Maine. A hole in the roof let out most of the smoke from the fire that burned in the middle of the dirt floor, for cooking and heat.

However, they did not stay home all the time. The men, of course, were more often absent than the women and children, on hunting trips or the warpath; but in summer, between the planting and the harvest, when the gardens could more or less look after themselves for a while, whole villages would go on excursions to the seacoast to fish and gather clams, oysters and lobsters. They traveled light, leaving their more cumbersome possessions at home under the care of watchmen, usually two or three ancients who were too decrepit to make the trip. With them they took fire, slow-burning punk placed between two large clamshells, the whole thickly encased in wet clay. For cooking they took, instead of their heavy pottery bowls, their beautifully made baskets, tight enough to hold water. Light and convenient as airplane luggage, these baskets served as carry-alls on the trip. Then, emptied of their contents, they could be filled with water, which was brought to a boil by dropping red-hot stones into it. The Indians were very skillful at the practical mechanics of comfortable camping.

Those interludes on the shore had much the same quality as a two-weeks' vacation from work does today. They were a change, a break in routine, a chance to see and do something different. There was a freedom from care about them, and an urgency, too, for the old Abenakis knew it couldn't last forever. The weeds grew in the gardens, and porcupines and woods mice would soon move into the empty lodges and wreak havoc. So the vacationers extracted from every minute the best and most that it held. They lived in light and airy temporary shelters of poles and brush, or in the open air. They did the least work possible around camp, spending their time swimming, fishing, feasting and playing games on the shining sands or singing shingle.

The Indians are usually pictured as wearing garments of leather. To a large extent they did depend on the hides of moose, deer, bear and caribou for their clothing. These they cured with great skill, so that they were soft and pliable, and they decorated their jackets and moccasins with intricate designs of dyed porcupine quills, colored moose hair and beads. Rawhide was used, too, for the webbing of the long, narrow snowshoes on which the tribes got about the countryside over deep-drifted winter snows. In addition, the Indians wove fabrics of moose hair, bark, milkweed fluff and other natural fibers, from which they fashioned clothes and blankets; and they made rugs and mats of reeds and rushes. They had developed to a remark-able degree what is mistakenly considered the purely Yankee trait of ingenuity in making use of the materials available, no matter how unlikely they might be.

Their extensive use of the lovely white birch, as closely as-

sociated with the lives of the Indians as the palm tree is with
the lives of the Polynesians, is an example of this ability. The
best-known birch product was, of course, the canoe, in which
light wooden frames were covered with large pieces of birch
bark, sewed together with root fibers, the seams sealed with
pitch. Some of these craft were large enough to accommodate
twenty-five or thirty persons, and seaworthy enough to make
possible voyages in rough seas to islands far off shore. The modern
Old Town canoe, considered the best-designed canoe in the
world, is modeled on the old birch bark canoes of the Abenakis.

But there were other uses of the birch. Light, strong tobog-
gans for hauling game or freight over the deep snow were
made of bark stretched over thin lathes. Every longhouse had
boxes, bowls and buckets of tightly sewn birch bark. The tissue-
thin, rose-colored inner layer of bark was painstakingly separated from the rough outer bark and used for paper on which
to record treaties, messages and historic events, in the written
language of symbols that the Abenakis had developed. It is
safe to assume that almost no new fire was kindled without the
aid of birch bark scraps as tinder, and birch was the common
firewood, since it split easily under the crude axes and even when
green, burned readily. Birch poles were used for the frames of
houses and the handles of tools.

The growing birch, so limber and lithe, was frequently used
in the setting of snares. A noose was attached to the top of the
tree, bent down and lightly anchored to the ground along a
game trail. When the triggering device was tripped, the tree
sprang erect, carrying with it the ensnared victim to dangle
high above the earth until the trapper came to dispatch it.

The same strong and graceful suppleness afforded the Indian
children the equivalent of playground apparatus. Just as the

country boys and girls of Maine do today, so did the Indian children of centuries ago swing the birches. They climbed to the feathery tops of the trees, hugging the trunks close in order not to disturb the delicate balance with their weight; and then, holding fast with their hands, launched into space for the quick, exhilarating ride back to earth. The birch set them down gently, and then, released, rushed upward with a leafy swishing.

The Maine Indians, in common with all other American Indians, practiced a democratic form of government. In spite of romantic references to beautiful Indian princesses and the persistent legend of Aaron Burr's affair with the Indian queen Jacataqua, the Indians had no royalty. They were governed by chiefs who were chosen by the people for their abilities and who held office only so long as they functioned effectively. If a chief's son in turn became chief, it was only because he was considered the best man for the office, not because of his lineage. That chiefs' sons did sometimes succeed them is true, but it's not a surprising truth. Some families in our own times and political structure possess outstanding traits of leadership or political savvy and thus make themselves conspicuous in governmental circles. So it was among the Abenakis.

An Abenaki chief was not an absolute monarch. He was assisted in his duties by a tribal council of mature and responsible men. There were at all times two chiefs: a war chief and a peace chief. The reason for this is obvious. A just, wise, level-headed man who could administer village affairs well might not have the fiery qualities or even the physical stamina desirable on the field of battle. We hear more about the war chiefs, because they were the more dramatic figures and the ones in charge during the grimmer and more lurid passages of history. War is better publicized than peace, but the peace chiefs were just as important, at least to the Indians, in their quiet, stay-at-home way.

It was they who kept things on an even keel in the villages during normal times—and peace was normal among the Indians until the white men came to disrupt it.

This, then, was the state of affairs in Maine when the first Europeans within history visited the area. These were the vikings under the leadership of Leif Ericson. We make much more of this fact than the vikings themselves did. There is hardly any reference at all to their American voyages in their sagas and records. Actually, they had known about the land southwest of Greenland for some time before anyone had the inclination to investigate it. In 986 A.D., Bjarni Herjulfson, blown off course on his way from Iceland to spend Christmas with his father in Greenland, had sighted an unknown forested coast which was probably a part of northern New England. He had not bothered to land, as he was late already and in a hurry. When he finally arrived in Greenland and mentioned his discovery, no one was particularly interested. New lands were all in a day's work for the roving, adventurous vikings.

Fourteen years later, in 1000 A.D., Leif Ericson remembered the tale he had heard from Bjarni as a boy and decided to check on the rumor. With thirty-five companions, he sailed to the west and in time raised the barren coast of Newfoundland. This was apparently not Bjarni's land, which had been distinguished by thick woods. So Leif turned to the south and in due course arrived off the shores of Maine. He and his crew explored the New England coast fairly thoroughly as far as Rhode Island, and at some place along the way they landed, built huts and spent the winter. This was probably in Massachusetts. Leif's account remarks on the milder climate and the noticeably longer hours of daylight, in comparison with Greenland. These observations would apply better to Massachusetts than to Maine or Nova Scotia.

This first band of explorers seems to have spent a pleasant and profitable time on North America, and subsequently other viking parties followed their lead. The land was much more fertile and the climate less rigorous than in Greenland or Iceland; so the question arises as to why they did not establish permanent colonies in this new and better land.

One of the reasons was that the vikings were primarily rovers and fighters, and not colonists. Their true home was Scandinavia, and that is where their hearts lay. They had left Norway to colonize Iceland in the first place only because Harald Fairhair had gained control of the country and was ruling it with a firmer hand than was acceptable to some of the more independent and recalcitrant chiefs, who moved out rather than submit to law and order. Then later Eric the Red, father of Leif Ericson, moved on to Greenland, not because he wanted to, but because he was banished from Iceland for killing a man in a drunken brawl. These Icelanders and Greenlanders had no desire to move even further from their homeland, which was still within visiting distance. If they went anywhere, they wanted to go back home.

For a century or two, however, they continued to make voyages to North America for the main purpose of securing lumber for their shipbuilding industry, on which their economy very largely depended. Both Greenland and Iceland were lacking in good stands of timber, and New England was closer than Scandinavia. So the many trips made across the stormy North Atlantic were actually as routine as the sending of a truck to the lumberyard would be today. The vikings did a little incidental hunting and fishing on these excursions, and they explored the country to some small extent, but their chief concern was in cutting and loading and transporting wood.

Eventually even these visits stopped. The native Indian pop-

ulation became more and more resentful of these strangers who
were cutting their trees and scaring their game, and began to
attack landing parties. They outnumbered the small Norse bands,
and their weapons—powerful bows of rock maple or ironwood,
stone-tipped arrows, long spears, heavy clubs and stone-headed
tomahawks—were as good as those of the vikings. The Abenakis,
moreover, had the moral advantage of fighting in defense of their
homes and on familiar ground. Fierce and experienced warriors
though the vikings were, they lost a great many battles that later-
comers, with the great advantage of firearms, would have won
easily.

At just about the time when things on North America were
becoming more and more difficult, famine struck Greenland.
The native Eskimos there, with whom the vikings had been on
very bad terms for four hundred years, seized this opportunity
to raise an army and sweep down on the famine-weakened Norse
settlements, wiping them out. The few survivors fled back to
Iceland and Norway. The distance to New England from these
places was too great to make the lumbering trips practical, so the
voyages to the west stopped altogether. In time the New World
was all but forgotten.

It seems very strange that so vigorous a people could have
frequented the Maine coast for so long a period and left so little
trace of themselves. Once in a while a bronze tool or weapon
of Norse origin is uncovered as evidence that they were indeed
here a thousand and more years ago. Occasionally, too, triangular
holes are found chiseled in ledges close to deep water, in which
the vikings once set pegs for tying up their ships while they
loaded the lumber. Near Pemaquid there is a deep-buried piece
of paved road that is thought to have been built by the vikings,
although that is not certain; and on Monhegan and the Outer
Heron Islands rock faces bear mysterious inscriptions in cunei-

form characters that are believed by some to have been made by the Norse. Others contend that they are simply natural weathering of the rock, or the scoring of the glacier. Since no one has ever been able to decipher them, their true origin is anybody's guess.

As far as the history of Maine is concerned, these early visitors might as well have stayed at home. News of their discoveries never penetrated to the rest of Europe to serve as a guide to future explorers, for the simple reason that the vikings were not on speaking terms with anybody else. No impression was made on the land they had found, nor were the lives and customs of the natives altered a whit. There seems not even to be any Abenaki legend or myth of bearded strangers coming in great, winged canoes out of the rising sun.

After the last dragon-prowed longship spread its square, crimson-striped sail and disappeared over the eastern horizon, it was as if it had never come. The long, green combers rolling in from Spain quickly obliterated footprints and keel marks on beaches, and the next high tide washed away the litter on the rocks. A little less quickly the temporary quarters the vikings had built fell into ruin and decay, and their traces were overgrown with wild morning glory vines, raspberry canes and blueberry bushes. The small gaps in the forest where ship timbers had been cut soon filled with new growth, and the boot-worn patches of earth about the landing places grew up to grass and sea lavender. The vikings had left as little lasting impression on the land that is Maine as do the great banks of fog that move in from the sea, shroud the countryside for a space in blowing veils of grayness, and then vanish under the sun as though they had never been.

2. THE NEWCOMERS

The first voyage of Columbus, in 1492, marked the break-through of the barrier of ignorance and fear which separated the New from the Old World even more effectively than the distance and danger involved. After it was over and he was home a hero, Columbus wrote, "Everyone who heard of this enterprise said it was a mockery. Now even tailors wish to discover."

There was a certain amount of justification for this rather bitter comment. It was perfectly true that, now that the way had been shown and the principal terror of falling off the edge of a flat earth found to be groundless, many were quick to enter the race for a valuable prize. This was the discovery and control of a westward trade route to the Orient. When in 1453 the Ottoman Turks captured Constantinople, they cut off the old overland routes to the Far East and stopped the highly profitable flow of silks, pearls, tea and other luxury items into Europe. More important, the spices of the Orient—nutmeg, ginger, cloves, mace, cinnamon and especially pepper—with which rich and poor alike disguised the taste of the ill-cooked and tainted foods of the time, became unobtainable. Great wealth awaited whoever restored this thriving commerce, and many, many expeditions were launched almost immediately, as Columbus so acidly observed.

As yet, the truth had not dawned on anyone. Among the scientists of the day, the fact that the earth was round had long been accepted, although it was a new idea to the general public; just as nuclear fission was known to be possible in the scientific circles of our day long before it came to the attention of the average citizen. But, oddly enough, the fifteenth-century geographers, working independently, all made the same error in their calculations and arrived at a reckoned circumference of the earth that was about one-fourth too small. The practical navigators of the time had no reason to disbelieve an estimate handed down from supposedly reliable sources, which placed the Spice Islands of the Pacific and the coast of Asia just about where Columbus found land. It looked easy—just a question of getting there first and seizing control.

Then, as now, governments often subsidized projects and ventures when it seemed to be in the public interest to do so. With what amounted to national prosperity at stake, each country rushed to outfit and man ships and to find competent mariners for the various explorations. The services of able seamen and trained navigators were at a premium. These men were professionals—mercenaries, if you like—who sold their talents to the highest bidder, undeterred by notions of patriotism. They had one loyalty, to the country that was currently paying them.

And that is how it happened that an Italian established the first claim to Maine for England. He was John Cabot, a Venetian navigator sent out by Henry VII in 1497 to see what he could see. Following approximately the old viking route across the North Atlantic, he sighted Nova Scotia and coasted down along eastern Maine. The forbidding aspect of the coast, with its guardian reefs and dark wall of forest, convinced him that this was no bargain. Upon returning to England, he made a written report describing his discoveries in some detail. There was nothing here to interest the British Crown, which had its mind on passages to China and a monopoly on the spice trade, so the matter was dropped. Cabot happened to be the European who rediscovered the vikings' Vinland, but that was unimportant, since someone else would inevitably have got around to it fairly soon. What makes his voyage important is the fact that his report in writing gave England a basis for her future claims to the territory.

Cabot's adverse findings discouraged exploration of the Maine coast for a quarter of a century. Then in 1524 Giovanni da Verrazano, another Italian from Genoa but in the employ of France, happened along the Down East coast and spent some time sailing in and out among the islands. He, too, gave the whole thing up as a bad job, but his brief visit established for France a rather tenuous claim that was to cause a great deal of trouble in the next two hundred years. Verrazano was followed the next year by the Spaniard Esteban Gómez, suffering from the Spanish itch for fabulous riches in gold and jewels such as had been found in Mexico and Peru. He soon saw that he had come to the wrong place and sailed away.

Gómez, however, made an indelible impression on Maine, which is more than any of his predecessors, including the vikings, had done. Probably for the simple sake of easy identification and reference among his crew, he gave names to places— names which, all unwitting and thoughtless of their origin, we use today. Landing on a pleasant island, he called it Lovely Country, Campo Bello. Observing the helmet shape of a great, island-dotted bay, he named it Bahia de Casco, Casco Bay, and a bay shaped like a sack was Bahia de Saco. When he came into the astonishing bay where the highest tides of the world run, he called it Bahia Profundo, Deep Bay, the Bay of Fundy.

The next visitor, Simon Ferdinando, a Portuguese navigator in the service of England, didn't arrive until almost fifty years later, in 1597. He, too, was looking for treasure, so his stay was brief. In the hundred years since Columbus, nobody had learned very much. Men's greedy hopes were still fastened on the discovery of spectacular stores of gold and emeralds, and their energies expended in the fruitless search for a northwest passage to the Orient. Their eyes were blinded to the beauty of a continent which they regarded only as an obstacle, and to the enormous though less obvious wealth in natural resources which that continent possessed. They were unable to see the country for what it was and could become, only for what it was not and failed to provide.

Of no help to the correcting of this shortsighted attitude was the myth of Norumbega. How this wildly improbable fantasy started isn't known. A hearsay account of Norumbega

appeared in Rasmusio's *Voyages* as early as 1539, but the tale
had been going the rounds for years before that. It was briefly
this: that somewhere in the wilderness up the broad reaches of
the Penobscot, or some other river of that general description
(everything about the story was very vague and hard to pin
down), there existed a great city, rich and beautiful beyond
even the fabulous cities which the Spanish had looted in Central
America. The walls of its palaces were overlaid with gold leaf
and surmounted by crystal towers. Even common cooking
utensils were of solid gold and silver, ornamented with gems.
Some of the gardens of its temples were planted, not with
ordinary flowers, but with shrubs and bushes of wrought gold
and silver wire, bearing fruit and flowers of jewels. The children
of Norumbega played jackstones and marbles with diamonds
and pearls. All these wonders and more had actually been seen
by someone, although by whom was indefinite. Probably by a
friend of a friend of a friend.

In reality, of course, the Indians of Maine were lucky if they
had a few crude iron or copper pots in which to cook, and a few
colored beach pebbles to string around their necks; and all they
asked of a building was that it be tight enough to keep out the
worst of the wind and weather. So the report about Norumbega
must have been some disappointed explorer's idea of a wry
practical joke. Or perhaps the Indians themselves started the
rumor. They had been known before, in the Southwest, to tell
tall tales of glorious cities further along, in the hope of inducing
their Spanish conquerors to go away and leave them alone.

Whatever the source, the myth of Norumbega came into
being, and was repeated, and grew, and was believed; and a
great many people wasted a great deal of time trying to find the
city. The most casual acquaintance with the land and its natives

ought to have dispelled forever the illusion; but people believe what they want to believe, and it was the temper of the times to want to think that wealth was to be had for the asking—or at most a little arm-twisting—in the New World. If the Incas could fill a room full of gold at Spanish insistence, it wasn't unreasonable to suppose that the Abenakis could do the same. Or so, at least, it seemed to the very early explorers.

The dream died hard, but it finally died. In the end, all that was left of the legend was the name, the first of many names by which Maine was to be known. About a hundred years after Cabot, Queen Elizabeth granted to a navigator friend, Sir Humphrey Gilbert, a charter to explore the New World, in recognition of various services he had rendered the Crown in its perennial troubles with the French and the Irish. Sir Humphrey outfitted a ship and hired John Walker to captain it. Walker came to anchor in Penobscot Bay in 1580. He went ashore, planted the English flag in the long shadows of the Camden hills, and took formal possession of the land in the name of his queen. He called the country Norumbega, and so it was known for years to come.

Captain Walker made a favorable report to his employer, Gilbert. To anyone who knows Penobscot Bay, it's difficult to imagine how it could have been otherwise. Accustomed as he was to the little harbors of England and the sluggish Thames with its crowded shipping, Walker could hardly have helped being impressed with this great and gracious basin of breeze-fretted, diamond-bright blue. To the west the hills rose in slow benediction against the sky, and to the south and east the lovely islands—Deer Isle, Vinalhaven, Isle au Haut—floated like sunning whales. From the north a wide river flowed down between stands of towering pines, and over all arched the brilliant Maine heavens. It must have seemed to Walker like a truly new world, a world fresh from creation.

His account was enough to fire Sir Humphrey and his half-brother, Sir Walter Raleigh, with enthusiasm. They promptly arranged to receive grants under an old establishment of Edward IV called rather elaborately and certainly all-inclusively "The mysterie of merchant adventures for the discoverie of regions, dominions and islands and places unknown, and the fellowship of English merchants for the discoverie of new trades." This amounted to a permit to the charter holders to go where they pleased and do business as opportunity arose, with the backing and protection of the Crown. It was a convenient document.

Operating under the "mysterie and fellowship," Gilbert and Raleigh ships made several voyages of exploration to the coast of Maine. Their *Speedwell* and *Discoverer* visited Monhegan—that wild and lovely outermost island—in 1603, and the captains, Martin Pring and Edmund Jones, were struck with the notion of taking back home a birch bark canoe that some Indians had left there. This was probably just a tourist impulse to collect a souvenir, but no publicity manager could have come up with a brighter idea for promoting his product. The little canoe, frail, tangible, curious and outlandish, accomplished more than pages of glowing words of propaganda could have done, when it was exhibited in England. It made the new land seem suddenly real and not impossibly remote.

Among those to be touched by its mute appeal was another of Elizabeth's favorites. She kept about her a coterie of dashing, handsome, brave and polished young men, for the adornment of her court and probably for her own entertainment; swash-buckling blades like Sir Francis Drake, Sir John Hawkins, Gilbert and Raleigh, and the Somersetshire Englishman with the darkly romantic Latin name, Sir Ferdinando Gorges. There was nothing foppish about any of this crew, in spite of the affected, overmannered life they may have led while at court. They were all tough and ruthless fighters, veterans of many military campaigns, widely traveled in dangerous places and men of intelligence and imagination. Not the least of them was Sir Ferdinando.

Gorges had known of the project in which his cronies were involved for several years, and he had taken in it the mild interest we all accord the activities of our intimate friends. But he had had problems of his own to occupy his more serious attention. He was captured and imprisoned in Lille at the time of the invasion by the Spanish Armada, and then he was wounded at the Siege of Paris. Then, although he had been knighted for conspicuous gallantry on the battlefield of Rouen by the Earl of Essex and was the object of a certain amount of hero worship, he came very near to being beheaded when he got home and became mixed up in politics. Only the fact that he had powerful friends in the right places saved him. This narrow escape may have inclined him toward less stormy and hazardous arenas than those of war and politics.

At any rate, when he saw the canoe and talked with Pring, Jones and another seasoned explorer of the Maine coast, John Smith of Pocahontas fable, his secondhand interest in Norumbega became personal and intense. His seems to have been a very complex nature. He had already proved himself to be a recklessly brave man of action and a smooth and beguiling ladies' man. Now he showed another side of his character, that of the hard-headed and cautious businessman. Sensing his new interest, Gilbert and Raleigh used all their considerable powers of high-pressure salesmanship to enlist his aid in their venture; but close friends as they were, and persuasive, Gorges committed himself to nothing until he had talked further with the down-to-earth trio with the down-to-earth names—Smith, Jones and Pring—who really knew the truth about Maine and its possibilities. He came out of the long conferences an almost fanatic convert. Gilbert and Raleigh were committed by their charter only to exploring and developing trade. The things he learned from the men who had been there convinced Gorges that these were limited objects. He was possessed—almost obsessed—with the new and original idea that Maine could and should be colonized.

By this time Raleigh had fallen from Elizabeth's capricious favor and was dividing his time between banishment in Ireland and imprisonment in England, and Gilbert had been lost with a ship off Newfoundland. Gorges therefore entered into partnership with the Earl of Southampton and the Earl of Arundel. They outfitted the *Archangel,* which arrived off the Maine coast in 1605. Her captain, George Weymouth, had been given instructions to explore the country with special regard to its potential as a site for future colonies. With an eye, possibly, to keeping the bosses happy and his own position assured, he made glowing reports. He said, for example, that some barley and peas he planted as a test of the soil and the growing conditions shot up to a height of eight inches in the sixteen days after they had first been put in the ground.

This seems unlikely, although under an ideal—but rare—combination of circumstances it was not impossible. Along the Maine coast, as anyone who has gardened there knows, the soil lies thinly over and around rocks and ledges which store heat from the sun. Often a slight haze which is not quite a fog prevails, concentrating the sun's rays and providing moisture. Nature thus provides the humid, evenly heated conditions of a hothouse or forcing bed, and while these continue, seeds do sprout and grow amazingly. "Drop 'em in, hoe 'em under, an' jump clear," the natives say even today at times like this. It is possible that Weymouth chanced on one of these halcyon exceptions to the usual cold and drizzly spring weather for his pea-planting, and that his report is not so disingenuous as it appears.

Weymouth was a busy man in his employers' interests. Besides conducting his little agricultural experiment, he made friends with five Indians whom he encountered at Allen Island, near the entrance of Penobscot Bay. He showered them with gifts and attentions and appealed to their vanity through a show of dependence on their local knowledge. Then, when he was ready to return home, he kidnaped them and took them back to England with him. This really reprehensible act of treachery sowed the first seeds of doubt of English goodwill in savage minds, but it also resulted in undeserved benefits.

With his apple-polishing eye still on a roseate future for himself, Weymouth presented Sir Ferdinando with three of the Indians as slaves, a quite handsome gift. Gorges, however, had more insight and imagination than did his agent. He saw in the three Abenakis a priceless opportunity for calling attention to his overseas interests. He treated them as honored guests in his home and arranged a really brilliant publicity coup in having them formally and with great pomp presented at court. They were the first North American Indians ever to be so distinguished. Trained since childhood to dignity and composure through the solemn ceremonies of their tribes, and to a noncommittal deportment when circumstances were puzzling, the Abenakis turned in a performance which even royalty found impressive. They became a vogue and were feted and entertained widely and elaborately in

London's best circles. They were a very valuable advertising property.

Their greatest value, however, was as a source of information about Maine, a fact that Gorges recognized immediately. In order to tap this source, of course, it was necessary to find a means of communication other than signs. With a tremendous patience that seems at odds with his previous fiery and impetuous behavior, Sir Ferdinando set about teaching his charges to speak English. It says much for his tact, charm and obvious goodwill toward these displaced, bewildered, homesick men that they learned the strange tongue in a surprisingly short time, and could speak it accurately and fluently enough to answer questions about their native, lost land fully and in detail. Their trust in Gorges was complete. They were willing and even eager to tell him anything he wanted to know, with no fear of a betrayal such as they had suffered at Weymouth's hands—an experience which must have left them suspicious of overtures. Or perhaps just talking about home brought it nearer to them in their exile.

There must have been in the Indians' manner of describing their native land a graphic poetry, a poignant nostalgia, that communicated itself to Sir Ferdinando. In the end he was in love with the country that he had never seen and haunted by visions of its dim forests and clean coast. What had started as a business matter had changed to something else, to a dream that was to possess him and direct all his actions for the rest of his life.

In 1606 Gorges and his associates hired Captain Henry Challons to sail a group of colonists in their *Richard of Plymouth* to Maine, there to establish a first settlement. With them went two of Sir Ferdinando's Abenakis, to act as emissaries to the tribes in the cementing of friendly relations. Inevitably, when there is a sudden great demand for specialists in any field, the incompetent ride in on the coat tails of the competent, and such a one was Challons. The trip to Norumbega had by now been made so many times by Smith, Jones, Pring and others that there was practically a groove worn in the North Atlantic by their keels. Nevertheless, Challons managed to get off course to an almost incredible degree and arrived at last in the vicinity of Puerto Rico. Here his ship was seized by the Spanish and everyone aboard taken into captivity. The would-be colonists never saw the coast of Maine and, worse still, the invaluable and irreplaceable Abenakis were lost forever to Gorges.

The third Indian, just to round off the record, was later repatriated. He was Tasquantum, called Squanto, who was of so great a help to the Plymouth Pilgrims in 1621. But all that was yet to come.

In spite of the Challons fiasco and the consequent loss of enthusiasm on the part of his associates, Gorges persisted. He found a new partner, Sir John Popham, the Lord Chief Justice of England, and the next year their company, called the Plymouth Company, sent out another group of colonists under the leadership of Popham's son George and Raleigh Gilbert, son of Sir Humphrey Gilbert. This party of about 120 men landed near the mouth of the Kennebec at what is now Popham in the autumn of 1607.

The fall of the year is unbelievably beautiful on the coast of Maine. The air is crystal clear and as heady as wine, and the whole earth shouts with color—crimson, gold, orange, copper and the dark green of the spruces—against the deep blue of the sea. But it is not the ideal time to try to establish a brand-new colony, with no shelter and not even the timbers to build a shelter, and with no ripening crops ready to harvest against the coming winter. In rural and coastal Maine even today, the five

months of the year from June through October are spent largely
in making preparations for the other seven. The Popham colonists had almost no time at all to provide properly for the gales
and blizzards to come. They probably had no conception, accustomed as they were to the relatively mild climate of England, of
how tough a Maine winter can get.

That winter of 1607-8 was unusual, even for Maine. The new
settlers recorded: "On the 18 of Januarie we had in seven houres
space thunder, lightning, raine, frost, snow, all in abundance, the
last continuing." The hastily erected buildings were far from
adequate to keep out the bitter cold, and many of the colonists,
including George Popham, died of pneumonia. The food that
had been left them by their ship ran low, and they were not
experienced enough in wilderness living to trap and hunt very
successfully. They lived in a state of semistarvation, and inevitably scurvy developed among them. Finally, in order to keep
somewhere nearly warm in their miserable and drafty hovels, the
men heaped so much wood on the fire that they burned down
the main building. When the ship returned in the spring with
new supplies, the sick, hungry and discouraged colonists wanted
only to go home and forget the nightmare. They abandoned
their colony without regret and left to Jamestown the distinction
of being the first English settlement in America. The tale they
took with them of the hideous Maine climate deterred further
attempts at colonization for some time.

One thing they did accomplish before illness and the weather
defeated them. They built a boat. This was the "pretty Pynnace"
Virginia, of about thirty tons. The *Virginia*, the first ship to be
built and launched by Europeans in the New World, might be
considered the mother of the American Merchant Marine. She
was a good, sturdy little vessel—rather surprisingly so, consider-

ing the general ineptitude of the Popham settlers in other respects
—and she long outlasted the ill-fated colony. Her first·voyage,
that very winter of 1608, was to England with a cargo of Maine
furs and sassafras root; and then for over twenty years she
shuttled back and forth between England and Virginia, carrying
supplies one way and tobacco the other. Finally she was wrecked
in a storm off the Irish coast. She wasn't very big and she wasn't
very showy, but she set a precedent of seaworthiness and de-
pendability for all the great fleet of Maine-built vessels to come.

Shortly after the Popham fiasco, Sir John Popham died and
the Plymouth Company failed. Interest in settling Maine sank to
a new low because of the adverse report. Sir Ferdinando, however, clung stubbornly to his belief that his Abenakis' picture of
the country was truer than that presented by the understandably
prejudiced ex-settlers. For years he tried to get backing for another attempt, without success. Finally, in 1616, he gambled all
his personal possessions and holdings on one more try. The sum
he was able to raise by mortgaging everything was sufficient for
only a very humble little expedition—one small ship under Captain Richard Vines and a company of only sixteen men. These
were mostly Gorges' personal servants, who had very little
choice but to go where they were sent.

This tiny, forlorn last hope unexpectedly justified Gorges'
faith. Perhaps he was lucky—in his captain, in the weather, in
the site chosen for the colony, in many imponderable factors.
At any rate, the party weathered the mild winter well in the
snug cabins they built on the Saco River near what is now Bidde-
ford Pool and had nothing but good to report back to England.
Vines, who had embarked on the enterprise simply as a paid
navigator hired for a job, was so enraptured with the country
that fourteen years later, when he could afford to retire from the

sea, he returned to spend the rest of his life near what is now Saco.

Apparently it required only this small demonstration to turn the tide of popular opinion. Within the next decade, before 1635, suddenly—or it seemed sudden in view of the long term of defeatist thinking on the subject of colonizing Maine—a rash of thriving little settlements sprang up along the western coast of Maine, which was now named New Somersetshire—at Kittery and Wells and York, at Pemaquid and Saco and Brunswick and Portland, and far out on Monhegan Island. From being considered a crackpot, Gorges leaped to fame, wealth and popularity. He was made Governor General of New England, as the place became known, and given a charter to all the land between the Piscataqua and the Kennebec rivers. This charter specified that the territory should "forever be called the Province and Countie of Maine and not by any other name whatsoever." This was the first official use of the name, the origin of which is not known. Gorges was the lord palatine of the province, which meant that he possessed the absolute power of royalty, and that Maine was actually during this period a feudal estate.

This overlordship, however, Sir Ferdinando exercised in absence. He never did get to see the beautiful land in which he invested the better part of his life. There was always too much depending on his presence in England to allow him to leave. He sent his son Thomas to represent him in the New World, and his nephew William Gorges, but he was never to visit the frontier for whose early development he was directly and almost solely responsible.

Several years later, at the time of the fall of Charles I, Gorges made the political error of espousing the wrong cause. He paid for his mistake. He was stripped of everything he owned and died in prison, an impoverished and broken-hearted old man. His bones lie somewhere in England in a lost grave. Even his name has almost disappeared from the map of the land that was so much his own. What was the village of Gorgeana is now York, and Gorges Island has been corrupted to Georges Island. All that remains is Fort Gorges, a disused, depressing octagonal stone structure on a low-lying, swampy island just outside Portland harbor. Gorges is now known as the Father of Maine, a title well deserved for the endless, tireless, self-sacrificing effort he devoted to his brain child. But he himself never had the cold comfort of knowing this future distinction.

Although Gorges' vessels were the only ones to visit the Maine coast with the definite object of colonization in the first half of the seventeenth century, there were plenty of others on different errands. There was Bartholomew Gosnold in command of the British *Concord* in 1602 on an exploring trip which he turned to good account by taking back to England a full cargo of furs, cedar and sassafras from southern Maine. There was Henry Hudson in 1609, who was off the Maine coast more or less by accident. He was an Englishman employed at the time by the Dutch, to find a route to the Orient across the top of the world. The polar icecap defeated this plan, so Hudson felt free to disregard his sailing orders and use up the rest of his allotted time looking elsewhere for a northwest passage. This decision brought him to the Maine coast, among other places, and he is given credit for cutting and stepping for his *Half Moon* the first of millions of masts of Maine pine. At least, he is the first who recorded such a repair, but it is likely that there were others before him who didn't consider so routine a chore worth entering in their logs. He also gave the Dutch an excuse for later raids along the coast.

Then in 1610 there was Samuel Argalls, driven off course by a storm while on his way from Virginia to England. His stay in Maine was as short as he could make it, but the voyage is of interest because of an entry in his log concerning a current offshore strong enough to bear his ship along rapidly against head winds. This is the first known observation of the Gulf Stream, although some of the earlier explorers certainly ought to have noticed a phenomenon having so direct an effect on navigation.

More important than any of the foregoing were the French. They had not been ignoring the New World by any means. At the time when James the First was granting to Gorges and his associates all of what are now Maine, New Hampshire and Nova Scotia, King Henry of Navarre and France was almost simultaneously issuing a patent to much the same territory to Pierre du Gast, the Sieur of Monts. While Gorges was trying to sell the idea of colonization, du Gast was doing something concrete about it. By persuasion, bribery and coercion, he quickly assembled a band of seventy men from all walks of life. Some were of his own class, noblemen whom he talked into the notion that it would be an exciting and interesting adventure to carry the flag of France overseas. Some were priests, influenced by the possibility of saving heathen souls by the hundreds. Some were soldiers lured by the vision of loot, and some were jailbirds who regarded any future as preferable to rotting in dungeons. In 1604, three years before Gorges got his Popham colony together for their abortive attempt, du Gast had this motley lot on Dochet Island in the St. Croix River, off what is now Calais, Maine.

Against all probability, this collection of incompatibles in background, viewpoint, culture and experience made an excellent team. Du Gast had not made Gorges' mistake of delegating his authority to some less convinced and enthusiastic agent. He was there himself to provide solid leadership and furnish an example of industry and optimism. Working together—some of them at tasks to which they had never before turned a hand—the colonists built a sound, well-planned community of comfortable cabins, workshops and a chapel, all enclosed in a strong stockade. There they lived throughout the winter, the only Europeans on all North America, and there in 1604 they celebrated Christmas as a religious holiday, the first such observance ever to take place in the Western Hemisphere. They found, however, that the island wasn't a very good site, being exposed to storms and often cut off from the mainland by floating ice in the river. So at the end of the winter, they decided not to go home as the Pophamites did in similar circumstance, but to move their settlement to a better location.

Therefore Samuel de Champlain, the navigator of the company, set out to the south and west along the Maine coast, looking for a location that met the requirements. He did not find one, although he devoted almost two years to the search. He explored Frenchman Bay, went up the Penobscot as far as the present Bangor, investigated the Kennebec and the Androscoggin and Casco Bay, and continued all along the coast as far as Hyannis on Cape Cod. Why he didn't recommend any one of a score of lovely harbors for the transplanting of the French colony is a mystery. Camden, Rockland, Portland—they all seem better than what was finally chosen: Port Royal on the Bay of Fundy. But he must have had reasons that seemed good to him. Champlain was nobody's fool.

He was, on the contrary, a remarkable man and very probably the greatest New World explorer. He excelled in a great many areas besides navigation. His carefully kept journals give us our best and almost our only knowledge of the New England and Nova Scotian coasts before the coming of the settlers. Champlain was of a scientific turn of mind; in fact, he was the first to suggest the Panama Canal, an idea so far in advance of the times that it was regarded as sheer lunacy. The same bent caused him to describe everything he saw in painstaking detail. He took a botanist's interest in wild grapes and cranberries and strange flowers, an ichthyologist's interest in the schooling of cod and the running of eels, a zoologist's interest in mink and foxes and moose, and the delight of an artist in the colors and contours of the land and sea. He was a good cartographer. His maps of this coast were the best of the era. Our own still carry names given by Champlain: Petit Manan, because its appearance from the sea reminded him of Grand Manan; Isle au Haut, for its bold, sheer cliffs; Mount Desert Island, l'Isle des Monts Deserts, island of the wild and desolate mountains; and others.

Among the other things he did on this voyage of exploration, Champlain planted crosses at various spots to mark the sites of future missions and monasteries. Like most of his compatriots, he was a devout Catholic, but more than personal religious feeling prompted this act. The French, like the English, were interested in both colonizing and fur trading; but unlike the English, they were almost equally interested in spreading enlightenment. The English made converts to Christianity when it was convenient to do so, but the French included as a part of their colonial policy the conversion of the Indians and the spread of Catholicism. Priests were conspicuous in any company sent out to North America, and they were charged equally with the spiritual welfare of the colonists and the saving of heathen souls. These priests were expected to cooperate closely with governmental agencies, and they were undoubtedly a part of a political plan, but they themselves were motivated by a deep and very real concern for the salvation and redemption of the native tribes.

Among them were the Jesuit Fathers, Pierre Biard and Enne-mond Massé. These men had been sent to join the Dochet Island colony by the wealthy and pious Marquise de Guercheville, Queen Marie de Médicis and other devout ladies of the French court, to whom the idea of Frenchmen falling into sin and error in the wilderness was evidently abhorrent. The du Gast com-pany, however, was not particularly receptive. They had their own priests, who had come with them and labored beside them through the early days of the colony. They hinted rather broadly that the Fathers would do better to spend their time and the Marquise's money in stamping out heresy among the Abenakis. So in 1613 Biard and Massé set sail in the *Jonas* to the southwest, with the intention of building a mission at one of Champlain's cross-marked spots.

Soon they found themselves lost in one of the dense and baffling fogs that frequently move in on the Down East coast. These are caused by the confluence of the warm Gulf Stream and the icy Labrador Current a short distance off shore and make this the foggiest area in the world, not excepting the Aleutians. The *Jonas* waited this one out, which is about the only thing a vessel can safely do; and when it lifted, the startled company found themselves close under the lofty peaks of Mount Desert Island. The good Fathers interpreted this as a sign from God that they should establish their proposed mission here. They went ashore, planted a cross, calling the place Saint Sauveur, and celebrated Mass. Then they built the first mission and monastery in the New World east of California and settled down to the life proper to men of their calling, a life of hard work, prayer and preaching to the Indians.

Their peaceful and industrious routine did not last long. Just as their little gardens were growing well and the Indians had accepted them as friends, Samuel Argalls, who had previously discovered the Gulf Stream and was now Admiral of Virginia, came along the Maine coast on an exploring and fishing trip. His standing orders from England were to discourage French colonization wherever he might chance upon it, and the unexpected sight of this orderly and thriving little mission where none had been before reminded him of his patriotic duty.

No man for half-measures, Argalls hastened ashore, burned the mission to the ground and took into captivity any French or converted Indians who survived the unequal battle. Those who appeared likely merchandise for the slave market he loaded aboard his ship, and the others he set adrift on the open sea in small boats. These finally managed to make their way back to Nova Scotia, where their tale did nothing to endear the English to the French. Thus ended the first conflict between the two nations in the New World.

By this time it was apparent to everyone that the new land held none of the more glamorous and obvious forms of treasure, and its true wealth was beginning to be recognized. Foremost for a time were the fisheries. The demand for fish in the Catholic countries of Europe was very great, and fishing was a highly profitable business. In fact, these fisheries became known as the New England Silver Mines, and it was an appropriate name. They brought to ships' owners as much or more wealth than actual mines might have done, and the cod, mackerel, pollock, haddock and herring really looked like molten silver as they poured in shining streams from net to skiff or flowed in moonglinting rivers into the sack-shaped weirs.

Going to New England to fish was nothing new. As far back as the middle 1500's, Spanish, Basque and Portuguese fishing smacks made annual trips to the Maine waters, setting up camps and drying stages on Monhegan and Matinicus and at Pemaquid and other places. Before the coming of either Gorges or du Gast, the scene was lively with the white sails of the French and English fishermen as well. All along the coast were the busy bases where the catches were dried and salted for transport home and where the crews lived during their stay in preference to the cramped, dark, malodorous quarters aboard ship. Here the men stretched their legs on the turf-covered ledges, washed their salt-stiff clothing in fresh-running brooks, snared rabbits in the thickets and picked berries to vary their monotonous fare. During stormy weather, when the little ships had to run for shelter, it was not unusual to find as many as forty moored in some deep, safe cove, with the crews snug ashore.

The original practice of owners was to send their vessels on three trips a year to the New England Silver Mines, but it was found possible and more profitable to keep boats on the Down East coast all the year round. It seems very likely that long before du Gast and Vines many of these ordinary, overworked, ill-paid seamen recognized that it was possible to live well and comfortably in this new land. They had done it. As a part of the season's work, they had sat out fogs, kept warm during winter gales and managed to dry tons of fish in spite of howling northeasters. They were not really settlers, because no matter how long they stayed, they knew always in the backs of their minds that they were going home; but they were habituated transients.

They make it a little hard to pin a date on the settlement of the Maine coast. The Vines colony in 1616 is supposed to be the first permanent settlement; and Kittery, settled in 1623, was the first town to be incorporated, in 1647. But history isn't really as clean-cut as that. There isn't that sharp a line between the time when Maine was not inhabited and the time when it was. Year after year the camps around the drying stages were occupied by crews who thought of themselves as being there for a few seasons and of the place as being a temporary convenience, but there was continuity over decades. There's no possible way of determining the moment when the temporary became the permanent. Some of Maine's present fishing villages were once only shore bases of the old fisheries, and there's no way of knowing when the one became the other. Monhegan is a case in point. The date given for the first permanent settlement there is 1620. Yet the island had been frequented continuously by fishermen for more than fifty years before that.

Thus, while it is convenient to set arbitrary dates, it is also a little misleading. Gorges and du Gast deserve great credit for promoting colonization as a definite aim. But perhaps almost equally responsible were all the nameless men who gradually over years, without realizing what was happening, came to look on the difficult, stubborn, bleak scene of their labors as their proper place; who, thinking often of the time when they would return home, finally awoke to the knowledge that they were at home.

That is mere speculation. The fact is that by the middle of the seventeenth century little English towns were springing up everywhere west of the Penobscot, just as little French towns were springing up east of the St. Croix. There was a sameness about these hamlets, wherever they might be. Each had its little store, and chapel—whether Catholic or Protestant—and its sawmill and grist mill and tavern. Along the shore of each were long-legged wharves and beached boats, and behind each were rough clearings, the beginnings of farms. The people of both nationalities lived similar lives, depending equally on the land and the sea for sustenance, fishing and hunting and trapping and tilling the soil as best they could. With all their traditional differences, they had much in common.

Many of the first Maine settlers came directly from England with their families. But many moved east from Massachusetts, which was by now fairly well colonized. The reasons why they left what was a comparatively advanced and safe area, throwing away the hard work they had put into their holdings, were various. Some were in trouble with the local Massachusetts authorities and found it prudent to move. Some were simply restless—true pioneer types who liked having space around them and liberty to do as they pleased on their own property. When people started crowding in on them, when they could see smoke from a neighbor's chimney and hear the barking of a neighbor's dog, they up and moved to Maine.

A great many came for the reason they had left England in the first place—to avoid churchly discipline. The same leaders who had high-mindedly brought their flocks across the sea to escape religious persecution by the Crown had somewhere lost sight of the ideal of freedom for each man to worship as he chose. They became extremely zealous in enforcing strict adherence to the observances of their own new protest-religion, and the less strongly convinced saw no percentage in having exchanged one form of restriction for another just as rigid and severe. They, too, pulled up stakes and headed Down East.

An explanation for the Maine character of today—self-sufficient, sometimes touchy and opinionated, and always independent—can be traced in some measure to this nucleus of first settlers. The odd-ones-out, the lone wolves, the tough and dogged noncomformists and eccentrics were selected by circumstance for the original peopling of the land, which nurtured rather than corrected, through its very nature, a heritage of inborn orneriness.

Fur brought other settlers. Some of Maine's present-day towns grew out of fur trading posts, just as others began as fishing bases. Fur was as valuable as fish and, like fishing, was older than any settlement. In 1615, Sir Richard Hawkins, son of the famous freebooting Sir John, picked up a cargo of pelts on one of his trips along the coast and disposed of it in Europe at a handsome profit. This gave impetus to the trade, but he was not the first. Before him were Gosnold and many others, as far back as the sailors on the trading ship *Virginia*, and even further. Fur was as standard an article of early commerce as was fish, but the manner of conducting the business was less systematized. Ships touching on the Maine coast simply bargained for any skins that the local Indians felt like bringing down to the landings and exchanging for knives, beads, bright kerchiefs or whatever other cheap trade goods caught their unsophisticated fancy. It was all rather offhand and haphazard.

But in 1628, fur trading underwent reorganization in the hands of the Plymouth Pilgrims. The Pilgrims had rented the *Mayflower* for their famous voyage on a go-now-pay-later basis, and the payments were now coming due. Although their colony was self-supporting, they had no spare cash and no way of raising any such sums as they needed. The way out of their dilemma was to go into the fur trade, and the best place to carry out this enterprise was Maine, which was at the time part of Massachusetts anyhow and which had much better trapping than that around Plymouth. They chose three locations for their trading posts. One, at Machias, did not last long. It was too near the French domain for comfort—French comfort—and was soon captured and dismantled.

Of the other two, one was at Pentagoet on Penobscot Bay, later to become Castine. This one continued for seven years, or until the French put it, too, out of business. The third fared much better, adding to Plymouth prosperity long after the *Mayflower* debt had been paid in full. This one was located about forty miles up the Kennebec at a place called Cushnoc, which later became Augusta and the state capital. Cushnoc means "the tide runs no further up the river," and because of some significance attached by the Indians to the fact of its being the tide head, Cushnoc had been from time immemorial a rallying place of the Abenaki tribes for political and religious pow-wows. It was an ideal spot for a trading post. It was out of French sight and hearing, the small ships of the period could ascend the river that far with no difficulty, and the Indians were already in the habit of forgathering there.

This post lasted for almost forty years, during which there was no trouble with either the French or the Indians. It had, however, the doubtful distinction of being the scene of the first recorded murder in Maine's annals of crime. Soon after the post was established, a free-lance trapper named Hocking moved into the vicinity and started running his own trap lines for his own benefit. For all their piety, the Pilgrims were ever alert to their own worldly interests, and it seemed to them that Hocking was threatening their security. The Cushnoc factor, John Howland, told Hocking to move on; and Hocking told Howland that the woods were free and he had as much right there as anyone else.

This classic Maine reaction to any attempt at pushing around did not work. In the fracas that followed, Hocking's head was blown off. No one seems to have considered this more than a meting out of just deserts, and no charges were brought against Howland or his agents.

This was not the end of the matter, however. At the time of the shooting, there was a trade ship anchored in the river near the post. She was captained by John Alden of Plymouth, later to become the shy hero of Longfellow's *Courtship of Miles Standish*. When Alden returned to Boston with his cargo of furs, he mentioned the killing of Hocking merely as an item of Kennebec Valley gossip. Although he was in no way involved aside from having been in the general vicinity when the affair took place, he was promptly jailed as a material witness and possible suspect.

Plymouth had always been jealous of Boston, and the leaders of the colony viewed this treatment of one of their own as a serious affront. They sent Miles Standish—an ironic choice—to Boston to effect Alden's release. Standish brought the full force of his dynamic personality to bear, and Alden was freed. But Governor Dudley was so infuriated by Standish's violent and intemperate language that he ordered Standish himself bound over to appear in court to answer to the charges leveled against Alden. This was ridiculous, since Standish knew even less than Alden about the facts of the case.

From there on, the main issue of fixing responsibility for Hocking's death was lost in a welter of charges and counter-charges and an airing of old grievances between Boston and Plymouth. Eventually the whole thing was dropped. Alden married Standish's lady love, Hocking's killer went unpunished, and the Pilgrims made the point that Cushnoc was their monopoly, as far as fur went.

But other things besides mink and beaver pelts were involved. It was fairly easy for the Canadian Indians to bring their furs down the great concourse of the Kennebec to trade, and this they made a practice of doing. The French knew it, but they didn't care much. They had already put into effect a system conceived by Champlain. This was the sending of French youths to live among the Indians as their foster brothers, to learn their language and customs. These young men were called *coureurs de bois*, and they were a class unique and without equal in the exploration and settlement of America. They did not try to civilize the natives, but only to understand them and win their liking and confidence. Wild, brave, restless, far more at home in the wilderness than in villages, they were almost Indian themselves. Singly and in pairs, they ranged as far west as the Great Lakes; and they were instrumental in securing all the furs the French could wish. There was no need of worrying about the few that trickled down the Kennebec to Cushnoc.

But when the Jesuit missionaries of Canada received reports from Indians who had been to Cushnoc that their friends along the Kennebec and on the Maine coast were being converted to Protestantism by the traders, that was something else again. Such a situation could not be disregarded by the dedicated Catholic Fathers. In 1649, Father Gabriel Druillettes set out to remedy it. With Indian guides, he left Quebec, ascended the Chaudière River, crossed the height of land and came out on the banks of the Kennebec, which he followed as far as Norridgewock. Here he established a mission. He was the first white man to trace the upper reaches of the river and the first ever to set eyes on Katahdin. Years later, the trail that he blazed was used by Benedict Arnold when he led his forces against Quebec, and today State Highway 201, used by countless motorists and tourists, roughly follows the same route through gorgeous wilderness country.

Father Druillettes was typical of the Jesuit missionaries, selfless, devout, capable and hard-working. Moreover, he was sufficiently tactful and urbane to win the friendship of the English Protestants of the region. This was no mean feat. Catholicism was viewed with horror west of the Penobscot. But such was the quality of the man that when he had occasion to go to Massachusetts on business, Father Druillettes was entertained in the home of John Winslow, a Cushnoc factor from Plymouth.

The Indians idolized him and one of his successors at Norridgewock, Father Sebastien Râle. Father Râle was in some respects an even better missionary than Father Druillettes. He was deeply and personally concerned with the standard of living as well as with the spiritual welfare of his Indians. He lived among them as one of themselves, sharing their problems and trying to improve their lot. He won their love and respect by intervening whenever he thought that they were being abused or cheated by white men, be they English or French. He worked constantly on a book about Indian culture, folkways and law, the only contemporary attempt at any record of their civilization. He spoke the language well and compiled a dictionary of Abenaki words. He trained a choir of forty Indians to sing church music; and their descendants still use today some of the prayers he composed in their native tongue. When later he was killed by the English, the grief and wrath of his Indians knew no limit, and they fought savagely to avenge him.

But for a time, despite isolated incidents, the French and the English managed to get along without too much friction in the New World. This was due partly to the fact that between their two territories lay a buffer belt of wilderness known as Acadia-in-Maine, consisting of everything between the Penobscot and the St. Croix from the coast indefinitely west. Although this was technically claimed by both countries, neither one had made any serious attempt to settle it. Colonization naturally begins on a coastline or the banks of a navigable river, and the coast of Acadia was too forbidding to be tempting, fringed with dangerous reefs and shoals, and possessing few good harbors of any size and no great rivers to serve as highways to the interior. Inland was rough country, covered with dense forest, not worth the labor of clearing and cultivating. It was a grudging region that nobody wanted particularly. It was not worth fighting over.

In addition, both the French Canadians and the English of the Massachusetts Bay Colony, which included Maine, were bored with the overseas quarrels of England and France and determined to ignore them. They seemed remote, pointless and irrelevant to the problems which the settlers of both nations were facing in their new lives. Besides, they were bad for business. If they'd been left alone by their respective governments, the new colonists might have worked out among themselves a practical arrangement whereby they could live peaceably with each other. By 1650, as a matter of fact, the French of Quebec and the English of Boston were negotiating for a free-trade and mutual protection agreement, an indication that their hearts were not wholly dedicated to the ancient enmity. Negotiations fell through, but it was an indication of a new way of thinking in a new land, which might, given a chance, have saved a lot of future bloodshed.

For, in spite of their different origins, the colonists on opposite sides of the no-man's land of Acadia-in-Maine had more in common with each other than they did with their compatriots in Europe. They were faced with the same problems of surviving and prospering in the same strange land, of outwitting the wilderness and the wayward Down East weather, common enemies of which their relatives across the sea knew nothing.

They all lived in much the same types of houses, evolved by the common conditions, whose architect was practicality and whose builder was necessity. These homes were constructed of hand-hewn and sawed timbers, with thatch or shake roofs and low ceilings to conserve heat. French and English alike used the thin membrane of pigs' bladders or oiled paper instead of glass in their small windows, and they all dug root cellars for the carrying over of vegetables through the bitter New World winters. They all cooked over open fireplaces, and they all dreaded the sound of crackling overhead, where sparks from the mud and wattle chimneys had set fire to the roofs.

Although they had brought their national cookery with them —Yorkshire pudding, *pot-au-feu*, English ale and French wines —they had adopted the same regional foods. They all ate hasty pudding and hulled corn, used maple syrup and sugar for sweetening and drank spruce tea against scurvy. They carried squares of corn bread, journey cake or johnny cake, as emergency rations on long trips, walked through winter drifts on Indian snowshoes, and wore moccasins and fringed jackets of deerhide, cured and fashioned the Indian way. They all learned the Indian tricks of planting fish under each hill of corn, beans and squash; of netting the running alewives in the spring at the mouths of brooks; of curing venison over slow fires of hickory wood.

They became wise in the weather lore of the gnarled granite fists of land they inhabited, thrust out defiantly into the cold, gray North Atlantic. The rumble of the rote on the outer reefs drifting over the sparse fields served as warning of a three-day northeaster brewing in Maine and Nova Scotia alike; cobwebs on the grass at dawn promised a fine day to come; and the borealis streaming up from the northern horizon foretold a change in the weather. French and English both learned to read this shared language of the land.

They spoke different tongues, but into the speech of both crept the same Indian words—"slologan" for a swampy place, "wangan" for a community house, "wampum" for the purple and white beads of quahog shell that the Indians used as money. Each kept their own folk tales, but they all knew that poplar trees were the souls of Indian women who had talked too much during life. For all their national differences, they adapted well and easily to a new frame of reference, meaningless to those left behind on either side of the English Channel.

So for a while all was quiet on the Down East coast; or as quiet as any place can be where people, human and fallible, live their daily lives.

3. DISCORD IN ACADIA

The generally peaceable development of the new frontier continued for about fifty-five years, from 1620 to 1675, broken only by strictly local fighting between French and English forces. These occasions arose for the most part from attempts to prevent settlement by one nation on territory claimed by the other, and took the form of sea-borne expeditions. They involved only the crews of the ships and the citizens of the small colonies in question. The large majority of the settlers of both nationalities, scattered thinly over the area, neither knew nor cared what was going on at St. Sauveur or Machias or Penta-goet, since it in no way affected their day-to-day living. If they heard about it at all, the news aroused little more than natural interest and possibly a mild righteous indignation, certainly neither fear nor rage red enough to call for taking up arms.

This happy state of affairs was finally disrupted by the French and Indian Wars. These brought the Indians into the lists and consequently shattered the security of everyone living between the Down East coast and the Great Lakes. The several con-flicts with their separate names—King Philip's War, King William's War, Queen Anne's War, Lovewell's War, King George's War and the Sixth War—can be considered as one long war interrupted occasionally by short periods of uneasy truce. It lasted for about eighty-five years, from 1675 until the Peace of Paris in 1763. Prescott refers to Maine during this time as "this unhappy frontier," and it is an apt phrase. Children born early in hostilities lived all their lives until they were old men and women in constant dread of being wakened in the dead of night by Indian war whoops, to see red against the sky the glow of a neighbor's burning buildings. Never in their life-times did they know easy sleep, or the certainty that morning would not find the results of all their labors reduced to ashes and ruin, and they themselves dead or in captivity.

The causes lay much less with the colonists than in Europe. The French and Indian Wars were only a side issue to the old struggle between Austria, France and Russia on the one side and England and Prussia on the other for colonies, trade areas and naval supremacy. To Europeans, they amounted to little more than a series of border incidents between a few settlers and the native tribesmen. But to the people on the scene, it was a time of peril, a matter of life or death. Though the Maine colonists did not fully realize it, concerned with immediate dangers as they must be, more than their personal futures was at stake. The future of the entire region and of the nation not yet conceived was involved.

Though the quarrel was between the English and the French, a great deal of the fighting was done by the Indians. Caught up in issues of which they were unaware and impelled by loyalties which were sometimes cynically used to their disadvantage, the Indians were tools in the waging of this New World conflict between Old World countries. That the English suffered much more at Indian hands than did their Canadian neighbors was their own fault. Compared with the long-standing French policy of befriending the red men, the English harsh and indifferent treatment of them was stupidly shortsighted. When the time came to stand up and be counted, the Indians, with few exceptions, had no trouble at all in choosing sides.

The Indian fighting actually did not start in Maine or Canada, and had nothing to do with French and English differences. It began in Massachusetts, where the Wampanoag sachem Metacomet, known as King Philip, was provoked beyond endurance by continued cheating and ill treatment of his people by the Massachusetts English. He led his followers in a massacre of whites in June of 1675. In the year that followed, until Philip was killed in 1676, the war spread all over southeastern New England as far north as Saco, which was destroyed and from which fifty-four prisoners were taken. At Philip's death, his wife and son were sold into slavery and the rest of his tribe was driven out of Massachusetts. Many of them joined friends and relatives in Maine, taking with them the bitter seeds of their hatred of the English. Their aggressive and inflammatory example infected the Maine Abenakis, and that same year Casco,

Pemaquid, Cape Neddick, Black Point and Arrowsic were all burned and their populations either killed or abducted.

By this time, King Philip's original grievance was forgotten, and the whole thing had become a full-scale war involving wholly different issues and people. It was no longer a small affair between Philip and Massachusetts, but a large affair between France and England and their respective American subjects and allies. It was not so much cause and effect that brought this about as it was contagion. Many Indians harbored germs of dissatisfaction over small injustices that might never have become active had Philip's war not provided ideal epidemic conditions.

Living as closely to the Indians as they did through their Jesuit missionaries and their *coureurs de bois*, the French very soon learned to abandon the rather formal and orderly plan of battle customary in Europe in favor of the Indian method of guerrilla fighting. In the whole eighty-five years of the wars, there were relatively few conventional battles—the sack of Castine, the siege of Louisburg, the Battle of Lovewell's Pond—and exercises of military strategy as understood among civilized nations of the time. Instead, there were Indian raids, frequently inspired and accompanied by French officers. These officers were not in formal command, but they did exercise a certain measure of control over the warriors. For this reason, and because most of the Abenakis had become converted to Christianity with its humanitarian effects, the raids were generally conducted with less senseless savagery than characterized Indian fighting further west. They were bad enough, of course. People on both sides were killed and scalped, women and children were carried off into captivity, property was destroyed and families were broken. But torture and other forms of deliberate cruelty were rather rare. It was something—though not much—for which to be thankful.

Indian raids seldom depended on sheer weight of numbers for success, but on either surprise or what was called treachery, although perhaps stratagem would be a better word for it. That at least was what the Indians considered it, as a legitimate tactic of warfare. A war party would send a distraught squaw or a half-grown child to an English homestead, to make the claim of being lost, ill, outcast by the tribe or otherwise in distress. More often than not these pitiful waifs were taken in and given food and shelter. When opportunity arose, usually at night when their benefactors were asleep, they unbarred the doors to their companions, who had been lurking in the woods and who now had no trouble in killing or capturing the dazed whites and burning or carrying off their possessions.

Another trick was to have two or three unarmed Indians approach a village under a flag of truce and ask for a parley. If the settlers complied by sending out representatives, these would be quickly surrounded by warriors who sprang up out of nowhere and either killed or taken captive.

These tricks and others like them worked often and over a long period because the English, well aware of the jeopardy of their position on the inadequately defended frontier, were willing to grasp at straws. When the English settlers learned to distrust such overtures, they did a complete about-face and refused to trust any unknown Indians at all. Thus they alienated some who were or could have been their friends. Even before active hostilities broke out, the English had a tendency to brusque and unimaginative treatment of the Indians, which drove them away. The French, on the other hand, even before 1675, encouraged the Christian Abenakis of the Maine coast to move to Canada and establish their homes near the missions around Quebec and at the falls of the Chaudière River, where they lived on easy and neighborly terms with the French. Thus the French formed what amounted to a permanent pool of fighting men to be drawn upon when necessary.

They used this ever-available strength for surprise attacks, the classic Indian method of conducting warfare, developed almost to an art. An Indian war party on the move gave no more warning of its coming nor evidence of its passing than shadows do. No dead leaf crackled, no twig snapped, no damp patch of earth held the imprint of a moccasined foot, no sentinel blue jay screamed. Silent as thought, the warriors drifted through the forest and over the height of land that lay between Canada and the Maine coast. They carried a little parched corn and jerked venison with them, but mostly they lived off the country, bringing down game with noiseless arrows, chewing on edible roots and leaves and berries. No fires which might give the alarm were built for cooking or warmth. The Indians were indifferent to physical discomfort. They were patient, too. Sometimes, unsuspected even by the dogs, they lay hidden in the woods around a hamlet for days, familiarizing themselves with the habits of their victims and planning their best mode of attack. They were a redoubtable enemy, particularly to those who had been conditioned to think of war in terms of armies marching in formation to the ruffle of drums and the blare of bugles.

The English in time developed a system of at least partial protection. For each man to try singly to defend his own home was recognized as foolhardy and useless. Instead, one large dwelling with an accessible water supply, a commanding site and a central location was chosen in each community as a rallying point for all in case of attack. To the natural advantages were added fortifications such as loopholes overlooking all approaches, overhanging upper stories to allow firing down upon those of the enemy who managed to come in close and sod roofs against the menace of fire-tipped arrows. The whole was surrounded by a high stockade of pointed logs, with a wide, barred gate. If there was time, cattle were rounded up and driven into this corral, and, in any event, it served to delay the raiders. All in all, these garrison houses, though private homes, looked very much like small forts; and in French reports of some of the raids under French officers, credit is taken for the capture or destruction of a fort where no fort actually existed.

The need to live within running distance of the community stockade limited the expansion of villages, and it prevented the settling of interior Maine. In theory, all these subjects of the British Crown were entitled to protection as authorized colonists. In practice, it was impossible to fortify adequately so long and straggling a frontier. England, moreover, was involved in conflict at home which tied up most of her fighting power and her money. For a short while when Sir Edmund Andros was Governor General of Massachusetts, regiments of soldiers were assigned to duty along the Saco and Kennebec rivers and at Casco Bay and Pemaquid, and things in those regions improved. But when the Bostonians rebelled against Andros, whom they considered arrogant and high-handed, and placed him in custody, these troops were withdrawn. The Indians and their French leaders took advantage of this to swoop down with renewed enthusiasm, and for a time Maine as an English possession seemed doomed. By 1691, all except four towns—Wells, Kittery, York and Appledore, clustered in the extreme south—had been destroyed.

Both the French and the English paid bounties to the Indians for enemy scalps, but the French also paid even larger sums for the delivery of captives in good condition. This accounts for the number of women and children who managed to survive the

raids. Usually the men were killed on the spot as being too difficult to handle on the long forced march back across the border.
But the women and children were easier to manage. The
Abenakis showed them a certain rough consideration during the
harrowing journey through the wilderness, not so much from
humaneness as from self-interest. The more healthy prisoners
they could turn over to the French, the greater the reward would
be. There is on record one instance where an Abenaki brave
himself carried a small infant for days after its mother no longer
had the strength to do so, rather than dispatch it by knocking its
head against a tree—the usual procedure in such cases. Whether
this infant was delivered to the French or adopted into the
tribe of its savior is not known. The Abenakis had a fondness
for children and not uncommonly kept back little captives to
whom they had become attached during the journey.

Even considering the relatively good treatment these captives
received, it is surprising that so many of them survived. Most of
them began the long trek in a state of shock at having seen their
male relatives brutally done to death and their homes burned.
Seldom were they properly dressed for hardship, but set out in
bare feet and insufficient clothing. As the days wore on, those
who fell ill or could not keep up the pace were killed or abandoned to a certain death by starvation and exposure. In addition
to the remembered horror of the immediate past and the harsh
demands of the cruel present, always there was fear and uncer-
tainty about the unimaginable future.

Eventually some of the survivors were ransomed and returned
to their families and homes, and some escaped and made their
way back. Some of the very small children who were adopted by
the Indians or the French grew up never knowing their true
antecedents. Many of them believed themselves to belong to

their foster parents and so were, in a sense, truly lost. Some of the women were taken into French families as servants, and some of the girls were placed in convents. Of these, more than a few became nuns. Of an impressionable age, these young girls were profoundly shocked by the ordeal they had been forced to undergo and the discovery that the world was not the fine, safe place they had imagined. So they renounced it willingly for a more secure world of prayer, service and discipline within the sheltering arms of the Church.

Mary Scammon's story illustrates a different fate. When she was eight years old, Mary went to visit family friends in Scarboro. While she was there, the village was raided and burned, and the inhabitants carried off to Canada. Mary was an unusually pretty and intelligent little girl, and Governor Vaudreil of Quebec picked her out of the lot of new prisoners and took her home. The whole family was charmed with her, and she was soon accepted as a member and treated equally with the Governor's own children. She received an excellent education and lived a life of ease and luxury such as she had never known before. When she was seventeen, she married a Monsieur Disnincour, a man of wealth and position. It was a very good marriage from a worldly point of view, and apparently from a romantic one as well.

About seven years later, one of the intermittent periods of peace occurred when citizens of both nationalities were free to travel and conduct business back and forth across the border at will. Among the traders was Humphrey Scammon, Mary's brother from Maine, who learned by accident that his sister was still alive. Naturally, he lost no time in seeking her out, with the idea of taking her back to her own people. He found a poised young lady, very much the mistress of her own elegantly appointed home, who spoke English with a decided French accent. She was glad to see him and politely interested in all the news he gave her of a home and family and neighbors whom she remembered vaguely or not at all. But when he proposed that she return with him to her rightful place, she was aghast. Her place was here among the French Catholics of Quebec. These were her people, whom she knew and understood and loved.

She did, however, agree to go back with her brother for a reunion with her family and a renewal of acquaintance with the scene of her early childhood. Apparently this visit was not much of a success, since it was of rather short duration. What actually happened we have no way of knowing. People of that day, if they kept diaries at all, had a maddening way of stating bald facts in few words, with no details or elaboration. But it's not hard to imagine how things went. First there would have been an emotional welcome, with cries of wonder and happy tears at seeing the long-lost lamb back in the fold. But after the first excitement had worn off, the family and old playmates would have found very little in common with Mary, who now called herself Marie. This would probably have been considered an affectation, and the first small criticism would have been followed by others. Marie (if you please!) put on airs, she and her French accent. She wore impractical clothes. Who ever heard of a velvet cloak on a Down East farm? She was worse than useless around the place. You'd think she never washed a floor or milked a cow in her life. She was spoiled, that's what she was, with her city manners and Frenchified ways.

Mary herself could not have been very happy. Although Quebec was a grown-up trading post in the wilderness, still it was a city and had much more to offer than a Maine coast farm. She missed the solemn joy of attending Mass with her husband at her side; and the quick ripple of French voices as she walked down the gray Quebec streets; and the dear French way of doing things. She must have found the food plain and uninteresting after the French cookery to which she was accustomed, and the surroundings rather bleak. She missed her comfortable home, and her husband and children, and her servants and her friends. She was plain homesick. So she cut her visit short and returned to Quebec. Probably nobody was very sorry to see her go.

Generally speaking, Indian fighting was a rather anonymous business, carried on by shadowy raiding parties in which names and faces merged and were lost. But there was one Frenchman who never hid his light under a bushel and who was probably personally responsible for more depredation along the Maine coast than any other dozen individuals combined. This was Jean Vincent de l'Abadie, Baron de St. Castin, a Basque nobleman whose family owned large estates in the French Pyrenees. Castin, as he is usually called, was a wild one, born—fortunately for him —within his proper century and early transplanted to his proper environment. Evidently he had been a problem to his family from childhood. Otherwise it is difficult to account for the fact that at the age of fifteen he arrived in Quebec already an ensign in the regiment of Carignan-Salières, assigned to overseas duty. Military service began young among the French, but surely not that young unless there was reason to suppose that a boy would be better off under army discipline, or that the family would be happier if his talents were employed elsewhere than at home.

If army regimen was supposed to lick Castin into acceptable shape, it failed. Instead of taming down, he became even more confirmed in his free-wheeling ways. According to old accounts, he spent much more time in the wilderness with Indian cronies than he did in the barracks polishing his boots and his buttons like a good little ensign. He had an affinity for the Indians, and his superior had very little control over his conduct.

Not long after his arrival in Quebec, Castin decided to inspect some land near the mouth of the Penobscot that was held through royal grant by his family. This was a long way from Quebec, and none of the family had to date shown any interest in these holdings. He set off in a canoe with three young Indian friends and in due course arrived at his destination. As soon as he saw Pentagoet, he felt that he had come into his own.

Pentagoet had had, up until this time, a rather stormy history. It was founded in 1629 as one of the Plymouth Pilgrims' fur-trading posts and was destroyed shortly thereafter by the vigilant French. An expedition under Miles Standish attempted to recapture it, with no success, and it remained in French hands until 1670, when for a brief spell Cromwell's English occupied it. Almost immediately the French took it back, and it was during this occupation that Castin made his appearance. So impressed was he with the possibilities of the site that a few years later, when his regiment was disbanded and he was free to return home to the Pyrenees, he chose instead to stay in the New World, making Pentagoet—which later became known as Castine in his honor—his headquarters.

In the meantime, he had so consolidated his position among the Indians that they made him a chief and even regarded him as a sort of minor god. The evidence is that he had more influence over them and better control of them than any other single agency, including the Church. They loved and respected him almost to the point of idolatry. The same could not be said of Castin's own countrymen, who regarded him as a renegade. Repeated reports and complaints about him were sent back to France, the mildest being that he "had need of spiritual aid to

sustain him in the paths of virtue." Governor Meneval of Mont-
real was specifically instructed to prevent Castin's consorting
with the Indians and to make him conduct himself in a manner
becoming a gentleman. Meneval tried. He kept Castin in jail
once for two months on what Castin himself called a "pretence
of a little weakness I had for some women."

Reforming Castin was a hopeless undertaking. So when he was
legally married within the Catholic Church to the daughter of
Madockawando, a powerful chief of the Penobscots, the French
authorities gladly washed their hands of responsibility for his
moral welfare. Or perhaps they recognized the truth—that
through this marriage, much as they deplored it, Castin was
doing the French in Canada a tremendous service. By con-
tracting family ties with the Indians, he was assuring the French
of the unwavering support of a vast network of tribal connections. The Indians were unswervingly loyal to their own.

Castin considered himself a fur trader, and he made a fortune
of over three hundred thousand gold crowns at it. His principal
trading post was Pentagoet, which, however, stood on such de-
batable territory that he spent almost as much time defending it
as he did bartering furs. On one occasion the place was captured
by Flemish pirates while Castin was away up country, and he
was obliged to round up a band of his relatives and take it back
again. But his usual enemy was the English. Since the French and
Indian Wars were interrupted by occasional periods of truce,
Castin was never sure what he might find when he returned
from one of his long sojourns in the woods. Sometimes everything was serene, nobody disputed his tenancy, and the English
were only interested in trade. Castin hated the New Englanders,
but not enough to refuse their money. Actually most of his
great fortune came from doing business with the Yankees.

At other times, when he had been out of touch with political developments for weeks or months, he would arrive home to find that all the land he called his own had been given by treaty to the British. On one such occasion, he found Pentagoet plundered of everything of value by Sir Edmund Andros, then Governor General of Massachusetts. To add insult to injury, Andros had left a message to the effect that Castin could recover his property by going to Pemaquid after it.

Castin was never a patient man, nor one to eat humble pie, and this insolence infuriated him. From that point on, his hatred of the English became fanatical. For twenty years he waged a personal vendetta against all New England. He started out with Pemaquid, which he completely destroyed; and before he was through, he and his warriors burned Falmouth, now Portland, to the ground. His name was spoken in whispers along the Maine coast, a name feared even more than that of the Devil. There were things you could do to placate or exorcise the Devil, the pious English settlers believed. There was nothing you could do about Castin and his Abenakis.

Time finally accomplished what neither Castin's French superiors nor his English enemies could do. Age slowed him down and dulled the edge of his bitterness and hatred. The old wrongs seemed far away and trivial. With late-come wisdom he saw that all this fighting had accomplished very little, much as he had enjoyed it. He was tired now, and all he wanted was quiet. During one of the lulls between wars, he persuaded his only legitimate son to undertake the cause of a lasting peace among all the inhabitants of North America.

A remarkable combination of qualities resided in this young half-breed. He possessed his father's brilliant mind and enormous courage and pride, and he also had the wisdom and patience of his mother's people. Moreover, his was the double prestige of being Castin's son and the grandson of the revered Madocka-wando. When he went among the tribes to induce them to lay down their arms, his words were listened to and carried weight. The British, however, mistook his intentions or mistrusted his good faith. They seized him as an *agent provocateur*, bound him with chains and sent him in humiliation to Boston, where he was kept in a dungeon for seven months.

They could not have hit on a more successful device for arousing the whole Abenaki nation to murderous pitch. All the members of the Castin family were worshiped among the tribes, and this treatment of one of them could not go unavenged. War drums sounded up the long valleys and through the tall forests of Maine, rallying the warriors for a full-scale, all-out war against the English. It was to be a war in the old manner of the days before the white man, when Christian mercy was unknown; and it was to continue until every English man, woman and child was dead, preferably by torture. It is quite possible that, had it come about, it would have succeeded.

Fortunately, before the massive attack could be organized and launched, the young Castin was able to persuade his captors of his good intentions and was set free. He returned to his people and, with unexpected forbearance, set about undoing the harm. He managed to convince the Indians that the whole thing had been a regrettable error, but not a serious one, and to talk them into continuing with his original plans for peace. So successful was he that the resultant peace lasted for twenty years, a remark-ably long time on that trigger-happy frontier. By 1740, when the truce was ended by the outbreak of the War of the Austrian Succession, the Castin family with its enormous influence had passed from the scene. The elder Castin and his wife were dead, their daughters were well married to Frenchmen and living in Canada or France, and the young Castin, now a baron, had gone to live on the family estate in the Pyrenees.

The Indian fighting serves as the background for the French and Indian Wars. It continued sporadically for the whole eighty-five years, and it was costly in life, property and the development of the frontier. But there were campaigns of a different character carried on by the English and the French against this background, more or less independently of the Indians. One of the first of these was against Port Royal, the old French colony in Nova Scotia.

Maine was still a part of Massachusetts, governed from Boston; and while Boston was safely removed from scenes of actual bloodshed, arson and general mayhem, she did suffer nevertheless in the pocketbook through the decline of the Maine fisheries and fur trading. The blame for this grievous hurt was attached by Boston authorities to Port Royal, with some reason. French cruisers based there constantly harassed the Maine fishing fleet, and the town itself outfitted and financed some of the Indian raids that wiped out Maine fur trading posts. The obvious remedy for this irritation was to take over the Nova Scotian trouble spot, and the obvious man to do it, Boston concluded, was William Phips, the Maine-born High Sheriff of Massachusetts.

Phips was of almost exactly the same age as the Baron de St. Castin, and they both had a great deal to do with the shaping of Maine history. In all other respects they could not have been less alike. Whereas Castin was born a nobleman in a castle on the slopes of the Pyrenees and ended by living among the Indians as one of them, Phips was born in a backwoods cabin, close neighbor to the Abenakis, and worked himself up to an

English knighthood. Castin had no great worldly ambitions. Born at the top, he could afford to go his own merry way and follow his own inclinations. Phips, the youngest of twenty-six children of a dirt-poor gunsmith of Nauseag (now Woolwich), Maine, was eaten with ambition. Wars always bring into prominence individuals who might otherwise have lived out their lives in obscurity, but no war was needed to call attention to William Phips. His was perhaps the first success story in the classic American rags-to-riches tradition.

With twenty-one older brothers and four older sisters to keep him in line, William still grew up undisciplined, willful, fearless —and lucky. Looking about at the hard lot of the salt-water farmers of his neighborhood, he decided at an early age that he wanted something better. So he ran away from home. He didn't run far—only across the Sheepscot River by canoe to Arrowsic, where he apprenticed himself to a shipwright. It was far enough, however. During the four years of his apprenticeship, he came in constant contact with seafaring men who had been all over the world and who enjoyed nothing better than to recount their lurid adventures in foreign lands to this wide-eyed listener. Phips decided that he was going to sea, too, but not before the mast. When he went, it would be in the captain's cabin. But first he had to get out of Arrowsic, where nothing happened, to Boston, where anything might happen.

He accomplished this by working his way on a Boston-bound vessel, and, once arrived, found a job as a ship's carpenter. The city enchanted him. This was where he belonged. When he was a captain, he would live here, in a big house of rosy brick, and everybody would know him and pay attention when he spoke. His colossal self-esteem and self-confidence did not, surprisingly, blind him to his own defects. His mirror told him that he was handsome, the approval of his employers told him that he was smart and competent, and the ease with which he made friends told him that he had great charm. But his inborn common sense told him that he was an ignorant, graceless, untutored back-woodsman from a Down East gunk-hole. So he set about teach-ing himself to read and write and to conduct himself with the air and manners of a gentleman. Because he was intelligent as well as ambitious, he soon made himself acceptable in society.

Through the Phips initiative, aplomb and charm, he met and married the beautiful daughter of Roger Spencer, a wealthy and influential sea captain. It seems unkind to suspect that her father's money and position in any way colored Phips's feelings for this girl, but the fact remains that through this connection he almost immediately secured a contract to build a ship on his own, thus rising from hired carpenter to independent shipbuilder in one jump. He prudently decided to establish his infant shipyard down on the Sheepscot, where he had grown up and knew the ropes, and where he could count on plenty of cheap labor and abundant, cheap materials. What happened next was a sample of the kind of luck that seemed to fall his way so often in his life. As he was preparing to sail his completed vessel back to Massa-chusetts for delivery to the owner, an Indian war party swooped down on the vicinity. Phips rallied the frightened settlers, in-cluding his own numerous family, loaded them aboard his new ship and whisked them all safely away to Boston.

Here he was given a hero's welcome, with parades, speeches and banquets. Then, although his only experience in command was this one short little coastal voyage, he was offered the cap-taincy of a ship engaged in the West Indies trade. Humility and self-doubt were never among his weaknesses, so he accepted the commission, thus terminating his brief career as a shipbuilder.

Not surprisingly, he made an excellent captain, hard-fisted, decisive and fair-minded.

After a few trading voyages to the Indies, however, he concluded that this was too slow and tame a way of acquiring a large fortune and a brick house in Boston. The islands were full of stories of lost Spanish treasure galleons, and he decided that the best way to get rich quick was to find one. Many people have had the same idea and grown only the poorer for it, but Phips actually succeeded in locating a sunken bullion ship and salvaging enough gold to pay him handsomely for his time and trouble.

His imagination now took a grandiose turn. If he entered into a partnership in his treasure hunting, he thought, his personal risk would be cut; and what more solidly financed partner could he find than the British Crown? Everything about Phips was slightly larger than life, and everything that happened to him tinged faintly with the unlikely. It was unlikely that Charles II would give an audience to an unknown colonial yokel, or that he would be in the least interested in any vague get-rich-quick scheme. But Phips talked himself into the King's presence, and then he blandly talked the King out of an eighteen-gun vessel, the *Rose*, a crew of ninety-five men and a special assignment to go looking for Spanish gold.

That was all he needed. Less than three years later he was back in England with over two million dollars' worth of recovered Spanish treasure, half of which was his own. This was an impressive fortune in those days. The King further rewarded him with a gold chain and medal for himself, a five-thousand-dollar gold cup for his wife, a knighthood and an appointment as High Sheriff of Massachusetts. This obliged Phips to return to Boston, where he at once contracted for the building of a brick mansion at the corner of Salem and Charter streets. Five years had elapsed since he had left the city for the Sheepscot shipyard, and now he was back with everything he had planned for himself accomplished, and more. He had his house, he had his fortune, and everybody knew him and listened when he spoke, because now he was even more important than a mere sea captain. He was Sir William Phips.

Clearly, he was just the man to conduct the expedition against Port Royal in 1690. It turned out to be an operation not quite up to the Phips standard of drama. His force of seven ships and seven hundred men encountered no resistance from the French Governor, Meneval, who surrendered the undergarrisoned port without firing a shot. Phips extracted an oath of allegiance to England from the population and set up a temporary government of six councilors and a president chosen from among the local inhabitants. He stayed long enough to make sure that all the other little hamlets along the Bay of Fundy accepted the new British rule without argument, and then he went home to Boston. The whole affair took less than three months. As a reward, Sir William was made the first Governor Royal of Massachusetts and received as spoils of war some of Meneval's personal effects that caught his fancy, including four pairs of silk garters and four lace-trimmed nightcaps.

This easy victory presumably delivered over into English hands all of Nova Scotia and eastern Maine; but to keep control of this area, a police force of some sort was necessary, and Massachusetts had neither the men nor the money to provide one. England showed a surprising indifference toward lending aid to her colonies, even though it would have been in her own interests to do so. France retaliated for the Port Royal seizure by capturing Fort William Henry at Pemaquid, during the same

year, 1690, a vantage point that the English could ill afford to
lose. To the colonists the whole thing was pretty futile. They
gave time and energy to securing advantages for their side, and
almost immediately the French were allowed to cancel out the
supposed victory.

This was the foreshadowing of an attitude that was to grow
until the Revolution. In place of unquestioning faith in England's decisions and actions, the colonists began to feel doubt.
They depended on England for protection, and that protection
was not forthcoming. They asked for troops, and all they got
was a promotion for William Phips. They were being treated
like stepchildren, they felt, so perhaps they'd better start acting
like stepchildren.

It was in this rebellious mood that William Phips as Royal
Governor decided to stop the nonsense along the border once
and for all by capturing the French capital of Quebec. He extracted a reluctant agreement from the Crown to help him in
what was a major and important project, and set off overland
to the north with a small force for the job. The affair was a
fiasco. Sir William waited around at Quebec for half the summer and all the fall for English reinforcements that never showed
up and then, with winter approaching, was obliged to retreat
ignominiously. He was not accustomed to having his plans turn
out in this shabby fashion, and it was a chastening experience.

Shortly after the unsuccessful Quebec expedition, Sir William
undertook a matter that required a great deal of tact and finesse,
qualities for which he had not heretofore been especially distinguished. He was able to persuade the Indians to sign over to
the English their land on both sides of the Penobscot. Probably
no one else could have accomplished this. The area in question
was the heart of Castin's territory, and these Indians were his

friends. But young Castin had been talking to them about peace; and, too, they had known Sir William when he was a youngster living on the Sheepscot, and the bond of liking and trust had endured over the great gap of the years, in spite of the differences that had developed in their ways of life. On his word they signed the treaty, and they kept its terms until his death.

Now it seemed that the worst of the border troubles were over. So sanguine was Massachusetts that she offered free land to anyone who would homestead in Maine, and by 1740 the population had reached twelve thousand. Little villages sprang up along the coast, and the whole feeling of the area was one of energetic optimism. Everyone was busy and happy. The Indians were behaving themselves, and the French had stopped disputing English claims to Maine and Nova Scotia and were concentrating their efforts on the St. Lawrence Valley and the land west to the Great Lakes. At last, it seemed, a man could put his mind on his work—on building a boat, or clearing a field, or setting up a saw mill; on fishing or farming or lumbering or trading or, more likely, a combination of any or all of these pursuits. War was a thing of the past, and the future looked promising.

Communications were, to say the least, extremely unreliable and chancy in those days. Thus it happened that when the War of the Austrian Succession broke out in Europe in 1740, the news arrived at the French stronghold of Louisburg, at the mouth of the St. Lawrence, weeks before it reached Boston. This quarrel actually was a European affair, having almost nothing to do with the settlers across the Atlantic. It could perhaps have been ignored by them, had it not been for the Governor of Louisburg, a zealous career man named Duquesnel. He saw a chance to snatch honor and glory and advancement by seizing all of Acadia for France before the British even knew there was a war going on.

He began by capturing the nearby English fishing village of Canseau, where there were only a few peaceable fishermen who didn't even try to resist. Duquesnel then moved on to Annapolis, the old Port Royal renamed by the British, the taking of which would give him virtual control of all Nova Scotia. This should have been as easy as Canseau. After two decades of peace, which the English still thought was in effect, the town's fortifications had been allowed to crumble away, and large gaps had been made in the rubble for the convenience of cows pastured in the surrounding fields. By pure chance, however, several English ships came into the harbor just about as Duquesnel was ready to launch his attack. Showing more prudence than valor, he beat a hasty retreat.

This whole campaign accomplished nothing, not even the serious inconvenience of the Canseau fishermen, who picked themselves up and went about their business as before. But the English settlers along the Maine coast, when they heard of Duquesnel's activities, failed to take this philosophical attitude. Considering the slight damage that had been done, their rage seems out of proportion, but enraged they were. It was time, the consensus ran, that the French were taught a good stiff lesson, and what stiffer one could be devised than the capture of Louisburg itself?

The French had spent thirty years and thirty million livres in making Louisburg the Gibraltar of the West, an impregnable fortress guarding the gateway to Canada and controlling the valuable off-shore fisheries. Here was based the French Navy in America, and here lay a fleet of privateers, semiofficial birds of prey that darted out to plunder North Atlantic shipping. The value of the citadel to the French was beyond estimate. They were not likely to allow anybody to capture it.

The Massachusetts authorities agreed with this opinion. They saw no point in wasting men and money on a fool's project. The fools in question were the Maine coast fishermen, led by William Vaughn of Damariscotta. They had all suffered from interference by the Louisburg French with their fishing vessels, and they wanted a stop put to the nuisance. When a Down East Yankee's means of livelihood is affected, he can become pretty persistent and pretty eloquent. Such was the case with Vaughn.

The Massachusetts Assembly had well-founded objections to the idea. They said that the city was far too well fortified, garrisoned and provisioned to be taken by even a very large force, which they did not have at their command. The British Crown refused to supply soldiers or ships for any such hen-headed scheme. Furthermore, Cape Breton, where Louisburg was situated, was notorious for terrible storms, tremendous surfs and dense fogs, making the landing of troops hazardous if not impossible. An overland approach would not be feasible, as a wide and open marsh lay behind the city, impossible to cross under the guns of the fortress. Moreover, the high walls could not be breached without heavy artillery, which, even if Massachusetts had owned any, could not have been transported all that distance. So, all in all, the plan was impossible. The Assembly voted it down.

But Vaughn would not be voted down. He kept coming back with new arguments and information, most of which was false. He said, for example, that he had direct knowledge from an unimpeachable source that the supplies of Louisburg were down to starvation level and that the garrison was on the verge of mutiny. He said that he knew for a fact that the Crown would reconsider and back the expedition, once it was definitely decided upon, with both ships of the line and regiments of infantry. He said that fog and storms and high seas never had and never would bother Maine seamen; and that if the swamp proved too difficult and the walls too high, they would just wait until winter, cross on the frozen mud and walk right up the drifted snow over the fortifications. As for artillery, it would be foolish to lug it all that way, even if they had it. When they got there, they would capture what they needed and simply turn it around against the French. He said a lot of things, and the reason no one refuted them was probably that they sounded so ridiculous and childish that they weren't considered worth refuting.

Either through sheer gadfly persistence or through some inexplicable form of mesmerism, Vaughn won his argument by one vote. On the day when the plan was adopted, an Assembly member who was fiercely against it fell down and broke his leg in his rush to get to the meeting and register his protest. Had it not been for this rather farcical misadventure, the matter would probably have dragged on and on and in the end died of inertia.

The whole campaign against Louisburg from start to finish had about it the improbable and unrealistic aura that distinguishes farce. Men suffered, and achieved miracles of courage and endurance, and died; and there is nothing absurd about that. But the circumstances surrounding the heroism and the dying were almost ludicrous.

England, in spite of Vaughn's sanguine predictions, refused any aid at all; so instead of a well-disciplined army of experienced troops, there advanced against the Gibraltar of the West a disorganized rabble of farmers, merchants, fishermen and jacks-of-all-trades. About the only thing that could be said for them as a military force was that at least they all owned guns and were expert marksmen, and most of them had had some experience with human targets during Indian raids. They were all volunteers, joined up of their own free will, so their morale was good. A thousand of them—one-third of the entire contingent—came from Maine. This was half the adult male population of the province at the time, a disproportionately large percentage compared to the number of volunteers from the Massachusetts Bay Colony as a whole. But seizing Louisburg was a Maine notion and, if successful, would benefit Maine most directly, so it was considered reasonable that Maine should contribute most.

The sea force was equally laughable. Lacking the support of the British Navy, the colonists scratched together about ninety boats of all sizes and types, placed them under the command of Edward Tyng of Falmouth, Maine, and armed them as best they could with whatever guns they could beg or borrow—neither very many nor very good. One heavy French ship of the line, according to informed authority, could have blasted this entire cockleshell fleet clean out of the water with no trouble at all, and it is hard to understand why this did not happen. Surely the French must have heard what was going on. Their spy system was efficient, and Vaughn hadn't been doing his promoting in a whisper. At any rate, no French battleship appeared on the scene, and this was the kind of luck that favored this idiotic endeavor.

Even the most inept troops can be licked into shape by competent officers, but here was the sorriest lack of all. Having no standing army of their own, the colonies had nobody trained in military leadership. Since somebody had to be in charge, Governor William Shirley of Massachusetts appointed to the post William Pepperell of Kittery, Maine. Pepperell was a merchant and shipbuilder, whose father had come early to New England and established a fishing business. Solely through their own efforts, father and son had managed to accumulate one of the first large New England fortunes. Pepperell was shrewd and capable in his own field of trade, but he had had no experience on the field of battle whatsoever. He was, however, universally popular, and this was a big asset in the peculiar and delicate conditions under which he was laboring. Terms of enlistment in the volunteer army were very loose indeed, and there was nothing to prevent a man from picking up his gear and going home, if he felt so inclined. Any number of things might so incline him, chief among them being bossed around by someone he disliked. Most of these frontiersmen had never taken orders from anyone in their lives and were too set in their independent ways to form the habit easily or gracefully. Pepperell was one of the very few men who could have assumed authority and made it stick.

On March 4, 1745, the makeshift expedition set sail for Cape Breton. Most of the members had only a vague idea of where they were going and none at all of what they would find there. The whole affair seems to have been governed by a most un-Yankee optimism. Usually Yankees, especially Maine Yankees, expect and prepare for the worst. Then whatever happens, they figure, they won't be disappointed, and they may even be delightfully surprised. Against all probability, this uncharacteristic lack of caution was justified. The ragtag fleet met a small English squadron patrolling American waters under Commodore Warren. Warren was apparently bored with a long and uneventful tour of duty. He knew he was not supposed to assist this feckless undertaking, but since he had not received specific orders forbidding him to do so, he decided that he might as well go along and see the fun. He escorted the colonists down the coast and set up a blockade of Louisburg that was of inestimable value.

Usually in early spring the coast of Nova Scotia is battered by furious storms. Winds of gale force howl in from the Atlantic, the tides run wild and high, the surf tramples savagely on the reefs, and all the land is lashed by driven rain and shrouded in dismal fog. This year, miraculously, the weather was lovely—calm and gentle, bright and clear. The expedition disembarked with all the ease and much the air of a Sunday school picnic, and set up camp in comfort behind the city. Then they looked around to see where to begin.

William Vaughn had said that the French were low on supplies. This was something he had made up out of whole cloth. The French had plenty of supplies, stored in a series of warehouses across the harbor from the main fortress. Presumably they were safe there under the guns of the fort proper and of a companion fort called the Grand Battery that guarded the opposite side of the harbor entrance. Vaughn undertook to make a truthful man of himself. With a handful of volunteers, he crept around the harbor under cover of night and burned the storehouses and their contents to the ground. This ticklish operation dealt the French a serious blow very early in the proceedings.

Vaughn had also been very reassuring about capturing artillery to turn against Louisburg, and before the night was over, he accomplished that, too. As the party was returning to camp in the early dawn, someone observed that there was no smoke rising from the chimneys of the Grand Battery. The little group detoured to investigate and found the installation deserted. The garrison on duty had heard Vaughn's scouts pass in the night, seen the blaze of the warehouses and concluded that they were about to be overrun. In panic, they had rowed across the harbor to the city, not even stopping to spike more than a few of the thirty cannon that comprised the battery. These were professional soldiers, so there is no excusing such conduct.

Repairing the spiked guns was child's play for men who had spent all their lives tinkering with broken farm tools and mending ship's gear. The real problem lay in moving the artillery into position where it could be trained effectively on the citadel. Louisburg was protected on three sides by deep water, and on the fourth by a treacherous marsh. This last was the only possible approach for the cannon, and yet it was impossible. So the French believed, and on this belief they had based their defenses. But to Down-easters, devising ways of doing things that couldn't be done was a part of everyday living. The swamp presented an interesting problem, but not an impossible one.

While some canvassed the farms of the surrounding countryside for teams of horses and oxen, others built sixteen-foot sledges of logs and mounted the cannon on them. Then they started across the marsh. The draft animals proved almost useless. Beasts give up sooner than men do, probably because they cannot understand the purpose of a cruel task and have no reason to continue beyond the point of exhaustion. When the teams foundered, the men cut them loose and took their places in harness. Two hundred men were needed to move one sledge a few inches, then a few feet, then a rod or two.

It was terrible and heartbreaking labor. The mud was soon churned into hip-deep soup, in which the guns were in danger of sinking out of sight. So causeways had to be built. The work had to be carried on at night or in the occasional thick fog, because of sniping from the city walls. The weather turned cold and raw, as only a Cape Breton spring can, and the men were wet and half-frozen all the time. Their shoes rotted off their feet from continual soaking in acid swamp water, and their clothing was worn to shreds and tatters. Sickness was common —fevers and hacking coughs, pneumonia and influenza, rheumatism and gunshot wounds. Many died and were buried there on the desolate cape. More survived to live the rest of their lives with disabilities contracted in the dreadful marsh behind Louisburg. But under the incredulous eyes of the French, who had done nothing much to halt proceedings because they were so sure that proceedings would soon come to a natural halt, the men from Maine and Massachusetts bulldozed and manhandled the guns into place and opened fire on the city.

Now it was too late for the French to act. They had overestimated the strength of their position and underestimated Yankee stubbornness and toughness. Food and ammunition were in short supply, and Warren with his squadron was effectively preventing the smuggling in of rations from along the coast by boat. The fire from the cannon in the swamp was a constant harassment, damaging every building in the city and wearing dreadfully on the nerves of the inhabitants. It was a shaken citizenry that defended the walls against what they had concluded were madmen, but they held on in the last desperate hope that help would arrive from France before it was too late.

Finally, in June, one of France's greatest fighting ships, the *Vigilant* of 64 guns and 560 troops, sailed majestically into sight. Warren's blockading squadron had, as it happened, gone off somewhere below the horizon, and the *Vigilant* had clear sailing and a good wind into harbor. Evidently her captain had no idea of the true state of affairs. Before the dismayed and astonished eyes of the beleaguered fortress, he changed course to pursue a tiny English privateer that was tacking along the shore. This must have been purely for sport, a sort of kicking-up-the-heels to celebrate the end of a long voyage. The little schooner headed out to sea, with the *Vigilant* after her; and then Warren's squadron came boiling up over the horizon with all sails set, spoiling for a fight. Five hours later, the *Vigilant* was a prize of war, and Louisburg's hope of deliverance was dead. In mid-June the strongest fortress in the two Americas capitulated to the scratched-together, patched-up apology for an army from the New England coast.

England viewed the surrender with rather mixed emotions, chief of which was probably surprise. She had withheld aid in the first place because the whole thing seemed like a waste of time and energy, and here the feeble little colonies had done what British might refused to attempt. The surprise was tinged with dismay. It occurred to some that the colonists were becoming a bit high-handed. Such a display of aggressiveness and independence ill became properly loyal and submissive subjects, and might prove dangerous if it became a habit. But of course appropriate gestures of gratitude must be made, so Massachusetts was refunded for her time and trouble with 217 chests of Spanish dollars and a hundred barrelfuls of copper pennies. William Pepperell was made a baronet, but he did not live long to enjoy the honor. His robust health had been so badly undermined by the miserable hardships at Louisburg that he died soon after his return home to Kittery.

A short three years later, Louisburg was given back to the French by the terms of the Treaty of Aix-la-Chapelle in 1748. The colonists were shocked and filled with bitterness. They had not yet had time to forget the horrors of the campaign, or the thousand New Englanders who lay buried "like rotten sheep" in the filthy swamp. Too many of them rose each morning with aching bones and went about their day's work under the handicap of ruined health to accept gracefully this throwing away of all they had accomplished at such cost. They felt that they were being abused and belittled, and that their interests were being neglected. It was an attitude from which they were never to recover. Although border fighting continued along the Maine coast for another ten years, nobody's heart was really in it. Indians were fought if they came around causing trouble; but no more did the settlers go out looking for fights in far places. They had had enough of that.

In 1759, British forces under General Wolfe, with the aid of Colonel Rogers and his famous Maine-born Rangers, captured the French capital of Quebec, and France surrendered all her claims to Canada. The Peace of Paris in 1763 brought to a formal close the French and Indian Wars. A century and a half after the first struggling English colony on the Maine coast, the settlers were at last able to get down to the business of living in peace on this harsh and beautiful land.

4. THE BREATHING SPELL

For a people who were repeatedly ravaged by Indian raids, and who perforce wasted much of their time and energy in the unprofitable business of fighting, the Maine settlers accomplished a surprising amount in their first hundred and fifty years. In 1625, the only colonies with any promise of permanence were at Saco on the mainland and on Monhegan far out at sea. These were small huddles of rough board shacks. By 1774, in spite of adverse conditions, the list had grown to the dozens. Southern Maine was thickly dotted with villages, real villages boasting churches, shops, painted houses and—of course—taverns. These far from luxurious institutions were a necessity of the times. They provided rather Spartan lodgings for travelers, but, more important, they served as social and political centers for the communities. Court and Town Meetings were usually held in the taverns, the only buildings large enough to accommodate such gatherings. Naturally, ale and rum—the drinks of the day —were consumed there, but such consumption was under control. Drunkenness was not only frowned upon; it was punished by a period in the stocks, during which the erring brother had ample opportunity to repent his ways. Moreover, the tavern was usually next door to the church, a constant reminder of the wages of sin. This was not accidental. The permit to keep a "house of Common Entertainment" usually ended: "provided he keep it near the meeting-house." This proximity was to confound the Devil, who presumably would flee the vicinity of churches.

The settlements clustered most thickly along the shore. This was natural, since in the total absence of roads the sea remained the thoroughfare. All up the ragged coastline they blossomed —Kittery, Wells, York, the Berwicks. Near South Berwick was one of the earliest sawmills in America, and the first to use gang saws. This innovation enabled the crews to speed up production prodigiously, or, in the language of the times, to "perform great works." The boasting of the sawyers about their prowess was so loud and continuous that the neighboring towns rather acidly referred to the little hamlet around the mill as Great Works, and that's what it is still called today, long after the saws are silent. Wiscasset, Rockland and Ellsworth; Hancock, Sullivan and Jonesport; further and further Down East they spread.

Furthest was Machias, on the site of the short-lived early fur trading post of the Plymouth Pilgrims. After the French had wiped that out, Rhodes, the pirate, used the sheltered inlet of the Machias River—which means Little Bad River—as an occasional base. The location lent itself very well to use as a hideout for pirates, who do not court attention. It was screened from observation from the sea by islands and a winding approach, and had a plentiful supply of fresh water and an excellent beach for careening ships. Rhodes touched at Machias only when he needed rest or repair work done, but he was followed by the notorious Samuel Bellamy, who had more ambitious plans for the place.

During the French and Indian Wars, privateering was very common on both sides. Cotton Mather, in one of his famous "hanging sermons," warned the English of Massachusetts that in encouraging privateering they were laying the ground for out-and-out piracy, from which they themselves would suffer equally with their enemies. He argued that the stopping and plundering of ships at sea for the benefit of the government was only a short step away from doing the same thing for personal benefit, a step that an agile and unscrupulous mind would have no difficulty in taking. He was absolutely right. A great many privateers turned their backs on the law and became real pirates. The advantage was much greater gain for themselves, but there was the slight disadvantage of having every man's hand, including that of their own government, against them and of being unwelcome in every port in the world.

Bellamy had no intention of spending the rest of his life on the run. Inspired by the example of Mission, who had formed his own independent kingdom in Madagascar, Bellamy planned to make the region around Machias an absolute monarchy where he would rule undisputed, living a life of ease on the loot taken by the vessels he would send out from time to time to prey on shipping. His first step was to fortify Machias strongly and to build comfortable living quarters for himself and his men. Then he sallied forth in the *Whidaw*, his only ship, looking for treasure, recruits and women—especially women. He aimed to provide his kingdom with a better-balanced social structure.

The first ship he sighted was a French corvette of thirty-six guns, bound with troops to Quebec. There was nothing to be gained by attacking her, since she carried neither women nor treasure, and she was much more than a match for the *Whidaw*. But attack her he did, in spite of his many years of experience, which should have taught him better. He was lucky to escape under cover of darkness in a badly damaged ship, with about half his crew dead. Instead of going back to Machias to repair his vessel, he decided to acquire a larger, better one, which he thought he'd probably find to the south in the more traveled trade lanes. Off Outer Cape Cod, he encountered the *Mary Anne*, an unarmed New Bedford whaler, which he captured easily.

Bellamy had somehow, over the years, managed to convince himself that there was nothing morally wrong with piracy, that it was simply a fair means of redistributing the wealth of the world. He was so enamored of this doctrine that he showed true missionary zeal in spreading it. He always addressed the crew of any ship he captured, explaining his viewpoint carefully and giving any who wished to do so an opportunity to join his organization. When the *Mary Anne*'s captain, an upright and honest man, heard the golden sales pitch, he concluded that Bellamy was insane and had better be humored. His talented enactment of the role of enthusiastic convert fooled Bellamy completely.

All this took place off Eastham, Massachusetts, in a dangerous area of shoals and tide rips with which Bellamy was unfamiliar. He asked his new recruit to hang a lantern over the stern of the *Mary Anne* to pilot the *Whidaw* into deeper waters. The *Mary Anne*'s skipper drove his ship onto the bars, and the *Whidaw* piled up beside her. With the aid of Cape Codders who came out from the beach in boats, Bellamy and his crew were captured, eventually to be tried and hanged.

No one returned to Machias until after the fall of Quebec, when a group of settlers from Scarboro moved down along the coast to the secret and hidden estuary. They found the old fortifications fallen into ruins and overgrown with grass and bindweed, and they built their tidy little town on the foundations of Bellamy's kingdom. But to this day the outlines of the pirate stronghold can be traced along a series of dips and mounds that were the old moats and breastworks.

In the very early days, the islands along the coast were often chosen by settlers as being the safest places to live, the least liable to surprise attacks by enemies. The first settler of the Casco Bay area, Christopher Leavitt, spent his initial winter of 1623 on House Island, simply because he and his ten men felt more secure where they could see what was going on around them. When the Indian raids were at their worst, colonists frequently fled to the islands for safety. Many returned to the mainland when the danger was past.

Some, however, found that they liked island living, and stayed on. They all handled boats well; that was a prerequisite of successful coastal living, where fishing was a principal means of livelihood. So the sea around them was never a barrier. It was in times of peril a protective moat, and at all times a safe and easy highway to wherever they wanted to go. There was no need to fence cattle, who could not roam further than the beach, or to worry about wolves and bears, who seldom swam across the channels. The sea with its rich harvests lay all around them, an extension of the unwalled fields of corn and squash. On an island, a man felt free and independent, at home in his own plainly bounded little world that he knew intimately. Everything he needed was there, almost within reach of his hand.

So many of the islands from the New Hampshire border to the mouth of the St. Croix River were inhabited years before the Treaty of Paris—Peaks Island and Great Chebeague in Casco Bay; Long Island and Vinalhaven in Penobscot Bay; far-out Matinicus and nearby Louds Island; and Beals Island, *way* Down East. They all have much the same history. Someone came, and saw, and fell in love with a sea-girt domain of ledge, fir copse and salt meadow; and he made it his own, clearing fields, building a low, staunch farmhouse, planting fruit trees and rafting cows and pigs across from the mainland. Friends or relatives joined him; or his sons married off-island and brought their wives home to live, until there was a small, congenial community, snug in its tight, tide-washed world. These were the happy islands, the islands that had no particular history.

Some islands, though, were special cases. The Isles of Shoals were one. There are eight islands in this pod—as they continue to say Down East—of which five lie in Maine. Undoubtedly they were used as fishing bases by the Portuguese and others long before Maine was settled. The fish schooled, or shoaled, there in vast numbers, so fishermen fell into the habit of referring to them for convenience as the islands where the fish shoaled, or the Isles of Shoals. The name stuck.

The treeless, rocky islands were ideal for drying fish, so the first inhabitants were naturally the seasonal fishermen, who lived a monastic life on the sun- and spray-drenched ledges. In fact, they had a rule forbidding the bringing of goats, pigs, cattle or women onto the islands. They didn't want livestock running loose and messing up their drying stages, and they evidently didn't want women running loose and messing up their peace of mind. They liked things the way they were. But in 1647, a man named Reynolds had the temerity to take to the isles a pig, a goat and his wife. The law was invoked, and the case finally went to the General Court of Massachusetts, which handed down the decision that Reynolds had to get rid of his animals, but his wife could stay as long as she behaved herself.

This opened the door to other wives, and by 1700 four or five hundred persons lived on the islands. Among them were the Pepperells, and it was here that Sir William Pepperell of Louisburg fame was born. Perhaps because the women, who usually set the standards of behavior, were there on sufferance and so felt that they had to make a special effort, the barren islands supported the best-run town in the Province of Maine. The government by Town Meeting was free from graft, the economy was sound, the church was active and influential, and the schools were so good that thoughtful parents on the mainland sent their children to the Isles to be educated. The Shoals were almost the Ideal Republic, where not even man was vile. Later the place was to fall on evil days, a byword and a hissing for immorality and dark practices. But up until the Revolution it was the perfect example of democracy at its working best.

Another island with an unusual history was Champlain's Isle des Monts Deserts, Mount Desert Island, where the Jesuit Fathers, Biard and Massé, had their ill-fated little Mission de St. Sauveur. At that time the island was owned by the Madame de Guercheville who financed the mission. She had bought the property from du Gast, the founder of the Dochet Island colony, who in turn had received it by grant from Henry of Navarre and France. When Argalls destroyed St. Sauveur, he also claimed Mount Desert for England. It was an uneasy possession. Owning it, the English thought they ought to do something about it, so the Pilgrims made a halfhearted attempt to establish fur trading posts there. They were unsuccessful. The Indian friends of Biard and Massé were not very cooperative, and the French were too close for comfort. So the great and beautiful island remained virtually uninhabited until about 1688.

Madame de Guercheville and Massachusetts both considered themselves owners of Mount Desert, but the King of France, with royal blandness, decided that it was really his, and that he would give it to one of his favorites, the capable and elegant Sieur Antoine de la Mothe Cadillac. Cadillac had dreams of establishing a feudal domain on Mount Desert and actually did live there for a while with his wife, a retinue of servants and a company of what were really serfs. The island proved ill-suited to Cadillac's plan, so he moved on to found Detroit and eventually to become the Governor of Louisiana. His brief stay on the spectacular island, however, made a lasting impression on him. To the day of his death, he signed himself *Seigneur des Monts Deserts*. He made a lasting impression on the island, too. The highest of the several peaks is still known as Cadillac Mountain, and a number of real-estate titles today trace back to Cadillac ownership.

When Cadillac vacated the island, some of the serfs remained behind, freemen who gained their living largely from the sea. The many little harbors—Seal, Northeast, Hull's Cove and others—were typical French fishing villages. It was in Southwest Harbor in the year 1753 that a French frigate rode out a storm. One of the ship's officers—according to legend, dashing and handsome—became involved with a village girl. When the frigate departed, she was pregnant and subsequently gave birth to a son. Like naïve and foolish girls everywhere who take up with sailors, she thought this was True Love. She spent the next seven years waiting for her lover to come back, marry her, legitimize their child and sail them triumphantly off to France.

When the boy was seven years old, another ship sailed in from France. Aboard her was an emissary of the family of the child's father, come to claim him and take him back to France. There he would receive the advantages due the scion of a noble family, if his mother would relinquish all rights to him forever. It is difficult to imagine any woman handing over her child to a stranger, to be sailed over the horizon and out of her life, but, perhaps overawed by the gold braid and lace, that is what she did. The boy grew up to be Charles Maurice de Talleyrand-Périgord, Prince de Bénévent, and one of France's greatest and shrewdest statesmen. Is it possible to credit the wiliness for which he is particularly famous to his mother's down-to-earth, crafty peasant stock?

When Quebec fell, Mount Desert passed into the hands of the Massachusetts English. Massachusetts gave the island to her Governor, Sir Francis Bernard, as a reward for his services to the Crown. All the French went away, and the English began to filter in. The first was Abraham Somes of Gloucester, Massachusetts, who had sailed Down East to cut barrel staves. He found the long, beautiful fjord winding deep into the heart of the island, and was so impressed that he came back with his family and settled there. Somes Sound and Somesville, which is one of the prettiest villages anywhere, are named for him.

Many of the new settlers from Massachusetts, New Hampshire or England were like Somes. They preferred living alone in a likely spot to the gregariousness of the villages. The whole Down East coast is fringed with fir-crested, rocky points jutting out into the cold North Atlantic, and it was on these that the individualists established themselves, with their backs to the wilderness and their faces to the sea. By walking a few miles down the trace of an old dirt road to the shore it is still possible to find the sites of some of these long-abandoned salt-water farms. They are romantic and fascinating places, lively with happy ghosts, beautiful in themselves and in the past that they evoke.

They are easy to identify, and they all have much in common. There is one that lies at the end of a road so long disused that it is almost lost in briers and brambles. The buildings have rotted away, and the fields are growing up to blueberries, meadow rue, steeple bush and little fir trees; but struggling bravely in the midst of the encroaching forest are a few ancient, unpruned apple trees, flying pennants of pink-and-white blossoms or bearing a scattering of gnarly, sour fruit. A lilac, grown to tree size and fully twenty feet across its sprawling base, stands beside the stone-faced cellar hole. It is a lovely thing in spring, its old branches heavy with purple spikes, splashed bright against the dark woods. Lemon lilies still grow along the old foundations, honeysuckle run wild spills over into the cellar, and old-fashioned yellow roses drop their petals in the stillness. Almost smothered in the weeds and matted grass there are still a few straggling sweet william, foxgloves, spice pinks and Johnny-jump-ups. The pioneer men brought their guns and axes with them; the women brought their courage and roots and seeds from the gardens back home to lend grace to their new life.

On the seaward side of the cellar hole is a huge, flat granite slab that was the step to the vanished door. All the early settlers were almost obsessed with what they called "sightly locations," locations with a view. With so little of luxury and loveliness in their lives, they had the wisdom to grasp one beauty that was free and priceless. Seated in the sun on the warm granite step, with the scent of southernwood, fennel and marjoram from the old herb bed sharp in the nostrils and the panorama of cove and islands and sea spread out before the eyes, it is easy to reconstruct the life that was lived in this place so long ago.

From the step what was once a path leads to the well. It can still be followed. So many feet traversed it so many times a day for so many years that the earth bears a permanent impression. The wooden housing of the well is gone, but the masonry is as sound and the water as cold and sweet as they ever were. Below are the pastures where the cows and the wiry scrub sheep and the oxen once grazed. The early settlers stuck pretty closely to the accepted, conventional names for their animals. Oxen were Bright and Star. Dogs were Rover or Tray. A horse not named Dobbin or Whitey was rare, and it was reasonably safe to address any cow as Buttercup or Daisy. At the bottom of the pasture is the cove, glinting empty in the sun now, the long-legged wharf that once stood on the shore long carried away by time and the tides. Once it was busy and noisy. A salt-water farm without a boat was as unthinkable as a modern farm without a pick-up truck, and for some of the same reasons. She provided a means of transportation for family and produce and often served as a source of added income. In addition, she was absolutely essential to a livelihood that depended on the sea as much as on the land.

So almost as soon as the house was finished, there was a boat

under construction on the ways at the foot of the pasture. The
farmer and his sons cut the timber in their wood lot up back
during the winter and dragged it down to the shore over the

deep snows. In the spare moments of the spring and summer between planting and haying and harvest, they worked on their
boat. When she was done, they launched her and named her, for
their sister or mother, or for a girl back home. One was named
The Ten Brothers, after the ten boys of the family that built her.
Thereafter the boat rode at her mooring in the cove below the
house, a matter of pride, a pretty sight, a margin of safety from

all sorts of dangers. She was bound to be a good boat, but if she had her little whims and crankinesses, they would be corrected in the building of her successor. Almost nobody stopped at building one boat.

In the building, the boys were learning. When it came time for them to leave home, they would be qualified, if they saw fit, to find good employment in the commercial shipyards to the west —at Kittery or Brunswick or Bath, where contract building was now being done. Bath was the big place, with its three-mile Long Reach, where the banks sloped at just the right angle for ways and launchings and the protected channel ran in close and deep to the shore. Ever since William Swanton had launched the first full-rigged ship, the *Earl of Bute*, there, the waterfront of Bath had rung with the sound of hammer and saw. More ships were built on the Long Reach than on any other three-mile stretch on earth; until finally the English shipwrights appealed to the King to restrict shipbuilding in Maine, because the competition was ruining them.

Sitting on the granite step, one can almost see the boys of that early family, sprawled on the ground, chewing long blades of grass, waiting for dinner and listening to the oldest brother just back from the shipyards tell about Bath. He describes the yards, and the busy streets, and the foreign ships, and the wild excitement of a launching. Then he lowers his voice so that his mother and sisters busy in the kitchen cannot hear him through the open door and tells of riotous sailors ashore after months at sea, and drunken sprees, and women no better than they should be. The brothers listen, goggle-eyed, until their mother calls them to dinner. "Fish chowder," she says. "Come get it while it's hot."

Fish was standard fare, since fishing was one of the family's occupations and fish was always available. What fresh fish they needed they ate, and the rest they dried or pickled in brine. Some they kept to see them through the lean winter, but most of it they sold to one of the big traders, who exported it to Europe or the West Indies. In return they received sugar, tea, rum, molasses, tobacco and other of the few things they did not produce themselves, and a little cash. The corned fish, or cor-fish, was packed in barrels of their own making from their own wood, and the dried fish was graded according to quality. The good, standard grade consisted of large, perfect specimens dried slowly until the flesh was almost translucent. The culls, smaller fish or those that had been salt-burned in the curing, were called refuse fish and sold at about half-price. There was a big demand for them, though. They were perfectly good and edible, and plantation owners of the West Indies bought enormous quantities for food for the slaves. Then there was the best grade of all, dun-fish or dark fish, produced with painstaking care in small lots and therefore very expensive. Dunfish was summer pollock, lovingly cured on the rocks with very little salt and then aged in a dark place under a mat of salt marsh hay. This darkened the color and gave the fish a special, subtle flavor. It was the fish of epicures. The family did not bother much with dunfish. It paid out well, but there was too much else to do around the farm to give it the time and care it needed. They left its making to such as William Pepperell, who had seen the business wisdom of catering to the European carriage trade, specialized in dunfish, and made a fortune thereby.

After dinner the family scattered about the never-ending tasks of the farm. A couple of the younger boys might go back to hoeing the corn, or to collecting hemlock bark for the tanning of the deer hides from which their womenfolk would make jerkins and moccasins, or to hauling rockweed up from the shore to mulch the gardens. If it was churning day, the girl who had the magic hand with butter brought the churn outdoors where she could talk as she worked with her sisters, sitting on the step as they knit stockings or did the mending. When the butter "came," she pressed it in cheesecloth, washed it with cold well water, salted it and packed in tubs of fir wood, the only wood that imparted no flavor to contents. The buttermilk, rich with yellow flecks of butter, was poured into stone jugs and lowered into the well for cool keeping. There was nothing like cold buttermilk—or a concoction of vinegar, molasses and water called switchel—to see a man through a hot haying.

Behind the girls, their mother stood in the open door for a moment before going back to the length of linsey-woolsey that she had on her loom. She could see over the heads of her daughters the open pasture, the sparkling cove, the islands that float like basking whales off shore, and the faraway, empty horizon. But if she was thinking with longing of the land where she was born, a world way below the curve of the earth, no one would ever know. This was her home now.

The older boys and their father had gone up back of the house to the wood lot. They walked with the stealth and talked in the hushed tones of conspirators in an illegal enterprise; and that was exactly what they were. They were planning to break the mast law, to destroy a huge white pine that had been marked by the mast agent's surveyor with three ax slashes roughly in the shape of the broad arrow that identified property of the British Admiralty. They felt no guilt at all. The pine, measuring thirty inches at the base and towering straight and flawless high above the lesser trees, was on their own land. It was in the way, right where they planned to clear for another pasture; and they needed the wood for the building of a new ell to the house. It was their pine, to do with as they chose, they felt.

But the King had decreed otherwise. For a long time the

Royal Navy had been suffering from a shortage of masts, a shortage acute enough to endanger national safety. So the King had first sent out a Surveyor of Pine and Timber to make an inventory of standing Maine mast pines within ten miles of the coast or any navigable river. The surveyor had reported that there were plenty of masts, but that the settlers were "causing great havoc in the tymber" by cutting down the giant trees and sawing or splitting them up for clapboards, shingles, floorboards and beams. Consequently, in 1691 a new restriction had been placed on the colonists. Thereafter all white pine with a diameter of twenty-four inches or over at a foot from the ground was reserved for the Crown. To prevent misunderstanding, such trees were plainly marked with the broad arrow, and anyone caught cutting one was liable to a fine of one hundred pounds.

It was fairly easy not to get caught. The vanished house that stood on these foundations had been floored throughout with beautiful wide boards, each one trimmed down to just under the illegal width, in case a spy of the mast agent came snooping around. The trees from which the house had been built had been felled with bold effrontery and quickly cut up to nondamning dimensions. The building of the ell was less urgent, so more devious methods could be employed. As they walked along in the shadow of the woods, the father and his sons discussed ways and means. They could start a brush fire at the base of the pine, and so ruin it for mast purposes. There would still be plenty of good wood left for planks and rafters. Or they could clear away all the smaller trees around the pine and leave it standing alone. Tall as it was, its roots had very shallow penetration. Below the thin covering of soil lay solid rock. Without the protection of the wind-breaking growth around it, it would come toppling down of its own accord in the next high gale. It would be so strained and weakened by the thundering crash that it wouldn't be fit for a mast, but it would serve nicely for the new ell.

The boy from Bath looked up at the tree. Seemed a pity, in a way, he told the others. A tree like that was worth five hundred dollars to the Admiralty. He had been up to Freeport one time, and seen them balking masts down to the harbor, masts not so good as this one. Twenty-six yoke of oxen it had taken to move some of them, and they had to build the village around a funny-shaped common to give room for swinging the masts down to the landing. They treated those pines like they were made of glass, up to Freeport. Spent days building beds of snow and brush to cushion their fall, lest they be racked. The King must need masts powerful bad. His agents paid good cash wages to any who wanted to go into the woods, masting.

His father probably looked at him impatiently. "The King's got a-plenty of masts. This here one's ourn. He don't worry none about us. We got no call to worry about him." All along the coast the settlers were beginning to think and say things like that in the years before 1775.

When it came time for the next oldest boy to leave home, he may have decided to go up to Rockland and try his hand at kiln-wooding. It was getting so that a man had a choice of occupation along the coast of Maine. Since 1773, when William McIntyre built the first lime kiln at Thomaston, the new industry of lime-burning had boomed. There were huge deposits of good limestone all through the Rockland-Thomaston area. Since it required thirty cords of wood to fire one kiln, a sister industry had developed—that of cutting and delivering kiln wood. It required little cash outlay. Any old slapped-together sort of boat would do. It didn't have to be very seaworthy since it never left the safe inshore waters, and in any event, its buoyant cargo would keep it afloat. The wood was piled so high on the decks of these makeshift craft that they looked more like floating wood piles than anything else. The helmsman could seldom see over the pile to steer his course, so he hired a boy for a few pennies to sit on top and shout directions. Kiln-wooding was one occupation that was reasonably safe as well as profitable.

Sailing in the lime schooners was another story. These vessels were built with great care, because lime, if it got wet, would smolder and smudge and finally burst into flame. So the bottoms of the schooners were built double to keep the cargo out of the bilge, and the decks were double to prevent seepage from above. Even in his sleep, a man on a lime schooner sniffed constantly for the faint odor of slaked lime. At the first whiff, the entire crew got busy sealing every crack in the vessel with calking, old rags or anything else they could lay hands on, to starve the fire of oxygen, while the captain made all speed to the nearest harbor. There he anchored well away from the other shipping, and all hands gathered their possessions and hastily abandoned ship. Ashore, they sat around and awaited developments. Sometimes the ship suddenly exploded into raging fire, and that was that. If she was still afloat after two or three months, it was generally assumed to be safe to continue the voyage. Transporting lime was a chancy business at best. The boy who chose that as a career had plenty of adventures to recount on his visits back to the farm.

He may have brought news of what happened in Falmouth, later Portland, when he was there with the schooner in 1765. For some reason that he never quite understood, a mob seized and destroyed all the tax stamps in town. They said that they could not be taxed without their own consent and that the tax was "a dark design framed to abridge their English liberties."

The words sounded strange and meaningless as he repeated them, here in this quiet, sweet-scented clearing with its view of the sea. The cattle grazed with their heads to the wind as always, the gulls soared over in shining spirals, the surf broke on the reef that guarded the cove, and bees from his mother's hive crawled heavily in and out of the hollyhock blossoms. Falmouth and the angry voices seemed very far away. Surely the winds of that little squall of violence would never blow upon them here.

5. THE ENGLISH TROUBLES

The burning of the tax stamps at Falmouth was a foreshadowing of things to come. In the next decade the colonists, who had been carrying chips on their shoulders ever since England gave Louisburg back to France, collected a long list of petty grievances that added up to a generally resentful, if not overtly hostile, attitude toward the Crown. By 1774, the citizens of more and more towns from Saco to Machias were registering protests against taxation, carrying the offending stamps about the streets at the end of ten-foot poles before the ceremonial burning, to indicate their repugnance. The temper of the times was tricky and unstable, and in 1775 it exploded.

By this time Falmouth was an active and rapidly growing city, the natural shipping point of the furs, fish, lumber, farm produce and masts from the whole Province of Maine. No other colonial city, not even Boston, was busier or more prosperous. The majority of the people harbored sentiments against the British, but there were a few there as elsewhere who remained loyal to the King. Among them was a shipbuilder named Coulson, engaged at the time in constructing and outfitting one of the specially designed vessels for transporting masts to England. Masts were very definitely vital war materials, and while war was not yet a fact, it was a strong probability. So a committee waited on Coulson and attempted to restrain him from completing his project, arguing that exporting masts was giving aid and comfort to the potential enemy.

The British sloop-of-war *Canseau* was in the harbor, as it happened, and Coulson appealed to her captain, Henry Mowatt, for help and protection. What Mowatt intended to do about it is not certain. The chances are that he regarded this complaint as just another local teapot tempest that would blow over if he disregarded it. Not taking the matter seriously, he was unaware that feeling in the city was running high against him and so saw no reason why he should not follow his usual routine, which included an afternoon stroll with the ship's surgeon about the streets on Munjoy Hill. Some hotheaded zealot spread the word that Mowatt was spying on the activities of the city, and he was roughly seized and thrown into jail. His incarceration was short. He was released as soon as he promised to return when summoned for trial.

Trial day came and went, but Mowatt was elsewhere, thinking

over the treatment accorded him by Falmouth and getting madder by the minute. Five months later he reappeared with a small fleet of fighting ships, intent on revenge. A state of war had now existed for several months, so Mowatt's actions were technically allowable. He issued a warning that he would start firing on the city in two hours, which time the residents would be wise to employ in evacuating themselves and their valuables. He refused to consider any of the truce terms offered him by a frantic citizenry and on the dot of 9:30 A.M., October 18, 1775, poured everything he had—cannon balls, bombs, grapeshot—into the city. After dark he sent ashore mopping-up parties to burn any structures still left standing. All the public buildings—the customhouse, the courthouse, the town hall—were destroyed, along with the great warehouses and valuable shipyards along the waterfront, and more than four hundred private homes. Two thousand people were left homeless and without means of support.

One building did survive, and not by accident. This was Greely's Tavern, owned and operated by the Widow Alice Greely. Tavernkeeping was no occupation for a lady, but Alice Greely did not pretend to be a lady. Toughness, muscle and a disinclination to take any back talk from anybody were necessary to the maintaining of order in a seaport public house in those lusty days, and Dame Alice possessed those qualities in good measure. No puffed-up British captain was going to order her around. While her neighbors were hastily gathering their belongings and fleeing into the country, she was filling all her buckets, pots and pans with water. Then she sat down and waited. When the bombardment began, she was ready. As soon as a flame broke out on the tavern roof, she hiked up her skirts, scrambled up a ladder and put it out, swearing and joking bit-

terly all the while. Her tavern was the only public building to
survive Mowatt's fire, and County Court and other such as-
semblies were held there throughout the Revolution and until a
new courthouse was built in 1787. The tavern continued to be
a landmark in Portland and a memorial to rough-and-ready Alice
Greely well into the present century.

The spirit of rebellion was not confined to the western cities
and towns of the Maine coast. Far to the east, in little Machias,
the same yeast was at work. Early in the Revolution, less than
two months after the Battle of Concord and Lexington had
brought matters to a fighting pitch, Machias stood up to be
counted. This is remarkable, really, because the village was remote from the trouble centers and, because of distance and the
slow and haphazard transmission of news, not at all sure of events
or informed as to the issues at stake. The citizens would have had
every reason for considering the war none of their business, a
faraway and unreal affair of Massachusetts origin that they
would do well to ignore. Nobody would have blamed them.

In June of 1775, the British sent to Machias for some lumber
required for new barracks for the troops in Boston, a routine
request. This time, however, there was some disagreement about
filling the order. While some saw no harm in sending the lumber
as usual, others wanted to refuse, if only as a token protest to
the King's policies. A summer gathering place of the men of the
vicinity was on the bank of a little brook that flowed through
the village, and here they all met, informally, to discuss the matter. The meeting was typical of all such to this day in Maine,
whether they take place at the town watering trough, in the
post office, or around the pot-bellied stove of the general store.
Everyone said his say and then said it again with variations and
ramifications and the reciting of precedent and the prophesying

of dire repercussions. This can go on for hours with no conclusions reached.

Finally a Benjamin Foster became impatient with the endless
talk. He gathered himself together and leaped across the brook.
The time for shilly-shallying was past, he said. Either a man
bowed his neck to the British oppressors or he had no dealings
with them whatsoever. He himself was one of the latter, and
those who agreed with him would so indicate by jumping the
brook and standing at his side. Some crossed immediately and
some had to think it over, but in the end all the male population
of Machias was on Foster's side of the brook, and the village
was committed to the Revolution. The stream is still known as
Foster's Rubicon.

Having made up their minds, the men went back into the
woods, cut a tall pine and erected a Liberty Pole in the town.
This was the customary way of declaring revolutionary lean-
ings throughout the colonies. A few days later there arrived in
the harbor the British cutter *Margaretta* and two sloops, the
Polly and the *Unity*, loaded with supplies owned by a local
merchant, Ichabod Jones. Captain Moore of the *Margaretta*
—described as "a snip of a boy"—ordered the Liberty Pole
taken down or else, the *or else* being that if it were not taken
down, he would not permit the supply ships to be unloaded.
This high-handed ultimatum infuriated the men of Machias, and
they determined to show Moore what was what by seizing the
sloops *and* the *Margaretta*.

Moore discovered the plan and put to sea rather than fight.
Forty men under an old Indian fighter named John O'Brien
promptly gave chase in the *Unity*. This was a foolhardy thing
to do. The *Margaretta* was armed with sixteen swivel guns and
four four-pounders. The colonists had twenty muskets with only

three rounds of ammunition for each. The rest of the patriots snatched up the first weapons that came to hand, which happened to be pitchforks, since it was haying season.

The *Unity* overhauled the *Margaretta*, and within minutes the short supply of ammunition was expended. This would have been the sensible time to give up and go home, but instead the *Unity* drew alongside the cutter and her crew leaped aboard. There followed a rather ridiculous hand-to-hand combat in which pitchforks in the hands of the farmers and fishermen were pitted against bayonets in the hands of trained troops. Unbelievably, the pitchforks won, and the *Margaretta* was sailed triumphantly back to Machias, a captive of war. She was rechristened the *Machias Liberty* and, manned by Machias citizens, went out looking for the British *Diligence*, suspected of being in the vicinity.

When the *Diligence* was sighted, she was attended by another sloop-of-war. This fact did not daunt the men of Machias at all. They captured both vessels while they were at it. Then, having more important things to do than chase the British around the ocean, they proudly donated all three ships to the new Continental Congress for the furthering of the war effort.

The actual value of the vessels was considerable, but even greater was the effect of their capture. At the moment, the Continental Congress was sitting in Philadelphia, arguing the feasibility of commissioning a navy. The success at Machias of a small group of untrained civilians swung opinion favorably. Thus Machias won the title of Birthplace of the American Navy; and during the years since, there have been several U.S.N. vessels of various types and classes named *Machias*.

It was during that same year of 1775 that Colonel Benedict Arnold received orders from General Washington to march on

Quebec through Maine and capture the city. The advantage of this approach was, of course, surprise. To carry out his orders, Arnold was given an army of about eleven hundred men from southern New England, Pennsylvania and Virginia. These were all tough and experienced fighters, expert in the use of the long rifle-barreled gun, the tomahawk and the scalping knife. They were good woodsmen, too, in their native bailiwicks. They had no idea, however, of what they were getting into when they undertook to reverse the journey made by Father Druillettes in 1646, when he traveled from Quebec, along the Chaudière, across the height of land and down the Kennebec to establish his mission at Norridgewock.

Arnold's force set out in eleven schooners from Newbury-port, New Hampshire, for Pittston, a few miles below old Fort Western on the Kennebec, where a Major Colburn was building two hundred bateaux on order for the expedition. On the way they were joined by a company of Maine men under the command of Samuel McCobb of Georgetown. These Down-easters had already tasted British blood. In June of the same year they had marched to Boston in an amazing six days to participate in the Battle of Bunker Hill. Now in September, hearing of Arnold's plan, they wanted in. They liked to fight and, more important, they knew Maine and had some idea of the difficulties that lay ahead. While the others were more or less in a state of euphoria about the whole thing, seeing it as a glorious adventure, McCobb's tight-lipped outfit viewed it more soberly. They had a chance of success, they figured, or they would never have come. But they alone knew that it was going to be difficult.

The fact that the expedition was launched by a giant, three-day barbecue at Fort Western on September 23-25 gives some idea of the pleasure-jaunt attitude that prevailed for the time being. This was quite an affair. The Indian girl Jacataqua, who was serving as a guide because of her infatuation with Aaron Burr, a member of the forces, shot three bears, which were roasted whole. There was plenty of venison, beef, pork and wild fowl as well. All the settlers of the neighborhood contributed green corn, melons, potatoes and smoked salmon, while their wives baked up hundreds of loaves of bread and pumpkin pies. Everybody for miles around attended the festivities, which were enlivened by frequent toasts and bursts of song. It was a very gay occasion.

Jacataqua was not the only woman to accompany the expedition. There were other Indian women as well, and many of the white men took along their wives. Almost everyone who owned a dog took it, too. Considering the supposedly secret nature of the mission, the company seems unusually large, various and cumbersome.

After the feast, the route to be taken was decided and a band of scouts and Indian guides was sent ahead to blaze the trail to the Chaudière River. There was a slight hitch when Dan Morgan, commander of the Virginians, announced that he and his men would either lead the way or not go at all. Since he could ill afford to lose so many able fighters, Arnold conceded the point, and the march began.

Almost at once it became apparent that the bateaux were not all that they should have been. Because he had not been prepared to build so many small boats on short notice, Major Colburn was obliged to use unseasoned pine and oak in their construction. Moreover, knowing that the plan called for their abandonment at the height of land, he built with less care than he would otherwise have employed. Therefore the seven-passenger craft were unreasonably heavy, handled badly, warped as they dried so that they soon leaked like sieves, and eventually went to pieces under strain. By the time Norridgewock, only fifty miles up the river, was reached, a great deal of the shine had rubbed off the adventure.

At Norridgewock more trouble developed. The army set out with a hundred tons of provisions—five hundred bushels of corn, sixty hogsheads of corned beef, scores of tubs of salt pork and salt fish, even more sacks of dried peas and hardtack, and hundreds of pounds of flour. Now it was discovered that the beef, killed and cured in hot weather, was rotten, and that continual soaking in the leaky bateaux had caused the peas and hardtack to mold and washed the salt out of the fish. Everything had to be thrown away except the salt pork and the flour, so before it was even well started on its way, the army found itself on half-rations. There were still occasional small pioneer farms where cattle could be bought for slaughter, and an occasional moose or bear was killed for meat, but hunting and dickering took time, and time was something they could not afford to waste.

Winter was coming on. Those who had proposed the expedition had not taken into account the climate of Maine. In their experience October and November were lovely months, dry, crisp and invigorating, ideal for strolling through the forest. Autumn in the highlands of Maine is not like that. By the first of October that year, ice in the swamps was as thick as window glass—the worst kind of ice there is, since it will not bear the weight of a man and cuts through clothes, boots and flesh like a knife. Soon it snowed. The Virginians and Pennsylvanians were not used to snow, nor to the iron cold. Many of them contracted pneumonia or dysentery. Those who could still walk were sent back, and the others left in a crude log hospital until they should recover or die.

The rest of the force labored on, cutting their way through dense tangles of blowdown, floundering in bogs, toiling up the height of land. More and more equipment was abandoned— heavy cooking utensils, chests of ammunition, even guns and axes. Game became very scarce, so now the dogs were killed and eaten. It turned suddenly warm, heavy rains fell and streams rose four or five feet in a single night. A third of the dwindling army gave up and turned back, taking with them more than their share of the scant remaining provisions. But at last the survivors—only five hundred now—came out on the Chaudière.

The French inhabitants of the area were sympathetic to the American cause and provided the scarecrow horde with food, shelter and care. Many by this time were barefoot or close to it, so enough moccasins to go round were found. Clothes were mended, illnesses were treated, and for the first time in almost two months the men began to feel halfway human. The rested army was reorganized and continued on to the St. Lawrence. They crossed over at night and stood at last on the Plains of Abraham, before the city they had come to capture.

The garrison stationed at Quebec and the citizens of the city came out on the walls and cheered the Americans, not in derision but as a tribute to the tomfool courage and tenacity that had brought them through the hell of the winter wilderness. This ragamuffin band offered them no threat, so they could afford to be generous. Even Arnold could see how hopeless the situation was. He reluctantly retreated twenty miles and sat down to await Montgomery, who was supposed to reinforce him by sea.

Montgomery arrived on the first of December, but still the invading force waited for a good blizzard to cover their attack. Finally, a month later, it came; and at two o'clock in the morning Arnold and Montgomery advanced on opposite sides of the city. Almost at once Arnold received a cannon ball in the knee and had to be carried to the rear on his men's shoulders, and Montgomery was killed outright. The leaderless men were trapped under the barricades, and two hundred of them were shot down from the high, overlooking windows. A few escaped over the ice of the river, and the rest were captured. Many of them died in prison of smallpox or scurvy. So all the agony in the forest was for nothing, and all the courage was wasted—if courage can ever be said to be wasted.

This march on Quebec was about the only military campaign of any consequence carried on during the Revolution on Maine soil. The war there simmered down to underground resistance in an area that was essentially a buffer between British-held Canada and the better-fortified colonies to the south. Maine was almost unprotected. More than six thousand of her men—a very high percentage of so small a population—were serving on land or sea. They fought at Ticonderoga in 1777 and at Monmouth, Stillwater and Saratoga, where they were present at the surrender of Burgoyne. Nearly every able-bodied man in western Maine took part in the siege of Boston. There is an old letter in the Massachusetts archives, written in reply to an urgent call for additional volunteers from Falmouth, which reads: "Every one who can leave home is gone or going to Cambridge. You must draw on this part of the province for women instead of men, for knives and forks instead of arms."

Over a thousand Maine men were at Valley Forge alone. The army of Washington that went into winter quarters there numbered about eleven thousand. Eleven of the regiments came from Massachusetts, of which Maine was a part at the time. Half the 11th Massachusetts and almost all of the 12th were Maine men. It is difficult to determine the exact number, since in many cases the regimental records do not give a soldier's place of residence. But, 1,008—almost one-tenth of the entire force—are definitely authenticated, and there were certainly more—men with names like Ichabod Hunt and Ebenezer Morton of Gorham, Benjamin Nason of Arundel, Shim Emery of Kittery; plain old Maine names that suited the men who bore them.

The settlers back home seldom knew which way the war was going, so difficult were communications. Most of the time they suspected the worst, since their own coast was constantly raided by British warships from Canada and later Castine, known then as Bagaduce. The British had long been aware of the potential value to them of a strong base midway along the Down East coast, and because there was a strong Tory element in the Penobscot Bay area, Castine was selected. In June of 1779, General Francis McLane set out from Halifax with a fleet of eight ships and a force of nine hundred men to effect the.capture. He encountered no resistance whatsoever from the inhabitants, and immediately began to fortify the place. Shortly thereafter, three sloops under Captain Henry Mowatt of detested memory arrived, so most of McLane's command returned to Canada.

As soon as the authorities in Boston heard about all this, they were filled with alarm. Without waiting for the consent of the Continental Congress, they organized an expedition of privateers to recapture Castine. This consisted of a land force under General Solomon Lovell with Colonel Paul Revere in charge of ordnance, and a fleet of nineteen armed vessels and twenty-four transports under Commodore Dudley Saltonstall. Learning of this plan through their spies, the British at Castine sent word to Halifax that their undermanned post was badly in need of aid, and hastily tried to finish their fort.

The Americans arrived early on the morning of July 28 and landed a party of four hundred men under cover of the dense fog common to the area. Divided into three companies, they closed in on the British position, killing or wounding thirty of the small garrison. If this action had been followed up by the fleet, the place would undoubtedly have surrendered with little further ado. For some reason, Saltonstall stubbornly refused to fight or to cooperate in any way with the land forces. All he did with his 19 ships and 340 guns for the next two weeks was sail up and down the bay, firing token shots from a distance safely beyond reach of the cannon of the fort.

At the end of this period, a British fleet from Halifax under Sir George Collier appeared. Lovell's troops re-embarked, and Saltonstall made tardy preparation to engage in battle. At the first broadside from the British, however, the American vessels, some of them without firing a shot, fled upriver without waiting for a second salvo. In the confusion that followed, most of them were driven ashore, burned or blown up. The demoralized American soldiery scurried into the woods to make their way as best they could back to the safety of the Kennebec settlements. For years, survivors of this farcical campaign were tormented by a snide little ditty that ran:

> We burnt up all our shipping,
> Gave o'er the jolly cruise,
> And through the woods came tripping
> From captured Bagaduce.

As a result of this inglorious affair, Saltonstall was court-martialed and declared unfit ever again to hold a commission, although General Lovell and Colonel Revere were rightly and honorably absolved of all blame; and, reinforced by fifteen thousand fresh troops, Castine remained to the British, who now had almost complete control of the eastern coast of Maine, with the exception of the Machias region.

Tiny Machias, already distinguished for her lack of respect for British might and authority, now made herself even more objectionable, chiefly through the leadership of a man named John Allan. Much has been said and written about the plight of the Tories in the colonies who, because of honest political opinion, overnight were judged to be spies and traitors, were abused and stripped of their possessions and were forced to flee for sanctuary to Canada. Less considered has been the other side of the story. There were in Canada many sympathizers with the American cause who were regarded by their loyal neighbors as equally suspect and who were also driven out of their homes to take refuge among the revolutionists. John Allan, a Nova Scotian, was one of these. He had reason to believe that the British were about to induce the Indians to attack the people of Maine, and he thought that by establishing a trading post where the tribes could be furnished with necessities at a fair exchange, he might possibly be able to keep them at least neutral. He chose Machias for this endeavor.

Allan first went to Boston to ask for support of his plan. When it was not forthcoming, he continued on to Philadelphia by horseback, where he presented his idea to the Continental Congress so persuasively that he was appointed Superintendent of the Eastern Indians and Colonel of the Infantry at Machias. He was promised goods for his trading post, and Machias was designated an official military station to be supplied with two ninepounders and a garrison of three hundred men. Although these promises were not fulfilled to the extent that Allan hoped and expected, armed with them he was able to control the Indians and to prevent the area surrounding Machias from abandoning the fight for freedom. Several times fleets were sent out from Halifax to destroy the defiant little outpost, but none was ever successful. Machias remained a thorn in British flesh.

Nevertheless, the eastern coast of Maine was constantly harassed by British raids. A letter from Allan to General Washington gives some idea of the situation. Allan had gone to Frenchman Bay to bolster the morale of the settlers of that locality and insure their support of the revolutionary cause. For this purpose he called a meeting of the people of the town of New Bristol, now Sullivan.

"These present," he writes in the style of the day,

Voted Unanimously to do their Utmost to oppose the Enemy if they came there. I promised them every Assistance in my power, depending that I should soon be able by assistance from the Westward. Matters appeared Settled & agreeable for the Present. I returned to Machias. But on the 24th the British Ship The Allegiance of eighteen Guns from Bagaduce arrived there. Landed a party of Men about Two in the morning & with most wanton & cruel agravation Burnt Mr. Beans & Capt Sullivan's Houses, taking the Latter Prisoner. A man & woman in an advanced age of Life, the Latter Infirm, both of them Threatened. Not permited sufficient Cloths to Secure them from the Inclemency of the weather. Thus a family in a new Country Rendered miserable by Those Bloody Wretches, nor was it in my power to give any assistance, any further than by promises to Encourage them. The Ship committed several other Depredations, plundered several people & threatened Ruin to every one who in any way opposed their Taking off Lumber.

An additional menace to coastal settlers were what were known as the shaving mills. There is no satisfactory explanation of the origin of this name. The shaving mills, which are mentioned in almost every town history of the area, were simply small boats or barges that plied up and down the coast and rivers

seizing food, livestock, clothing, guns, powder, bullets and anything else that might be useful to the British. No payment, of
course, was forthcoming. While the British were blamed for
all this plundering, evidence points to the regrettable fact that
some of the shaving mills were owned by unscrupulous persons
whose only loyalty was to their own pocketbooks. They were a
type of war profiteer. The majority of the settlers were helpless
victims. They were not in any great physical danger, so long
as they offered no resistance; but it was heartbreaking to have
worked hard raising a crop or a herd, only to have it snatched
away.

The British were behaving in a rather shortsighted manner
that demonstrated a lack of understanding of the Down East
character. The colonists of the Maine coast had no great love for
their Massachusetts sponsors and might have been won over to
the Crown by more liberal treatment. As it was, the policy of
confiscation made these stubborn and independent settlers so
mad that they went to great pains to undermine and sabotage the
enemy. To keep them in order, the English were obliged to
maintain large garrisons in Maine that could have been used to
advantage elsewhere.

The chief reason for this need of policing was the shipyards.
The new American Navy leaned heavily on Maine for fighting
ships. In spite of the British, the Down-easters managed to build
and launch a respectable number of naval vessels, including the
first line-of-battle ship ever to be constructed in this country. She
was the *America*, built at Kittery and presented to the French
Government in appreciation of France's support of the colonies'
cause.

Probably the most famous of these ships was the *Ranger*, a
sloop-of-war carrying eighteen six-pounders, launched at Kittery in 1777, manned largely by Kittery seamen and placed im-

mediately under the command of John Paul Jones. Part of the romance surrounding the *Ranger* undoubtedly arises from the association of her name with that of her first captain. Jones was a far from ordinary man. Handsome, daring, endowed with intelligence and initiative and carrying a faint air of mystery about him, he was of the breed that attracts excitement and adventure, that is bound to move in a haze of legend and glamour. The *Ranger* reflected this glow.

Born John Paul in Kirkbean, Scotland, Jones came to Virginia at the age of fifteen as cabin boy aboard the *Friendship*. Before the voyage was over, he had fallen in love with the sea and ships, a devotion that lasted all his life and dictated his career. The name of Jones was added to John Paul as the result of a confused episode in Tobago, when he was forced to flee the island under an assumed identity to avoid being arrested in connection with the death of a mutinous sailor. The new name stuck, and it was as John Paul Jones that he acquired a reputation as a brilliant shipmaster and tough and resourceful fighter.

When the Continental Congress was considering whom to place in command of the yet unfinished *Ranger*, Jones was an obvious choice. The resolution for his appointment was passed on June 14, 1777, the same day on which the new flag of the United States was officially adopted. One of the very first appearances of the Stars and Stripes was aboard the *Ranger*. On her maiden voyage, she was sent under Jones to carry word of Burgoyne's surrender to the American commissioners in France. There, in Quiberon Bay, her flag received the first formal salute ever given the American colors by a foreign power.

Jones's sailing orders were liberal in the extreme:

We advise you, after equipping the *Ranger* in the best manner for the cruise proposed, that you proceed with her in the way you shall judge best for distressing enemies of the United States, by sea or otherwise. . . . We rely on your ability as well as your zeal to serve the United States, and therefore do not give you particular instructions as to your operations.

Jones took full advantage of this latitude. He sailed the *Ranger*, disguised variously as an English merchantman and a Dutch transport, into the Irish sea and lurked about in wait for British shipping. His list of victims is long, including the very valuable *Lord Chatham* and the revenuer *Hussar*, sent to the French port of Brest under prize crews. Furthermore, in observance of the *or otherwise* clause, he conducted frequent land raids on coastal towns and villages, distressing the enemies of the United States by burning warehouses and other important installations.

This was incidental to his true purpose. He was looking for the English ship of war *Drake*, considered invincible. No American vessel had ever defeated a British warship, and Jones intended to prove that it was possible to do so. He finally caught up with the *Drake* outside Belfast Lough and engaged her in battle. By ignoring accepted rules of sea fights and employing such unorthodox tactics as concentrating fire on the *Drake*'s rigging, rendering her unmanageable, and then raking her decks with musket and pistol fire, he succeeded in capturing her. This first American victory over an English ship of war was a tremendous booster of colonial morale.

Jones went on to an even more flamboyant career which included command of the *Bonhomme Richard* in its victory over the *Serapis*, and the rear admiralship of the Russian navy under Catherine the Great. The *Ranger*, much to Jones's disgust when he heard about it, was scuttled along with other ships of an American squadron to avoid capture by the British during the siege of Charleston in May, 1780. It was an ignoble end for the Maine-built vessel that had taken so proudly the salutes at Quiberon Bay.

It is a little ironic that after the surrender of Cornwallis at Yorktown and the signing in 1783 of the Treaty of Versailles, these dogged patriots of the Down East coast very nearly found themselves Canadian citizens after all. It was agreed that the English should keep all of the old French Acadia which they had acquired at the close of the French and Indian Wars. The English insisted that the western boundary of this area had always been the Penobscot River, although they had flatly refused to entertain this suggestion in former times of French possession. The Americans stood firm on the terms of the original 1621 grant given to Sir William Alexander by James I, in which the St. Croix River was specified as the western boundary of Nova Scotia. Confronted with the actual document, the British felt it unbecoming to dispute a ruling of one of their own kings, so the St. Croix it was and is.

This still left undetermined the ownership of some islands in Passamaquoddy Bay and the Bay of Fundy, a matter that was not resolved until almost sixty years later by the Webster-Ashburton Treaty of 1842. It is hard to understand why Daniel Webster conceded the ownership of Campobello, Grand Manan, and Deer islands to England. The rumor is that he was dined and especially wined so lavishly by his hosts of the British commission that he was operating with somewhat less than his usual clear-eyed efficiency. Whatever the reason, the islands belong to Canada, even though Campobello is only 250 yards from Lubec, Maine, a distance now spanned by a bridge. Actually, the territory involved is insignificant, and our relationship with the Canadians is such that no obstacles are ever put in the way of American visitors to the islands.

6. GOOD-BYE, MASSACHUSETTS

The idea of independence was in the air. Now that the colonies had won their freedom from the remote and often unsympathetic government of England, Maine began to consider the analogy of Massachusetts as an overlord. The two territories were separated by a wedge of New Hampshire soil, and a much greater gap existed between the ways of thinking and living of the populations. The government in Boston had as little understanding of the problems of the Down-easters as the King had had of those of the colonies. Laws designed for Massachusetts had little application to Maine. To all the old grievances that Maine remembered against Boston were added new ones, none of them very serious but all adding up to a sense of being slighted and put upon in the Maine mind. In less than two years after the Treaty of Versailles, the first newspaper in Maine, the Falmouth *Gazette*, was established for the express purpose of promoting separation from the parent state. The object was not accomplished for another thirty-five years, but the *Gazette* was a straw that showed which way the wind was blowing.

In the meantime, Maine grew. The Indians no longer constituted a menace, and millions of acres of ungranted land were now open to safe homesteading and undisputed title. The water privileges, the fertility of the land, the resources of forest and sea and the opportunity for the development of a variety of enterprises fired the imagination of many. Moreover, a Committee of Lands, set up to encourage the Maine-ward trend, was authorized by the Massachusetts government to sell to any would-be settler at a dollar an acre his choice of 150 acres on a river or navigable body of water, or to give him a hundred acres elsewhere on the condition that he would clear sixteen acres a year. This bait proved effective.

The population, which had been 24,000 in 1764, leaped to 229,000 in 1810—almost an explosion. After the adoption of the United States Constitution, Maine became a political district of ninety-three towns and plantations—or unincorporated townships—with eight Congressional representatives. The remnants of the Indian tribes were made wards of the state, as they are today. This served the double purpose of soothing the public conscience and opening up large tracts of land for safe homesteading. Portland Head Light, today the oldest and very likely the most frequently photographed and painted lighthouse in the

Western Hemisphere, was built in 1791. In 1801, the first Maine public library was founded at Castine, and the next year Bowdoin, Maine's first college, opened her doors. In 1809, the first cotton and woolen mills in North America were built at Brunswick and shortly thereafter Maine's first paper mill went into operation near Bangor.

As we know, Maine's economy had always since earliest times depended to a very great extent on the sea and shipping. Before the Revolution, Maine ships engaged in the three-cornered rum-molasses-and-slave trade between Africa, the West Indies and the home ports, and even more widely in the transportation to Europe of general cargoes of fish, cotton, grain, lumber, tobacco, furs and manufactured goods. At the end of the war, this commerce was in a bad way. A great many vessels had been sunk or captured by the British, so that a new Merchant Marine had to be built almost from scratch. This in itself was not too serious a matter, since Maine shipyards were quite capable of restoring the fleet. All it took was time.

The real problem was where to send the new ships. According to the old English Navigation Laws of 1651, no foreign ships—and American ships were now foreign—were allowed to trade with England or any of her many possessions, which included the West Indies. This put an end to the rum and slave trade and to much of the other trade as well. The new Merchant Marine was in the position of being all dressed up with almost no place to go, or at least none of the old familiar places. It was absolutely vital to find new markets, and the only possible place to look for them was the Orient.

Oriental trade had long been a monopoly of the British East India Company, so large and powerful an organization that heretofore no American trader had even dreamed of attempting to infringe upon its territory. Now, however, things were different. Now we were independent and desperate, a good combination for the making of progress. In 1784, Captain John Greene sailed the *Empress of China* from New York on the first direct voyage ever made by an American ship to Canton. China was barely a name to most Americans, and even the highly civilized Chinese nobility, the most cultured people of the world of the day, had never heard of the new little nation on the far shore of North America. But the great merchant princes in their silk robes and black skull caps showed a lively interest in the foreign ship with the unknown flag, seeing in it the promise of a new market for their tea, silks, porcelains and spices. Captain Greene came home with a rich cargo, which he sold at such tremendous profit that all shipowners, including those of Maine, at once determined to go and do likewise.

Thus began a fabulous period in the history of Maine shipping, the glamorous era of the China trade. The first of the Maine ships was the *Portland*, owned by Ebenezer Preble and Joseph Jewett of that city and captained by Seth Storer of Saco. She sailed for the Orient in 1796 with a cargo of beef, salt cod, pickled salmon, barrel staves and "shugar." The invoice of her return cargo is fascinating, if a little baffling. It includes, along with comprehensible articles like bandanna handkerchiefs, items with such wonderful names as Beerboom Gurrahs, fine and coarse Policates, Allabad blue and Chittabudy Baftas.

Some of the old Maine ships that became classic references in the history of the China trade had beautiful names: *Atahualpa*, the famous *Red Jacket*, the *Water Witch*, the *Flying Dragon*, the *Black Squall*. It is no wonder that they cast a spell over Maine coast boys, so that they lived for the day when they would be old enough to sign on a ship and sail off to the other side of the globe. Some of them rose to be captains of their own ships, some came home to settle down ashore, and some never returned at all. There were a great many dangers—typhoons, uncharted reefs, Cape Horn, Malay pirates, to list a few—to be faced by American seamen engaged in the China trade.

European trade had its perils, too. For years the Barbary states of Tunis, Algiers, Tripoli and Morocco had controlled Mediterranean shipping, demanding and receiving tribute from vessels trading in those waters. Even France and England paid annually up to $300,000 in gold for immunity, figuring that this was cheaper and easier than fighting for their rights. While the states were still English colonies, their ships came under the cloak of British protection; but once they achieved independence, this protection was withdrawn. The Barbary pirates took a very contemptuous attitude toward the new, weak little republic, considering its vessels fair and easy game to be preyed on whenever opportunity offered. American ships were confiscated with impunity, and their crews were held for ransom or sold into slavery. There seemed to be little that could be done about it.

The fate of the crew of the sloop *Squirrel* of Saco is a good example. In 1783, the *Squirrel* sailed from Casco Bay, and a few weeks later she was captured by an Algerian corsair. Her captain, Alexander Paine, and his men were taken before the Dey, who gave them the choice of becoming Mohammedans or slaves. With stiff-necked Yankee stubbornness, they refused to have their religious affiliations dictated to them, so they were stripped of most of their clothing and sent to the galleys. Here they were chained to benches and forced to row the pirate galleys, sometimes against their own countrymen, for five years, subsisting on a near-starvation diet of bran bread, goat meat and water.

Finally, during Christmas week of 1787, their galley encountered a French frigate that proved too much for her. As soon as the Algerians realized that they were about to be overpowered, they started butchering their slaves. Seven Americans, although seriously wounded, managed to stay alive until the French rescued them. They were taken to France, nursed back to health, and provided with passage to New York, arriving there in the middle of the winter of 1790. Having no money and no friends in the city, they started walking to Saco, begging food on the way. At last, seven years after they left home, they came back, old and broken men before their time.

A Maine boy was largely responsible for subduing the Barbary pirates. He was Edward Preble of Falmouth. Like many Maine boys before and after him, he ran away from his father's farm to sea at the age of sixteen. It immediately became clear that this was the life for him. When he was only eighteen, he was in temporary command of a sloop-of-war which, during the Revolution, captured against great odds a British vessel lying in the Penobscot. After the war he rose rapidly until in 1803 he was given command of the famous *Constitution* and made commodore of a fleet of seven ships assigned the task of disciplining Tripoli.

Preble first brought the Sultan of the less powerful Morocco to terms and then proceeded to his main objective. The throne of Tripoli was occupied at the time by a usurper, and Preble diplomatically formed an alliance with the rightful heir, who had a small army of faithful followers. While Preble's fleet bombarded the palace, these loyalists, reinforced by a detachment of the United States Army, attacked by land. The pirate pasha recognized the impossibility of his position and capitulated quickly.

In recognition of this service to his country, Congress gave

Preble a vote of thanks and a gold medal; and the Pope, who did not usually concern himself with the activities of Protestant Yankees, said that this young American commander, with a small force and in a short space of time, had done more for the cause of Christianity than the most powerful nations of Christendom had accomplished in ages.

Even before the Tripolitan campaign was over, Preble's health began to fail, and he retired upon his return home. But in the short space during which he had commanded the *Constitution*, he made his mark.

This iron man had a softer side. He fell very much in love with a girl named Mary Deering. Having spent most of his life at sea under rough conditions and in rough company, he was not at ease in the role of ardent suitor. When he was ordered abroad, instinct told him that he should not leave without making his sentiments clear, but he did not know exactly how to go about it. In desperation, he wrote a really touching letter to the girl's mother, ending: "If I possessed a world, I would give it freely for one hour with your family before I go, but that, alas, is impossible. Should Mary Deering bless another with her affections, and not me, I am lost forever—for Heaven's sake, plead for me!" He and Mary were married almost as soon as he returned home.

So many officers later to distinguish themselves in the service of their country received their early training under him that he became known as the Father of the U.S. Navy. He died when he was only forty-six, his health ruined by the rigorous demands he made on himself. His was the longest funeral procession ever seen in Portland, stretching on and on without a single carriage, only sincere mourners on foot, humbly escorting his body.

In 1793 France declared war on England, and the normal hazards of the American sailor—innocent by-stander though he might seem—were immediately increased. Both sides at once started preying on American shipping for sorely needed supplies. In addition, England, fighting for her life and suffering from a manpower shortage, began stopping American ships at sea and kidnaping sailors into her own service. The fiction maintained was that the men impressed were British subjects evading duty by hiding on American ships, but anyone not able to prove conclusively his citizenship was apt to find himself serving under the flag of Great Britain. Even the carrying of what amounted to crude passports—birth certificates and detailed descriptions of the bearer—offered little protection. An English commander in dire need of men to work his vessel simply chose the most likely-looking sailors of an American crew and removed them summarily to his own ship.

It was in the hope of stopping this abuse that the United States Congress pass the Embargo Act of 1807. Supposedly, cutting off supplies would induce England and France to treat American subjects better. The new law was hardest on those it was designed to protect. Maine commerce would have been completely crippled if Maine men had seen fit to comply with it. They complained bitterly, of course, but they also acted on the Down East principle that talk butters no parsnips. They turned their energies and talents to smuggling and blockade running. Almost overnight the tiny town of Eastport, on the Canadian border, became the busiest harbor in the whole United States. Flour was in particular demand in Canada, and in a single week over thirty thousand barrels arrived in Eastport. There was so much that the warehouses would not contain it, and it had to be piled in mountains on the beach. This was more than Eastport would consume in thirty years, yet it all disappeared within a few days. All night and every night a swarm of boats of all types and sizes, from schooners down to rowboats and even canoes, shuttled back and forth across the narrow bay, transporting flour. It was worth four dollars a barrel in the United States, but it brought nineteen dollars delivered on Canadian soil. The police assigned to preventing this traffic were out of sympathy with the law they were upholding and, for a small consideration, were glad to turn their backs. In addition, the British stationed armed vessels just over the international line in Passamaquoddy Bay to protect the American smugglers from their own revenue agents. It was a silly business, but very profitable.

Sometimes, too, a vessel would clear a Maine port with her papers all in order for delivery of her cargo at a destination within the United States. Then she would become disabled, or her captain would find that his compass was out of kilter, or adverse winds would blow her far off course. At last she would be compelled to take refuge in a West Indian port, where the cargo had to be sold to provide money for repairs and passage home. Nobody was fooled by this gambit, but nobody could do much about it either. It was so obvious that the Embargo Act was futile that it was soon repealed and a Nonintercourse Act was substituted. This did not materially change matters. Smuggling continued, and so did the stopping and searching of American ships and the impressment of American seamen.

By 1812, the situation had become intolerable. More than six thousand Americans had been seized and were serving on British warships, and all appeals in their behalf were ignored. The United States was driven by a group of "War Hawks" in Washington to declaring war on Great Britain. This war was obviously going to have to be conducted chiefly at sea, and on the

face of it the declaration appeared rather like the defiance of a
new-born kitten toward a full-grown tiger. The American
Navy consisted at the time of six first-class frigates and six
smaller ships, while the British had almost a thousand fully
armed ships-of-war.

This disparity was not so great as it sounds. England already
had one war on her hands and could not turn her full attention
to smacking down the Americans. Furthermore, within a week
of the declaration, Congress started issuing letters of marque and
reprisal to anybody who applied. These could be considered
licenses to practice piracy, being legal permits for the holder
to capture any English vessel he ran across and felt big enough
to tackle and bring into port, where he would receive prize
money.

This was like finding gold in the street to sea-minded Maine.
Everyone who owned a boat immediately applied for a letter.
From Casco Bay alone a fleet of forty-five vessels sailed forth
under the new sanction. The largest was the *Hyder Ally* of
367 tons, with a crew of over one hundred men and 16 mounted
cannon. But lack of size was no deterrent. There was also the
little *Lark* of four tons, manned by four men with four muskets.
She, too, brought in her prizes and collected her money. Those
who had no ships hastily set about building them, so that the
Navy was very soon augmented by a huge fleet of privateers. In
the first seven months of the war, Americans prowling the trade
lanes of the world captured over thirteen hundred prizes valued
at millions of dollars.

In spite of the great activity of the Maine shipyards and
the Maine privateers, the British did not at first bear down too
heavily on the Down East coast. They entertained the notion
that Maine, which had always been a little wayward, might

remain neutral or even prove helpful. It's a little hard to understand on what this notion was based, since Maine had suffered perhaps more than anybody else from the impressment of seamen. However, actuated by wishful thinking, the British exempted Maine from the blockade that went into operation elsewhere, allowing Maine vessels to pass freely in and out of port. Occasionally British warships even acted as convoys for Maine merchantmen. This is what the brig *Boxer* was doing when she became involved with the American sloop-of-war *Enterprise*.

The incident began when a group of merchants along the Kennebec sent a trading vessel, the *Margaretta*, to St. John, New Brunswick, for a load of the good English wool blankets. This, of course, was in direct defiance of the Nonintercourse Act and was also trafficking with the enemy, facts which the persons involved chose to ignore as being attempts to "prevent a cat from getting hungry by drowning it in a well." This is why the *Margaretta* went stealing along the coast like the smuggler that she was.

An arrangement had been made whereby the *Boxer* would convoy the *Margaretta* back to her home waters to prevent her from being captured by other English warships not in the plot, and for a fee of $500 in gold, the *Boxer*'s captain, William Blythe, undertook a further service. When the *Margaretta* entered the wide mouth of the Kennebec, he opened fire on her. This was to give the impression that she was being hotly pursued and to provide a good excuse for her not to stop at customs, where the nature of her cargo would require considerable explaining. The device worked perfectly. The *Margaretta* flew past Fort Popham with shot splashing in the water all around her, and the garrison at the fort, forgetting all about inspection, opened fire, giving the *Boxer* ample reason for abandoning the chase. And there the matter should have ended, with everybody happy and nobody hurt.

Unfortunately, some fishing vessels in the vicinity heard all the commotion and fled posthaste to Portland, where they knew the *Enterprise* lay. The *Enterprise* had been at Tripoli with Commodore Preble, and had an excellent fighting reputation. She would soon straighten out anybody who was picking on Maine merchant vessels, the fishermen were sure. As it happened, all her older and more responsible officers had been sent to the aid of Commodore Perry at Lake Erie, and she was under the command of Lieutenant William Burrows. He was only twenty-eight years old, had never been under fire, and would probably not have been left in sole charge if there had appeared to be any likelihood of the ship's becoming involved in battle.

When the fishermen came boiling into harbor with their report of firing up the coast, everyone, including Burrows, was carried away with patriotic zeal. Since there were no tugboats at the time, scores of small vessels volunteered to tow the *Enterprise* out to where the light breeze would give her steerageway. The next morning she sighted the *Boxer*, loafing along off Pemaquid without a care in the world. Her captain, Blythe, was only a year older than Burrows, and just as impetuous and full of fight. The two vessels were very evenly matched. To the young captains, the encounter seemed more of a sporting event and a test of skill than a deadly serious business.

All day long they jockeyed for position, and late in the afternoon they engaged near Monhegan Island. Within five minutes Blythe lay dead, and a few minutes later Burrows was fatally wounded. He lived long enough to see the *Boxer*'s masts come crashing down under the expert fire of his batteries, and to receive Blythe's sword in surrender. Then he died, and the *Enterprise*, her flag at half-mast, towed her adversary into Portland harbor.

Although it may seem strange in this unchivalrous day and age, the two boys were given a double funeral of great impressiveness, sharing equal honors. The bodies were brought ashore on black-draped barges, rowed with muffled oars and followed by a slow and solemn procession of all the ships in the harbor. The bells of the city tolled, and the guns of the artillery company saluted at one-minute intervals, all day long. The entire population of the city stood with bowed heads along the route of the cortege. Burrows' coffin was followed by the American seamen, and Blythe's by his own sailors. Everybody wept at the death of youth and courage. They were buried side by side in the old Eastern Cemetery on Munjoy Hill. The stones marking their graves may be seen today standing in the long grass on the quiet, sun-dappled knoll overlooking the sea.

Preferential treatment having accomplished nothing, England then decided that it was time to put on the pressure. A strong blockade was established along the entire coast, effectively putting an end to most shipping. Some trade with Boston was carried on by slow and tedious oxcarts and horse-drawn wagons inching along through dust or mud or snow over impossible dirt roads. The Down-easters retained enough of their wry Yankee humor to refer to this assemblage of snail-slow vehicles as the Mud Clipper Fleet or the Horse Marines, but in spite of the rather lame joke, they knew they faced ruin.

They were further aggravated when Moose Island, on which Eastport is located, was seized by the British on the grounds that it was a part of New Brunswick which they were merely reclaiming. They then resurrected the old boundary quarrel, deciding that the Penobscot was after all the western boundary of Nova Scotia. So they "reclaimed" Castine, which they made into a naval base, and all the towns upriver to Bangor. This gave them possession of all of eastern Maine. From their new strongholds they were able to police the coast thoroughly enough so that Maine was obliged to sit out the rest of the war, contenting herself with minor acts of resistance and brooding all the while on the failure of Massachusetts to provide her with protection during Mr. Madison's War, as it had come to be called.

The War of 1812 ended on December 24, 1814, with the signing of the Treaty of Ghent. Both countries got back the territory they had owned at the beginning of hostilities, but Maine never regained her tolerance of Massachusetts' indifference to her welfare. On May 20, 1816, Maine seceded from the Commonwealth and so informed the Massachusetts Legislature, which refused to take seriously any such childish and irresponsible nonsense. Washington, when appealed to, quoted Article IV, Section III, of the United States Constitution: "New States may be admitted by the Congress into this union; but no new State shall be formed or erected within the jurisdiction of any other State." That should have settled the matter.

But it did not. Maine, existing now almost as a small, independent republic, continued to make such a nuisance of herself for the next four years that finally both Washington and Massachusetts gave in, perhaps from sheer exhaustion. She was admitted to the Union as the twenty-third state on March 15, 1820, a day celebrated throughout Maine for many years thereafter with ceremonies comparable to those of the Fourth of July. These have been largely abandoned, but Maine has not forgotten her long fight for independence, nor entirely forgiven Massachusetts. Often when an unidentified out-of-state car is involved in an accident, I myself have heard the native Down-easters say flatly, *"More'n* likely they come from up Massachusetts way!"

And I have never heard a native give the place of his birth as just plain Maine. It is always the *State* o' Maine, with just that proud emphasis.

Part Two

THE STATE OF MAINE

7. THE FIRST FIFTY YEARS

Maine was a province for well over fifty years longer than she has been a state, but somehow those two centuries of provinciality seem now only a brief and long-ago preparation for Maine's coming-of-age, when her true character would emerge and her true nature be revealed. To some, the Province of Maine seems a wild and dangerous place where settlers were always fighting something—the Indians or the French or the English or Massachusetts or, all else failing, the climate. The people seem almost mythical, though there is ample evidence that they existed in flesh and blood, working hard, suffering, laughing and weeping, loving and hating, just as people do today. Their houses still stand in proof, full of articles that they made with their own hands and used every day of their lives. All kinds of progress was made during those two hundred years—in education and politics and public works and industry. Yet the words "The Province of Maine" evoke visions of log cabins in clearings by the sea, with men in fringed buckskins and women in long homespun skirts going about their simple chores.

That minute in March of 1820 that Maine achieved statehood nothing changed visibly. The log huts were not instantly replaced by gracious mansions, good roads did not immediately penetrate the wildernesses, and the pioneer people did not vanish in a flash, their places to be taken at once by an entirely different breed. Everything went on just as it had been going, in everyday respects. Ships loading in harbors at the fateful moment continued to load and sailed on the next fair tide. Carpenters sawed and pounded nails without a pause. Fishermen continued to set their twine or bait their trawls. Back in the woods, lumberjacks watched the shrinking snow and began to entertain thoughts of the bright lights and gay women of Bangor, at the end of the spring log drive. The same people who had been living in the province went right on living in the state, doing just about what they had always done. No light shone down from Heaven to illuminate the dawn of a new day, and no great chasm opened to divide the past from the future.

Yet the words "the *State* of Maine," spoken with quiet pride, imply that just such a chasm does exist. On the far side are the frontiersmen, the Indian fighters, the unlettered fishermen, the fellers of the King's mast pines. On this side are—well, what *is* the State of Maine?

It is a place, of course. It is over two thousand miles of surf-battered coast, and Katahdin and the Allagash and Moosehead. It is thousands of acres of potatoes in pink and white bloom, and the stately aisles of the Bowdoin pines, and a hill full of semi-precious gems, and veins of silver running under starved fields of

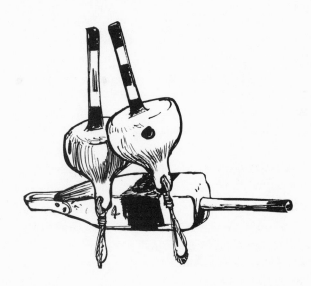

poverty grass. It is shoals of herring glinting in the moonlight, and snow sifting down into silent woods, foot upon unmarred foot, and bears eating raspberries in sunny August clearings and mountainsides ablaze with autumn color.

But Maine is more than a place. It is a way of life. It is getting up before dawn and eating apple pie for breakfast; and painting lobster buoys bright colors and spreading them on a warm ledge to dry; and catching stray cats to cut up for fox bait; and working in an office that looks out over low buildings to the hills or the sea. It is molasses doughnuts and blueberry dumplings, and carrying a glossy horse chestnut in the pocket to ward off aches and pains. It allows for such diversities as Bar Harbor and Bailey's Mistake; as the Jaffa Pilgrimage and New Sweden; as the gentle poet Longfellow and Hiram Maxim, inventor of the modern machine gun; as a horse-drawn plow and the Telstar Earth Station.

The State of Maine is people. They alone did not make the state—not the granite ledges and the eight-day fogs and the lovely lakes stepping like stairs down to the sea—but without them Maine would not exist. So the place to begin is with a person, one who was born in the province and died eighty-four years later a distinguished citizen of the state. He provides an excellent bridge over the imaginary chasm.

William King, born in Scarboro in 1768, was accustomed to making his own way in the world. He had learned early that no one else was going to do it for him. His much older half-brother Rufus, who assisted in the framing of the Constitution of the United States and has been called one of the dozen who contributed most to that document, was a graduate of Harvard and a man of culture and polish, as well as of great intelligence and purpose. By the time little William came along, however, the boys' father had lost all his money and, when William was seven, died. So William went to work in a sawmill, in order to live.

He never went to school. To the end of his life, William King could neither spell correctly nor speak grammatically. He never had time to master these unnecessary refinements. But there was nothing the matter with his intelligence nor his ambition. After a few years, while he was still in his teens, he decided that he was getting nowhere. He had never managed to accumulate the price of a pair of boots, although he had somehow paid the feed bill of a yoke of black steers that was his father's only legacy to him. Arithmetic and the adding of pennies into dollars he had learned, through necessity. Now, seeing no future for himself in Scarboro, barefoot he drove his cattle forty miles along the coast to Topsham, where he found a job doing the only thing he knew, sawmill work.

Things were as different in Topsham as he had hoped they would be. Nobody here knew him or remembered him as the dirty-faced little boy who could be ignored. In Topsham he was accepted at his own evaluation, which was pretty high. Through industry and Spartan frugality he soon owned half a saw, then a whole one, and finally the mill itself. Then he branched out. He bought some timberland and a store, instigated the building of a profitable toll bridge, and became one of the incorporators of the first cotton mill in Maine. He saw that the economical way to ship his lumber, cotton and store merchandise would be in his own bottoms, so he built five vessels. One, the *Reunion*, paid for itself on its first voyage, again on its second, and yet again on its third. Then it, along with its sister ships, settled down to making good and steady money for the owner.

Part of the secret of King's success was his ability to conceive an excellent idea, and then to delegate complete responsibility for carrying it out to someone else. For example, at a time when there were no cotton mills in Maine, because there was no cotton, he saw no reason why raw cotton could not be imported directly from the South and processed locally. So he built a mill and instructed Captain Nathaniel Harding of his *Androscoggin* to go to New Orleans and pick up a load of cotton for it. Harding, who had never been far south, inquired where New Orleans was. King himself had only a vague idea. Another owner might have scurried around trying to find out, wasting his time on a relatively trivial detail, but not King. He told Harding that that was his problem, and Harding—not surprisingly—managed to locate the place and in due course came back with the cotton. The *Androscoggin* was the first Maine vessel to engage in this trade, which continued to flourish for eighty years thereafter.

Topsham became too small for King eventually, and he moved to Bath. Here he acquired stores, warehouses, wharves and shipyards. In order to fill the holds of his rapidly growing fleet, he bought up huge tracts of land and planted them to potatoes, which he sold in the West Indies. He also developed great orchards, chiefly of apples, and exported the fruit to Europe. He organized the first bank in Bath, the notes of which bore, according to denomination, pictures of the various classes of sailing vessels then employed—schooners, sloops, brigs and the like. He was instrumental in founding the first marine insurance company in Maine, represented Bath in the General Court of Massachusetts and was made an honorary general of the Army.

At one time he owned the entire township of Kingfield, in Franklin County, and used as a summer place an old stone farmhouse there. His town house in Bath was one of the most elegant in the country, furnished with treasures brought home by his ships from all over the world—brocades and fine porcelains, priceless rugs and objects of art, French wallpaper and furniture, rare paintings and exquisite silk damask draperies. Here he entertained the intellectual, political and social leaders of the new America. He even acquired, through his cultivated wife, a certain degree of polish, although the cloak of manners never rested very easily on his shoulders.

During the War of 1812, King gave generously of both time and money for the carrying out of measures to protect the Maine coast from the British, and for promoting the idea of separation from Massachusetts. This was not entirely altruistic. As he walked in his bare feet behind his great black oxen on the dusty road from Scarboro to Topsham, King had dreamed the improbable dreams of wealth and power that bemuse all the young. Now he was wealthy and powerful, and it was not enough. Now he had a new ambition, to be the first Governor of Maine. It was toward this goal that he was working with a deviousness rather foreign to his forthright and businesslike nature. He may have been a little too devious. When separation became a fact and the question of governorship arose, some of King's adversaries accused him of violating the embargo and trafficking with the enemy during the war.

King was righteously outraged. With crushing and ungrammatical eloquence he denounced his detractors, showing them to be unreliable and furthermore very probably guilty of the same crimes they were attempting to prove against him. This was almost certainly a case of the pot calling the kettle black. During that war, the embargo was generally violated by Maine traders, smuggling was a blameless and almost respectable occupation, and the voyages of some of King's ships were highly suspicious. But King screamed his innocence so loudly that the matter was dropped as being at the worst not proven. King was duly elected the first Governor of Maine, an office he filled ably and vigorously. He was by no means the only one to contribute to Maine's severance from Massachusetts, nor to her new prosperity, but as first Governor he has become a symbol of the spirit of the time and occasion.

Early in her statehood, Maine was faced with an emergency rising out of the highly ambiguous Treaty of Versailles of 1783. This was the Aroostook War. Very few histories mention this little war at all, and yet it was a real and serious matter that nearly plunged the United States and Great Britain into full-scale conflict. The bone of contention was the boundary line between what were at the time of the treaty Nova Scotia and Massachusetts, but what became New Brunswick and Maine. The second clause of the treaty caused the trouble. It reads:

. . . the said frontiers are and will be as follows:—

From the northwest angle of Nova Scotia, which is the angle formed by a marked line in the North direction, from the source of the Saint Croix River to the plateaus or highlands, and from there along the highest points which part the basins of the rivers which flow into the St. Lawrence from the ones of the rivers which flow into the Atlantic Ocean, to the source nearest the Northwest of the Connecticut River and from there following the middle of this water course as far as the 45th degree of North Latitude.

This was just as vague and confusing as it sounds. The British provincials said that the heights mentioned ran through Mars Hill, about twenty miles south of the Aroostook River, an interpretation that gave Canada more than half of the present Aroostook County. The Americans said that Mars Hill did not divide the waters of the St. Lawrence from those of the Atlantic, so that an entirely different watershed was meant. To this the British retorted that the Bay of Fundy, into which the St. Croix flows, was no more a part of the Atlantic Ocean than was the Gulf of the St. Lawrence. It was perhaps only a question of definition, but over twelve thousand square miles of the richest stands of yellow pine in the world were involved, a treasure that neither country would willingly sacrifice. Although neither maintained it, both were eager to claim it.

In 1817, before Maine became a state, a small group of Americans penetrated the wilderness far up the St. John, to form the little settlement of Madawaska. This hamlet on either side of the river was under nominal British dominion, but it was so isolated that for about ten years neither the British nor the American government paid any attention to it. It existed almost as a miniature republic. A lumberman and builder of frontier sawmills named John Baker, a very forceful character, became the unofficial leader of this remote outpost.

Baker had received a title to his land from the Governor of New Brunswick, but in order to make doubly sure of his rights in this doubtful area, he also applied later to the Maine Legislature for a patent to the same land. This was granted him. He thereupon decided rather high-handedly that since he was an American, anywhere he chose to live automatically became United States territory. On the Fourth of July, 1827, he invited all the American settlers of the surrounding countryside to a celebration of the holiday, one feature of which was the ceremonial raising of the Stars and Stripes over Madawaska.

Word of these goings-on trickled back to the New Brunswick authorities, and there very shortly appeared on the scene a deputy, demanding an explanation of the flag.

"Why, it's an American flag," John Baker told him, "and if you've never seen one before, by God you can stand and look at it just as long as you please."

The deputy was not amused. He ordered Baker to haul down the flag. Baker defied him and New Brunswick and, while he was at it, the King and the British Empire as well. Indignant, the deputy's men chopped down the pole and took the flag off to Fredericton, the capital of New Brunswick. Before they were well out of sight, Mrs. Baker was hurrying off to the Canadian village of St. Basil to buy cloth for a new flag.

New Brunswick retaliated first by accusing John Baker and the other citizens of Madawaska of rebellion against British law, second by taxing heavily all foreign residents of the territory claimed by the province, third by seizing all the timber the Americans had cut along the St. John, and finally by arresting Baker, carrying him to Fredericton and throwing him in jail. Before the boat bearing her husband away rounded the bend of the river, Mrs. Baker started cutting out still another homemade flag. Baker was fined and sentenced to three months in the provincial jail, where, as a concession to his personality, he was allowed the best cell. This, he later reported, was not so comfortable as might be desired, but was probably as habitable as most ordinary prisons. The Bakers, as can be seen, were difficult people to daunt.

Maine complained to the Federal Government, and the Secretary of State, Henry Clay, promised to back the infant state if New Brunswick refused to free John Baker and some companions subsequently arrested. Enoch Lincoln, Maine's third governor, promptly threatened New Brunswick with invasion by the United States Army if "Americans captured on American soil" were not immediately released. Actually, neither England nor the United States wanted to get into another war, so Baker was freed; and King William of the Netherlands, as a neutral and disinterested party, was asked to arbitrate the affair of the border. In 1831 he presented his decision, which was immediately rejected by everyone concerned.

Nothing having been settled, Canadians and Americans alike continued to settle on soil claimed by the other country. Lumbering had now become a huge and profitable business in the disputed area, and too much money was involved to allow things to drift along as they had been doing. In 1839, Governor John Fairfield of Maine submitted a report to the Legislature calling attention to the value of the timber—which he estimated to be over $100,000 in a single winter—being cut and sold by Canadians on Maine territory. He recommended that a land agent be sent to Aroostook with a large enough force to seize the Canadian teams and provisions, break up the lumber camps and "disperse those who are engaged in this work of devastation and pillage."

Such an expedition, headed by the land agent Rufus McIntire, set out, but no sooner had they arrived in Madawaska than they were captured at gunpoint by New Brunswick militia and sent to the Fredericton jail. Infuriated, Maine seized two unwary Canadians, the New Brunswick Warden of Public Lands and a Captain Tibbets of Tobique, and bundled them off to Bangor. Here they were paraded through the streets, but they were not jailed. Instead, they were held in custody at the Bangor House, famous for its fine food and lodgings, where by all accounts they fared extremely well. Maine newspapers made a great point of the difference between gentlemanly Maine and uncouth New Brunswick in the treatment of prisoners.

Up to this point, the whole affair had been a rather schoolboyish calling of names and getting even for real or fancied insults. Now matters took a more serious turn. Since Washington evidently intended to do nothing about Maine's troubles, the state sent ten thousand of her own militia to protect her border. At the same time New Brunswick militia, reinforced by regiments of British troops from Quebec, gathered along the St. John River. Both armies constructed breastworks and mounted cannon. Then they sat back, each force eying the other grimly and waiting for one false move. It would have taken very little— one itching trigger finger, one accidental shot—to blow the situation sky-high and precipitate a real war.

Fortunately, the Federal Government rather tardily awoke to

the gravity of the situation. Congress hastily passed a bill authorizing the sending of fifty thousand troops to support Maine, and the spending of ten million dollars to meet expenses if war became inevitable. The commanding officer was General Winfield Scott, under orders to fight if necessary, but not until after he had exhausted every possibility of arriving at a peaceable settlement of the difficulty.

As it happened, Scott knew Sir John Harvey, the fiery old war horse Governor of New Brunswick. They had fought against each other at Stony Creek and Lundy's Lane, not the worst basis for mutual understanding and even a kind of friendship. Between them, they worked out a highly nonofficial agreement that Aroostook should remain under the jurisdiction of the United States, and all land north of the St. John should belong to Canada. Natural products of the region should be exempt from duty to either nation. Actually, the provisions made and later ratified were almost identical with the proposals of the King of the Netherlands ten years before.

So ended the Aroostook War, without a drop of blood being shed. It is a war that has been laughed at often, and more often ignored. Yet it was a serious matter involving the vital issue of whether the United States Government would allow infringement by any foreign power on the rights of any one of the member states.

And what became of John Baker, so determinedly and aggressively an American? He, of all people, woke up one morning to find himself a Canadian citizen. Madawaska lay on both banks of the St. John, and he happened to live on the wrong one when the river was finally agreed upon as the boundary. He resigned himself to his fate, declined to continue what would be a one-man war, and turned his considerable energies to piling up a fortune in the lumber business. He is, however, buried in the American soil of Fort Fairfield, under a monument erected by the State of Maine to commemorate his flamboyant patriotism.

It would seem that Maine, which lay so far from the Mason-Dixon line and in which not a single slave was owned, might escape any deep involvement in the Civil War. She would, of course, send her quota of men and money for the preservation of the Union; but aside from that, it would appear at first glance that she need not be seriously affected either economically or emotionally.

This was not the case. Through the cotton trade, close ties had been formed between Maine and the South. It was said that Bath and New Orleans were closer neighbors than Richmond and Washington, and in some ways this was true. Many Southern businessmen owned shares in Down-east vessels and mills, and many Maine men had money invested in Southern enterprises. Out of these partnerships, true friendships of fifty years' standing had arisen. Families of the two areas had intermarried with all the confidence of mutual understanding and regard that usually attends a wedding between next-door neighbors' children who have known each other all their lives. These people had known each other all their lives, and well. Although the distance was great, it was possible for them to visit back and forth frequently and easily on the trade ships, and to become thoroughly familiar with each other's backgrounds. Such close ties could not suddenly be broken without a great deal of heartache and bitterness.

The story of Ruggles Sylvester Morse is an example. He was a Maine businessman who, like many others of his kind, found it convenient to establish his headquarters and to live in New

Orleans. Here he married one of the lovely Southern girls, and for a while the young couple was very happy indeed. Their home in New Orleans was as beautiful as wealth and taste could make it, and during the hot summer months they sailed north to Portland, where Mr. Morse had built his wife what is now considered the finest Victorian mansion in America. It was almost an idyllic life, full of gaiety and the companionship of a large circle of friends in both the North and the South. The Morses were to be envied their felicity.

Then the Civil War broke out, and feeling in New Orleans turned against this Maine man, who was now regarded with dark suspicion. He moved to Portland, but here, too, he was suspected because of his long residence in the South. He and his wife were shunned by Portland society, and Mrs. Morse was in addition genuinely homesick in the bleak Northern climate for the warm, easygoing land where she had been born. The two lived almost as recluses in their luxurious and elegant mansion, truly displaced persons who were never to regain their lost happiness. They were as much victims of the war as any soldier on the field of battle.

This mental agony because of divided loyalties is common in all wars, of course. Many of the Maine coasters suffered the less romantic but equally real distress of losing much that they possessed. Four days after the firing on Fort Sumter, the Confederacy began to issue letters of marque and reprisal. Maine shipowners should have anticipated this and taken the normal precaution of arming their merchant marine, but they did not. As a result, hundreds of Maine vessels fell into the hands of Southern privateers in the first six months of the war. In only ten days, the Confederate *Calhoun* alone captured Maine ships valued at more than $150,000. Before the war was a year old,

Maine shipping was so badly crippled that it was a question whether it would ever fully recover.

Even Maine's principal and well-fortified harbor of Portland was not safe from marauders. In 1863 the Confederate privateer *Tacony*, captained by Lieutenant Charles Read, was sent out under a roving commission to do as much damage to Northern shipping as possible. Read was a bold and resourceful young man, and he managed to wreak quite a bit of havoc along the sea lanes before it became clear to him that his ship was achieving too much notoriety for safety. Rather than return home while the returning was good, he captured a small Southport fishing vessel, the *Archer*, transferred his guns and crew to her, and burned the old, incriminating *Tacony*. This gave a brand-new lease to his privateering life.

Soon thereafter another Maine fisherman, the *Village*, was sighted. Preliminary to capturing her, Read hailed her and started a long, disarming chat with her skipper. The soft, slurred speech of the South gave the captain of the *Village* the mistaken impression that everybody aboard the *Archer* was drunk. In a neighborly spirit of helpfulness, he offered to pilot his supposed fellow fishermen into Portland Harbor and to see that he came safely to mooring. Abandoning all thought of bothering with so picayune a victim as the *Village*, Read accepted the service.

Once at anchor off Fish Point, Read discovered nearby the revenue cutter *Caleb Cushing*, preparing to put to sea in search of the *Tacony*. He was at once possessed with the mad idea of capturing her, sailing her out under the guns of the forts, and then returning to burn all the rest of the ships in port. It was a preposterous plan, but it almost worked. By pure chance, the *Cushing*'s captain had died the day before, and most of the crew had gone ashore to attend his funeral. Now, in the evening, they were still ashore, recovering from their grief by the sailors' usual method. The few watchmen were quickly over-powered, and the *Archer* and her big prize sailed safely out of the harbor. There must have been tense moments aboard the two vessels as they slipped past the forts, but those young and foolhardy enough to participate in such a scheme must certainly have enjoyed every minute of its execution.

Then, when success seemed certain, the breeze failed and the two ships were becalmed. No amount of whistling up a wind or of scratching on the masts was of any use. At seven o'clock the next morning, the absence of the *Cushing* was discovered, and a whole fleet of steam-powered vessels boiled out of the harbor after her. A few token shots were exchanged, but Read saw the futility of putting up any real fight. As a last service to the Confederacy, he blew up the *Cushing*. Then he surrendered himself, his men and the *Archer*.

Maine contributed money to the war effort—eighteen million dollars, which was a huge sum for so small a state. She contributed men—72,945, or over 10 percent of her entire population of all ages and both sexes. One of her regiments is credited with saving the Union line at Gettysburg.

It was a typical Maine regiment, made up of men and boys from farms and small towns. At the start, none of them had the least notion of military discipline, nor in fact of military bearing and behavior. Given an order, they were as likely as not to ask, "Why?" If the explanation was reasonable—and the officers were perfectly willing to explain and if necessary to argue—the order was carried out. If not, men and officers talked it over together—more often than not leaning on posts or squatting comfortably on their heels—until a better course of action had been decided upon.

This regiment was commanded by Colonel Adelbert Ames, who, although a Maine man himself, had had the benefits of a West Point training and who had already distinguished himself at the first Battle of Bull Run by conduct so gallant that he was later awarded the Congressional Medal of Honor. When he first saw his new command, the 20th Regiment Infantry, Maine Volunteers, at Camp Mason, he was thoroughly disgusted. "This is a hell of a regiment," he said. That was in August of 1862. Less than a year later, in July of 1863, as he watched the thin, tough line of the 20th Maine withstand assault after assault on the rolling fields of Gettysburg, he said it again. "This is a hell of a *regiment!*" There was no disgust in the words then, only a great and respectful pride.

Lincoln's wartime Vice President was a Maine man. This surprised no one in Oxford County. Everyone had been expecting something of the sort for over fifty years, since the winter of 1809. During that winter an Indian squaw named Mollocket, more commonly known as Molly Ockett, set out on foot from Andover toward Paris. She was a familiar character in the country, a remnant of the tribes who wandered around the area in a rather lost manner. Some people thought she was slightly touched, some considered her a witch, some had great faith in her herbal cures, and everybody agreed that she was harmless. On this occasion she was overtaken by a blizzard, and when she came to the mill at Snow Falls, on the Little Androscoggin River, she asked for shelter. The miller, who was new to the district and unacquainted with Molly Ockett, drove her away, probably through fear. Furious, she cursed him, his family and the very ground on which the mill stood, declaring that nothing would ever prosper there.

Then she struggled along the snowdrifted road until she came to Paris Hill, where she found refuge in the home of some settlers. There was in the household a sickly infant, and Molly, after she had been warmed and fed, picked him up, crooning strange Indian phrases to him. He would be all right, she told the anxious young mother. Moreover, he would grow up to be a very distinguished man, well known beyond the boundaries of the state. So no one in Oxford County expected anything less of Hannibal Hamlin than that he should become Maine's twenty-third governor, a United States Senator and finally, in 1861, the Vice President of the United States.

It is easy to dismiss this as an old wives' tale; but the mill at Snow Falls burned soon; and in the century and a half since Molly Ockett cursed the place, no enterprise has succeeded there, although many have been attempted. It is a beautiful spot, besides being an excellent mill site, with a slender white falls plunging forty feet from a ledge into the gorge below and a pleasant growth of trees all around. But nobody has ever had any luck there since the day Molly Ockett was turned away.

The close of the war found Maine almost drained of men and money. Shipping had declined sharply because of the heavy losses incurred at the hands of the Southern privateers. Recovery was uncertain in view of the competition offered by the new railroads. The postwar depression felt by the entire country was especially acute in Maine—so acute, in fact, that a great many people saw no sense in staying on in so poverty-stricken an area, but moved on to what they hoped would be greener pastures. This tide of emigration reached such serious proportions by the late 1860's that Maine's future became a matter of great concern to her leading citizens. Among these was William Widgery Thomas, who now came forward with what at the time was a unique proposal.

During the Civil War, Thomas, who was only twenty-three

at the time, had been the United States Consul to Gothenburg, Sweden. In those years he developed a great admiration for the Swedish people, whom he described as being "fair-haired, sturdy, honest, industrious, law-abiding and God-fearing, polite, brave, hospitable and generous." Many of them, he knew, were emigrating to the Middle Western parts of the United States. It seemed to him that an effort should be made to induce some of these desirable citizens to settle in Maine, which was in many respects very much like Sweden. He preached his conviction persuasively enough so that in March 1870 a bill was passed by the Maine Legislature to encourage Swedish immigration by offering free land and state aid to those willing to come. Thomas was made Commissioner of Immigration, an office created for this particular occasion.

He immediately went back to Gothenburg and set about enlisting a pilot group. There was nothing hit-or-miss about his methods. Feeling that a great deal hinged on the success of this initial experiment, he took every precaution to insure its success. All candidates—and there were many—were carefully screened, in regard not only to their characters, but to their health and abilities as well. All the men must be farmers, or at least have a working acquaintance with the soil, since the proposed settlement must necessarily be agricultural. All the women, in addition to the usual accomplishments of country wives, must be able to spin and weave. Other basic occupations had their representatives, too. There was a pastor, of course, and a civil engineer, a blacksmith, a basket-maker, a wheelwright, two carpenters, a baker, a tailor and a maker of wooden shoes. Any normal requirement could be met within the limits of this self-contained community.

The party of fifty-one men, women and children arrived in

Halifax, Nova Scotia, on June 13, 1870. By wagon, by river-steamer, by horse-drawn flatboat and on foot, they proceeded across Nova Scotia, and up the St. John River to Tobique Landing, a distance of several hundred miles. Teams took them across to Fort Fairfield, Maine, where a welcoming banquet was held for them. Then they followed the Aroostook River into the deep forest until they came to what seemed to these land-wise people an ideal spot for their new homes. It is significant that the first thing they did was to kneel down and pray, although this was in no sense a religious pilgrimage. Then they formally baptized the yet unborn town New Sweden, rolled up their sleeves and got to work. Everybody worked, the strong Swedish women heaving and hauling alongside their men, and the children laboring according to their size and strength. Land was cleared with almost incredible speed, lots were drawn for farms, and log cabins sprang up almost literally overnight.

During the next three years, more colonists arrived, until the population rose to six hundred souls. Illness was virtually unknown, perhaps because of Thomas' insistence on a clean bill of health in his group. By 1873, 22,000 acres had been cleared, a prodigious feat. At this time, state aid was withdrawn. It was no longer necessary, if indeed it ever had been. The office of Commissioner of Immigration was abolished, having served its purpose. Today New Sweden is a prosperous and orderly community of about seven hundred descendants of the original settlers, a tidy little village with a distinct flavor of Sweden in its appearance and customs. It is proof of what can be done with a little forethought and planning and a wholehearted willingness to work.

The times were changing. New attitudes were springing up everywhere and new ideas were abroad. The comparative simplicity of the world before the Civil War was lost in the complexities of the coming twentieth century. In order to survive in the modern day, Maine had to change, and she did. But, stubborn as her own granite ledges, she did it in her own way. Maine, in spite of Progress, continued—and continues—to be almost defiantly Maine.

8. TWENTIETH-CENTURY MAINE

If it were possible for a state to have a split personality, that would have to be the diagnosis of Maine in the present century. Some of the reasons for this lie in the nature of the country, some in the character of the people, and some in the impingement of modern times on an almost anachronistic scene. Maine is fundamentally fitted for and geared to her original industries of fishing, farming and lumbering, which, although new methods may be employed, still remain among the primitive occupations that depend directly on the land and sea, the wind and the weather, and that place man in a close relationship with nature. The way of life implicit in these occupations tends to be simple, a matter of fairly immediate and discernible rewards in proportion to the amount of labor and judgment expended. That's the way since earliest days that the people of Maine had lived and thought—in terms of the individual's ability to cope with his natural environment. This demanded courage, patience and stamina, but very little subtlety or sophistication.

Late in the nineteenth century, something happened to change this pattern of living. Bar Harbor was "discovered." Some time before this, the artist Thomas Cole, founder of the Hudson River school of painting, visited Mount Desert Island. The Hudson River school derived its name from the fact that the members began their work along the Hudson at a time, shortly after the Civil War, when there was a general back-to-nature movement in the literary and artistic worlds, and picturesque landscapes were the vogue. Cole felt that he had exhausted the possibilities of the Hudson and the Catskills, so he ventured to the coast of Maine in search of further inspiration.

Cole was no impoverished and socially unacceptable dauber. He was a polished gentleman with a wide circle of friends among the very wealthy, and he was also of a volatile, articulate and enthusiastic temperament. He talked so much and so rhapsodically about the beauties of Mount Desert Island to such of his friends as the Morgans, the Rockefellers and the Tracys that they were impelled to go and see for themselves. It became the fashion to summer in this remote spot that Cole had found. Staying in lodgings and hotels—which soon sprang up—proved rather unsatisfactory in the long run, so large tracts of land were bought and summer "cottages" were built. These were actually huge and elaborate mansions, staffed by large corps of servants and kept on the grand scale. By 1900, Bar Harbor rivaled or excelled Newport as the summer social capital of the United States.

These visitors were by no stretch of the imagination tourists. Tourism as we understand it today did not exist at the time. It was not easy to get to Maine and even harder to travel about the state. The automobile was in its infancy, an expensive toy of the rich, not dependable for long or continuous jaunting over miserable dirt roads. The common carriers, the railroads and the steamships, gave access only to focal points like Portland, Bangor and Ellsworth, whence horse-drawn vehicles were taken to destinations. Having made the long and rather grueling journey to Maine, summer people were content to settle down in one place for the season. Ordinary working men and those of moderate means could not afford the time or the money necessary for a Maine summer. Therefore the summer people were almost exclusively those of wealth and its companion, leisure.

These often called themselves "rusticators," which meant that in spite of their costly establishments they tried to live pastoral lives. They entertained themselves in self-consciously simple ways, going on bird walks, making collections of flowers and shells, observing the stars, classifying mosses and lichens. Although they gave elaborate dinner parties in their mansions to the same people that they entertained in Boston, New York or Philadelphia, they offset this necessary nod to convention by building little cabins in the woods of their estates to which they could escape from the regimen they had brought with them. Here they gave themselves over to the simple life, both hearty and contemplative, that they felt to be appropriate to this wild and lovely island. They "roughed it," carrying buckets of water from springs with their own hands, picking berries for their plain wooden tables, chopping wood and telling themselves that they were really in communion with Nature. Some of them thought about Life and wrote philosophical essays which they read to their intimate friends, or even had privately published.

It was a synthetic approach to the simple life. Always their wealth stood in the way of the rusticators' coming to grips with reality. At any moment they could drop their pose and return to luxury. The rigors that they underwent were self-imposed and could at any time be self-terminated. But their effect on Maine was considerable. Seldom has so small a group influenced an entire population so drastically under peacetime conditions.

It started in a small way, with the providing of a new type of employment for the native residents. Although the key positions on the staffs of servants were usually filled by trained employees whom the rusticators brought with them, these were augmented by local help. Girls and women, hired as second maids or cooks' assistants, had their first inkling of the life of a world far removed from the one they had always known. Men and boys serving as grooms, gardeners, boatmen and caretakers discovered that it was possible to earn good money without working themselves to death and without risk. It was a revelation that changed their lives.

It has been suggested that the wealthy summer people were unintentionally and unwittingly guilty of a form of insidious corruption, changing a class of self-sufficient, independent, hardworking individuals into a group of parasites and lackeys. To a degree, this may have been true. But surely no one can be blamed for offering opportunity, or for exchanging a difficult, dangerous and sometimes impoverished life for one that was easier, more secure and more profitable. All that one had to do to share in the bonanza was to learn to say "Yes, sir." This was not always easy for men and women whose chief pride had always been that they were their own bosses. To some, the difficult lesson was not worth learning, but to more, the compensations made it worthwhile.

Several of my native friends used to work for the wealthy summer people of Mount Desert Island, and to them the summer of 1914 stands out as an especially memorable season. The war—World War I—was still safely overseas, but its existence was brought home by the internment of the German liner *Kronprinzessin Cecilie*, carrying a cargo of gold, in Bar Harbor. The passengers dispersed to their various destinations by rail, but the ship's captain and officers remained with their vessel. This was not the hardship it would seem. Travel in Europe being for the time out of the question, the summer population was larger than usual, and the unexpected presence of this glamorous band of foreign gentlemen acted as a spur to gaiety. There were parties for the strangers almost every night, and picnics on the mountain, and moonlight sails on Frenchman Bay. Everybody had a marvelous summer, a last feverish fling before the winter of war closed in. Maine contributed $116,000,000 and 2,094 casualties to that war, but many people remember it better as the war that stranded the *Kronprinzessen Cecilie* in Bar Harbor.

Several factors brought this early phase of the summer people business—and business it is—to an end. Increasing taxes made inroads on great wealth, so that many could not afford to keep up the huge summer estates any longer. Then there was the servant problem. Wartime wages had spoiled capable men and women for being on constant call for a mere twelve or fifteen dollars a week. They could do better than that elsewhere. The big summer houses could not be operated without servants, and servants as a class no longer existed. So a great many of the estates were closed, or sold for inns, private schools or sanatoria, or torn down. Many of those in the Bar Harbor area went up in flame during the terrible fire that swept the island in October of 1947, a not too grievous loss to the owners of what had become white elephants. But in some other localities they still stand, shuttered and shabby, their once beautiful gardens grown up to hay and raspberry canes, monuments to a past glory.

Before they gave way to the modern version of the summer people, the vacationers and the tourists, the rusticators performed for Maine a great and lasting service that stands forever as a reminder not only of their wealth, but more of their foresight and generosity. As early as 1910 two of them, George Bucknam Dorr and Dr. Charles Eliot of Harvard, became very much disturbed about lumbering operations on Mount Desert Island. A great deal of the charm of the place lay in its first-growth forests. If these were cut, as seemed inevitable, the scenery would be ruined and erosion would complete the disaster.

The two men went among their wealthy friends soliciting funds to buy the imperiled land, and succeeded in acquiring about fifteen thousand acres, one-fifth of the island, most of it on and around Cadillac Mountain. They then offered the land to the Federal Government to be used as a National Park. It was accepted by Congress in 1919 under the name of Lafayette National Park, changed in 1928 to Acadia National Park. Subsequently, private owners of land across the bay on Schoodic Point and out at sea on Isle au Haut gave additional territory, so that now the park consists of about 27,860 acres of beautiful, unspoiled mountain and coastline. This was the first National Park east of the Mississippi and the only one to be purchased with private funds and given to the people by individuals.

The value of the park cannot be overestimated. With more and more shore and wilderness property being bought by persons who promptly—and understandably—post it with no-trespassing signs, it becomes increasingly difficult for those who dislike crowds and wish only a quiet place in which to sit and look at a tree or at the sea to find one. Acadia provides this opportunity. There are within its confines over two hundred miles of beautiful roads and fifty miles of separate bridle paths —the personal gift of John D. Rockefeller, Jr.—as well as trails for hikers, free public campgrounds with modern conveniences, and facilities for boating, swimming, fishing, cycling and golf. Park naturalists are on hand to give free instruction and advice, and an archaeologist to explain exhibits in the Abbe Museum. The park is used each year by thousands who quite possibly do not realize that this is testimony of the sense of responsibility that usually goes hand in hand with wealth and privilege.

The greatest factor in the change from the old type of summer people to the new was the development of relatively cheap, dependable automobiles. They made it possible for people of every income bracket to visit Maine and gave rise to the tourist class. For a long time, automobiles were barred by local ordinance from Mount Desert Island, Long Island in Penobscot Bay and some other islands in a geographical position to enforce this ruling; but finally even these last outposts of conservatism bowed to the inevitable. Bridges were built or car ferries established in recognition of the fact that what once was called the "summer complaint" was now a profitable business. It seems a little cold-blooded to consider eager, enthusiastic, flesh-and-blood people as an industry, but in Maine they are a major source of income on which many enterprises depend directly or indirectly for survival.

Once this was recognized and accepted, official Maine lost no time in adopting businesslike attitudes and procedures toward the new trade. A Maine Publicity Bureau was established for the aid, comfort and guidance of the visitors who brought so much outside cash across the Piscataqua. Roads were improved to facilitate their travels, rest and recreation areas were built, and every effort was made to insure their happiness. The little local radio station near where I live in Hancock County, for example, several times a day during the season broadcasts an appeal to the natives to be nice to the summer people. Although the wording is a trifle veiled, the message is clear—that we will all benefit if the tourists like us well enough to keep on coming and spending their money. As a constant reminder of our duty, the registration plates of motor vehicles in the state, including those of hearses and ambulances, bear the word "Vacationland."

These summer people bring much more than money into the state. In the olden days of the clipper ships, wide travel all over the world acted as a broadening influence for Down-easters. Now they stay at home more, and the world comes to them, bringing new viewpoints, new attitudes, new practices. Most of these summer people are not wealthy, but are vacationing on limited budgets, something that the native mind can easily comprehend. They are human and approachable. It is no effort to be nice to them, and out of what may start as purely business relationships, many true and lasting friendships arise. This is not a one-way deal. It is impossible to be exposed for any length of time to Maine realism and horse sense without effect, and most of the summer people find that they go home with a revised sense of values. The association is good for all parties concerned.

For a state that has so well adjusted to the modern phenomenon of a footloose public and developed it into a large industry, Maine's handling of her water-power possibilities has been a little puzzling. The water power available through her countless rivers, streams and tidal basins is one of the state's most valuable natural resources. It has been exploited since earliest days, when every little brook had its dam and grist or saw mill. Most of Maine's larger cities owe their growth from hamlets to being situated on rivers with natural falls or good dam sites. Maine ranks seventh among the states in developed water power, with an enormous potential still undeveloped. Recognizing the value of this resource, the state in 1929 passed laws forbidding the distribution of Maine-generated power outside her boundaries. This was in the hope of luring new industries to locate in Maine. Maine is the only one of the fifty states to have such a law.

The plan did not work. While a few industries did move to Maine, more considered that the disadvantages of climate and a remote location with consequent high shipping rates were greater than possible benefits. The law conclusively cut off any revenue that might have been forthcoming from large hydro-electric plants designed to furnish all northern New England with cheap power. This was the idea behind the Passamaquoddy Tidal Power Development Project, undertaken in 1935 by the United States Government, financed with federal funds and supervised by Army engineers.

Quoddy, as it came to be called, was based on an old principle. Since early colonial days, tidal power had been harnessed in Maine, chiefly to turn grist mills. This project, however, was to be on a gigantic scale, the first of its kind ever undertaken. Passamaquoddy Bay, in fact, is one of the few places in the world where it would be possible. Here ocean tides with a range of from thirteen to twenty-four feet ebb and flow with tremendous velocity through narrow guts between islands into an almost completely landlocked basin. By building dams across the channels, great waterfalls would be formed which would operate generators during seven hours of each tide cycle, or fourteen hours a day. The hiatus in generation would be filled by the construction of a pump-storage reservoir. More electricity would be generated than is supplied by all the power stations in the state combined, and cheap power would be available throughout northern New England and possibly parts of eastern Canada. Living conditions would be greatly improved, and new industries would be attracted to the area, providing better livelihoods for all. What the TVA had done for the Tennessee Valley, Quoddy would do for barren eastern Maine.

None of this materialized, partly because the state stood firm on her right to uphold even an unsuccessful law, even against Washington, and partly because of political currents and cross currents. An enormous sum of money was poured into Quoddy, not only into the dams, but also into the building of an elaborate and costly housing development for the engineers, workers and their families, called Quoddy Village. Then almost overnight the whole thing was dropped, the construction abandoned without serving any purpose, the houses left to stand empty. The whole area was plunged into a worse condition than it had ever suffered before. The little town of Eastport, which had been getting along all right in a modest way, was left bankrupt. To meet the demands made by the sudden influx of thousands of men and their families, it had gone deeply into debt for new schools and public facilities. Now many of the five thousand thrown out of work so abruptly became public charges and the responsibility of a town without funds. There was acute distress from cold and hunger, even actual starvation, about which little or nothing could be done.

The worst result, though, was the destruction of the dream of better times that had been promised, and the growth of an extreme cynicism in regard to the good faith of a government

that could treat its own people in such a manner. It strength-
ened in the lobstermen and farmers, the lumbermen and sardine
packers, a deep and abiding distrust of outside interference and
of newfangled notions.

Therefore it is a little ironical that because of an accident of
geography the state should be the scene of the development
of about as newfangled a field as there is—that of modern communications. During the First World War, when radio was
young, great difficulty was experienced in maintaining constant
communication with Europe. The best and most powerful stations of the time were subject to periods of complete blackout.
Then a naval officer, Alessandro Fabbri, discovered that clear
reception was always possible at Otter Creek on Mount Desert
Island. The Navy decorated Fabbri for his service and established at Otter Creek a station which proved to be of incalcu-
lable value. This was later moved across the bay to Schoodic
Point, where it continues to function efficiently without interference or blackout. It was then learned that the stretch of
Maine coast from Frenchman Bay eastward for about sixty miles
offered the best sending and receiving conditions in the Western Hemisphere.

So when the Navy decided to build the world's largest and
most powerful radio station, they chose Cutler, a tiny fishing
hamlet that lay within the zone, as a site. At a cost of seventy
million dollars, twenty-seven towers were erected. Each is as
tall as the Eiffel Tower in Paris, long considered one of the
Wonders of the World. Always within the memory of man,
the top of Mount Katahdin has been the first point within the
territory of the United States to catch the rays of the rising sun.
Now for a period during the summer when the sun reaches its
northernmost limit, the towers of Cutler have that distinction.

Their nine-hundred-foot tips are ablaze with light when Katahdin and all the rest of the nation lies in the shadow of the earth.

These towers, rising incongruously from the flat and sparsely settled coast, serve as a communications link between the mainland of North America and ships on and under all seven seas, especially Polaris-armed nuclear submarines. Within sight of the installation, which has a rather frightening Buck Rogers aspect, men alone in small gasoline-driven boats haul lobster traps of the identical design used for well over a century. The air about them is full of the vibrations and waves that are signals to aircraft carriers off Hawaii or submarines beneath the polar ice, yet they are out of communication with mankind until they return to harbor. Maine is a country of contradictions.

Nor do they stop there. Far back in the mountains of Oxford County there is a little village called Andover. Once, many years ago, I spent a winter in Andover. It was the prototype of all sleepy crossroads hamlets. There was a general store, a post office, and a barbershop that was open for business one evening a week. The chief and almost only form of amusement was to go over to the store of an afternoon and swap gossip and tall tales with the occupants of the Liars' Bench, drawn close to the cherry-red-hot, pot-bellied, wood-burning stove. It snowed and sleeted a lot that winter. Sometimes the back street on which I lived remained unplowed for days, and my children had to go to school on skis. Once we had a blizzard that knocked down all the telephone wires, filled the only road to civilization with hard-packed, ten-foot drifts so that neither provision trucks nor the mail stage could get through, and left us completely cut off from the outside world. That is how I remember Andover.

The village itself is still very much like that, I understand.

It is still occasionally impossible during a winter storm to call one's next-door neighbor on the telephone. But up in a great bowl in the hills only a mile or two from the same old general store, men are talking directly with Europe by means of a satellite in space. When the Bell Telephone Company decided to experiment with direct overseas telephone and television service by use of Telstar, they chose Andover as the site of the first and to date only earth station. Sending and receiving conditions in Maine had already been shown to be superior, and the wall of mountains that surrounds the Telstar station acts as an additional screen against interference.

So there it is, a precursor of the fantastic future in the middle of an area that is still mainly populated by deer and bobcats, foxes and bear; an area where some men still make a large part of their livings by trapping mink and beaver, where lumberjacks still put up their cords of pulpwood with two-man crosscut saws, and farmers continue to turn over their tip-tilted acres with horse-drawn plows and harrows. The 210-foot bubble of inflated dacron and synthetic rubber rises weirdly from a clearing in the forest, and inside it the gigantic "ear" turns and strains for tiny signals from a twenty-eight-inch man-made sphere whirling in outer space.

During the summer of 1962, sitting before a portable set in my shack on the Down-east coast, I viewed the first live television program ever received in this country directly from Europe. I kept reminding myself that this was not a rebroadcast, not a film; that I was seeing these things as they happened, hearing these words within the same moment that they were spoken on the other side of the world; that the images and voices, before they came into my little living room, had traveled at incredible speed millions of miles through the cold and dark of interstellar space to Telstar and back to earth. It seemed to me truly a marvel.

But when I said as much the next morning to a fisherman friend of mine, he was unresponsive. "May be marvelous," he admitted grudgingly, "but so's a two-headed calf. Both of 'em are unnatural. 'Twasn't intended we should talk to Europe direct, and no good'll come of it. Been my experience that talk leads to trouble. We need less of it, not more. I'm agin the whole works."

That is, I suppose, the predictable reaction to Telstar of a breed that has always maintained that what you don't say can't be held against you, and that newness is a suspicious quality.

Once it is clear that an innovation has value, however, Downeasters are not too hidebound and inflexible to change their attitude. The Jackson Memorial Laboratory, which represents Progress in the field of research, has understandable goals and meets with approval. The laboratory was established in 1929 and is the world's foremost center of cancer research, with which it is usually identified, although its work is not limited to cancer. The stated purpose of the laboratory is "to increase man's knowledge of himself, of his development, growth, and reproduction, of his physiological and psychological behavior, and of his inborn ailments, through research with genetically controlled experimental animals." This research includes the effects of radiation, tissue grafting, muscular dystrophy, heredity, cell behavior, blood variations and similar matters as well as cancer. The institution is supported by grants from such bodies as the American Cancer Society, the Atomic Energy Commission, the Ford Foundation and the National Hemophilia Foundation, and by contributions from private individuals and organizations.

Mount Desert Island was chosen for this significant and important work because of ideal conditions of cleanliness and quiet. There are no earth tremors there to disturb delicate instruments, and few free-floating impurities in the air to defile cultures. The island life is calm and slow-paced, allowing the technicians to work without pressure or distractions. Many of them are Down-easters, sons and daughters of Maine farmers and fishermen who were first employed because they were available. Then it was found that they were unusually good at the type of tasks set for them. Brought up to wait on the turning of the tide or the sprouting of a seed, to note and interpret small weather signs and odd bird behavior, to recognize that a properly done chore is insurance against loss or disaster, they were patient, observant and thorough. With their native intelligence and their lifelong familiarity with all kinds of animals, they make excellent laboratory assistants.

The experimental animals are mostly mice and rabbits, good for the purposes because they are small and breed rapidly. Many can be housed in a small area, they eat comparatively little, and several generations of a strain can be studied within a short time. During the great fire of 1947, a hundred thousand mice with recorded cancer histories for many generations were destroyed. This was a shocking loss that might have ruined the project. Fortunately, it had been—and still is—the policy of the laboratory to supply mice freely to like institutions all over the world. Hardly had the ashes cooled before descendants of the original specimens with their complete histories started arriving at Jackson, so that the research continued almost without interruption, and money poured in from public and private sources, including some from the natives of New Guinea. Remote from the world though it might be on its island, the Jackson Laboratory was a concern of all humanity.

In colonial times the usual and indeed almost the only means of transportation to Maine and between the settlements, which were confined to the coast, was sailing ships or small boats. As the interior was developed, roads were built and travel was by horse or horse-drawn vehicle. Around the turn of the century came the railroads—the Maine Central, the Bangor and Aroostook, the little Belfast-Moosehead Lake Municipal—covering much of the state with their network of tracks; and as the number of out-of-state visitors increased, a steamship line operated between Boston and Portland.

It was fairly easy in those days to get into and around the state by public conveyance. When I was a child attending summer camps in Maine, we used to take the overnight boat from Boston, debark early in the morning at Portland, breakfast in the restaurant of the big and noisy Union Station, and then board a little combination mail-baggage-and-passenger coach for our destination. There was no problem at all, except for those subject to seasickness. The course of the steamer was parallel to the coast, so that its motion was a combination of rolling and pitching extremely unsettling to the queasy. The rest of us had a lovely time fraternizing with the other passengers and staying up long past bedtime to watch the distant lights of Massachusetts, then New Hampshire, and at last Maine slide past on the western horizon. This was the classic approach to Maine, and it was exciting and good.

The journey into the interior was equally delightful. The trains were locals that proceeded in a leisurely manner from milk stop to whistle stop, where the entire crew—conductor, engineer, fireman and brakeman—got off to carry on long conversations of a personal nature with idlers on the platforms. People would enter the coach, greet acquaintances—and everybody knew everybody else except us outlanders—exchange family news and neighborhood gossip, and then leave the train two or three stations further along. By that time even we knew that the woman with the straw suitcase was going to stay a spell with her sister, who was poorly; and that the man in the plaid shirt and high boots was bound upcountry to look over a stand of timber he cal'lated to log off come winter. All the while the lovely Maine scenery unrolled slowly enough so that we had time to note barns that had been painted since last year, individual apple trees in late bloom, and even the color and breed of cats lying supine on sunny farm doorsteps. When we came to our station, the conductor wished us a happy summer as he handed down our baggage. It was all very folksy and heart-warming.

Things aren't like that any more. For a long time now there has been no steamship service into Maine, although there is one out of the country. This is the *Bluenose*, the huge ferry that plies between Bar Harbor and Yarmouth, Nova Scotia, every day in summer and twice a week in winter. This is a really big boat, capable of carrying hundreds of cars, including great refrigerator trucks, as well as throngs of passengers. It saves those bound for Canada 750 miles of driving and a great deal of time and wear-and-tear. One of the few excitements in the movieless, diversion-free, *way* Down East area where I live much of the time is to drive over to Schoodic Point in the evening to watch the *Bluenose* go by on her return trip. First there is a faint glow to the east across the restless wastes of the dark and empty sea, and then she looms up over the horizon like a gigantic fire balloon. The air throbs faintly with the steady heartbeat of her engines, and as she changes course majestically into Frenchman Bay, snatches of music drift across the water. Her passage is impressive and strangely moving.

She is not loved along the coast, however, great a boon as she may be to tourists and shippers of produce. The first count against her is that she is an innovation within the past few years. That alone is enough to damn her. In addition, she brings thousands of pounds of Canadian lobsters into this country on each trip to flood the market and lower the price. Ninety per-cent of the men of the area derive their livings entirely from lobstering, so this is a serious threat to the regional economy. Finally, she sometimes drifts slightly off course, and her propel-lers cut the lines of the buoys that mark the location of lobster traps, so that they are lost, along with whatever catches they may contain. This does not happen often enough to constitute a threat to the solvency of the lobstermen, but as one of them contends with some heat, "That ain't the point. It's the principle of the thing. My Pa and my Grampa and *his* Grampa before him, all of us has *always* set our traps any place we damn well please in the whole Atlantic Ocean. And we'll keep right on so doin', *Bluenose* or no *Bluenose*. If anybody's got to give way, let her do it. We were here *first!*" Maine logic leans heavily on precedent and sees nothing odd in cutting off the nose to spite the face. That operation is one of a man's inalienable rights.

Now the railroads have gone the way of the steamship lines. There is no longer any passenger service on Maine trains. It was discontinued in 1961, because the railroad officials claimed that they could no longer afford it in this age of the automobile. Freight, yes; people, no. They were only an expensive nuisance to the railroads, with their insistence on adherence to timetables. There weren't enough of them using the trains to be worth the bother.

Without question, the railroads had a point. Most people do drive their own cars about Maine, or rely on the expanding bus lines. But it is sad, all the same. There is a forlornness in the sight of the rusted tracks and the boarded-up old stations. They mark the passing of something that was as comfortable and safe as an old friendship, something that was more than a means of getting from one place to another, something that held the state community together just by being there. The sound of a train whistle echoing up the long Maine valleys was more than an indication that the 11.28 was on time. It was assurance to lonely women on farms back in the hills that their isolation was not complete and irrevocable, that at any time they could take the train down to Lewiston or Portland to spend a day among people, to see the pretty things in the store windows, to eat a meal not of their own cooking. It was a tocsin to boys and girls daydreaming in rural schools, sending their minds on long journeys they would make to far places and stirring them with visions of the great things they would accomplish once they got there. It was a promise to aged parents that the children would be home for Christmas, no matter what the weather. You could depend on the trains.

The same cannot be said, unfortunately, for the planes that have tried to take their place. As you drive along U.S. 1, you are confronted at well-chosen intervals by signboards erected by the airlines: "Getting tired? You'd be there now, if you'd flown." I used to find this infuriating. By that time I was indeed getting tired and would have liked nothing better than to be there, changed into my old clothes, with my feet up on the rail of a porch that overlooked the sea. Now I know better than to indulge in that particular regret. It is possible to fly from Boston to Rockland, Bangor or Bar Harbor in a very short time. It is also possible to spend much of the day flying around and around, only to find yourself back in Boston. The Maine coast is subject to sudden dense fogs that make landing a plane highly inadvisable or downright impossible. I have spent too many hours waiting in fogbound airports for guests who finally arrived the next day by bus to be impressed any longer by "You'd be there now." The airlines themselves are beginning to have their doubts about the practicability of imposing the air age on a region whose very meteorology and climate are hostile to the whole idea. They are currently asking permission of the Civil Aeronautics Board to discontinue most of their Down East flights. Maine is a place where it is wise to keep your feet on the ground.

So she remains a state a little out of step with the rest of the world and a little at war with herself. Her geographic position, her climate and terrain, the nature of her industries and the character of her people make this inevitable. Her clinging to the old way of doing things, to the old viewpoints and values, is neither sentimental nonsense, stubbornness nor simple nostalgia for the past, as it might be in other regions or societies. In Maine, the old way often remains the only possible way, and who is to say whether this is a shackle or a salvation?

9. THE WORKADAY WORLD

No one knows exactly when the original Indian inhabitants of Maine began to clear little patches of ground and plant them to corn, beans and squashes, but it was long before any European dreamed of the existence of vast continents across the western sea. Within historical times, a thousand years ago, we know that the vikings sailed their dragon-prowed longships across the uncharted North Atlantic for the chief purpose of securing lumber; and that five centuries later the Maine waters were lively with fleets of Portuguese, Spanish and French vessels, come to fill their holds with the cod and mackerel, pollock and herring that shoaled so plentifully on the continental shelf of North America. These—farming, lumbering and fishing— were the original industries of Maine, dating from before the earliest colonies. Surprisingly, they continue to flourish today, when so much in the world has changed. Methods are very different, but a great many people still make their livings from the soil, the sea and the forests of the state.

In colonial times, the only agricultural product exported from Maine was corn. For a while it was even used as currency in a land that had little or no actual cash. Corn is still an important crop in the south-central part of the state, where it is grown for canning factories. The first canned corn was what is now called niblet-style, whole kernels packed in water. Maine developed the cream-style pack, often still called Maine-style, when the kernels were sheared from the cobs with sharp knives and canned in their own milk. To maintain a uniform product, the packing companies supply the grower with their own preferred hybrid seed, tell him how large an acreage to plant, and guarantee purchase of the entire yield at a predetermined price, if it is up to standard. The same arrangement applies to the growing of other vegetables, especially peas and string beans, for commercial canning. This system takes some of the risk out of farming by assuring the farmer a market, always providing, of course, that the weather cooperates. The whim of the weather is an occupational hazard that has so far not been eliminated from agriculture.

After the Civil War, new crops began to be raised on a commercial basis. Chief among these were apples and potatoes, both of which are still important. At first, most of the apples were Baldwin, Ben Davis and Greening varieties. Now the growers have largely switched to the McIntosh, Delicious, McCoon and Northern Spy, which are exported in large quantities either fresh, as cider or canned. It is still possible in Maine to get a good hot argument started at the local Liar's Bench—the long bench for loafers in every general store—on the relative merits of apples. The Northern Spy, not especially well known outside New England, is usually a favorite; but there is always at least one old die-hard who maintains against all comers with vehemence and, if necessary, profanity that nothing has yet been developed that will come near to touching a good Baldwin apple. Normally taciturn men become downright lyrical on the subject of the Baldwin, dwelling lovingly on its firmness and juiciness, its remarkable keeping qualities, its adaptability and its subtle, tart-sweet flavor. For an all-round apple, give them a Baldwin every time!

Aroostook County is said by its citizens to be the greatest concentration of high-yield potato land in the world. Whatever else is raised there, except for vegetables in family plots, is almost entirely for rotation, to rest the land for further potatoes. There is a reason for this. As one grower says, "Aroostook ain't a potater country just for the hell of it." The deep, rich soil will grow practically anything—good hay for the big dairy herds and fine work horses that were once raised there, or beautiful lettuce, green peas and commercial fruits, for example. But Aroostook is so far from city markets and shipping costs are so high that perishable vegetables and dairy products cannot be sold at a profit. The day of the work horse is past, although Aroostook farmers still raise trotting horses for their own amusement. So the great, level, fertile fields are given over to potatoes, for which the lime-rich soil is especially suited and which can be stored for reasonable periods without spoilage.

The normal annual value of the Aroostook potato crop is over $25,000,000, or half the agricultural income of the state. It is not unknown for a farm to net $100,000 in a single year, although overnight this can turn into a $25,000 loss or more. The weather, for once, is not to blame for this. Unlike the rest of Maine, inland Aroostook is blessed with amazingly uniform and dependable weather, with just the right amounts of rain and sunshine for successful potato culture. What ruins the Aroostook farmer is market fluctuation resulting from production in other parts of the country. If the nation as a whole grows over three and a half bushels per capita, then Aroostook is in trouble. If the figure falls under that, Aroostook makes money; and the lower it drops, the more money it makes.

Perhaps because the economy of the area is based on what amounts to a gigantic speculation, the whole atmosphere of Aroostook is very unlike that of the rest of Maine. It seems both in its appearance and in its people like a different country altogether, more like the early West than conservative and cautious New England. The land is flat and almost treeless around the little towns, most of which are distinguished by strikingly broad streets, like those of the West, and rather heterogeneous architecture. Things are bright and new and breezy and loud. After a profitable harvest, Cadillacs and Lincolns appear everywhere, driven as often as not by men in overalls, disreputable old sweaters, battered felt hats and worn work shoes. These are the owners, who feel that clothes do not make the man. Following a disastrous year, there are no new cars, but neither is there any complaining. Everyone has been flat broke before and managed to survive. It's only a temporary condition anyhow; only until next year, when the market is bound to improve. Optimistic is the word for Aroostook farmers.

The wives of the early settlers of Aroostook, determined not to let backwoods living lower their standards, learned how to make starch out of the potatoes that grew so well in the burned-over stump land of their clearings. It was a simple process. Raw potatoes were grated fine into clean, cold water and left to stand for a while. Then the water was drained off and used for a final rinse of petticoats, best dresses and decent white shirts, so that the family would make a proper appearance at church or on festive occasions. Soon this home expedience grew into a business which consumed the bulk of the potato yield. Starch sheds were built near rivers and streams, and churn graters beat the potatoes to a pulp that was stirred into vats of cold water. This paste was dried in kilns, and the result was a smooth, white powder—starch. At the time of the Civil War and a little later, Aroostook produced 90 percent of the starch made in the United States.

Now the starch industry uses other sources, chiefly corn, and has moved elsewhere; and Aroostook potatoes are sold for seed, especially to the South, for table use and for industrial alchohol.

A name prominent in the annals of potato raising is that of Elisha E. Parkhurst, who first went to Aroostook as a tinware peddler and tinker. He was impressed with the possibilities of the soil, so he sold his horse, wagon and stock in trade, and bought wild land, which he cleared at the rate of ten acres a year. At the time he was interested in growing grass and clover, a profitable crop, since hay was as necessary to a horse-drawn generation as gasoline is today. It was he who imported from England the first alsike clover seed, unknown at the time in the United States but now one of the nation's foremost legume crops. In time Parkhurst was converted to potatoes, along with everyone else in the county. He is sometimes mentioned in textbooks as being the first to use Bordeaux mixture as a potato spray. Less than half a century later, in 1936, his grandson Edwin Parkhurst introduced the dusting of crops by airplane, now standard procedure, not only in the raising of potatoes in Aroostook, but of almost all other crops everywhere as well.

The competition in the potato business is terrific, especially from the West with its famous Idaho baking potato. Therefore it is not enough to raise superior potatoes. They must be promoted as well. Aroostook spends a great deal of time, thought and money on selling potatoes. They are washed and graded by size to save the housewife time and trouble, and then they are packaged in attractive containers designed to catch her eye and appeal to her artistic sense. A great deal of emphasis is placed on the fact that potatoes are not in themselves fattening, for the benefit of a weight-conscious nation, but are a good, sound food, low in calories and high in vitamins and minerals. It's all that butter and cream added by the consumer that does the damage. To preserve proteins and minerals in potatoes, Aroostook advises baking or steaming them with their skins on. The worst way to cook a potato, nutritionally speaking, is to drop it into cold water and bring it to a boil. If you must boil it, at least start with hot water.

All this advice and information is to be found in little booklets distributed by the potato growers associations. They also include odd items from the history of the potato, a native of Peru, Ecuador and Bolivia. It found its way to Europe through the Spanish Conquistadors and soon spread all over the known world. In some countries it met with fierce opposition, as innovations are almost bound to do. It was considered a bodily poison by some and a cause of insanity by others. If these arguments failed to hold up, it was condemned because it is not mentioned in the Bible. It is inconsequential, but to me engaging, that in 1785 Louis XIV sported potato blossoms in his button-hole at a royal fete, and Marie Antoinette wore them in her hair.

Another important crop in Maine is blueberries. Eighty per-cent of the nation's canned or frozen blueberries come from the wide and desolate barrens of Hancock and Washington counties. This is a semicultivated crop. Wild berries have always grown profusely in the shallow soil with no help from man. They still do. It is possible to go out and pick enough for a pie in a very few minutes along almost any roadside during the season. All the commercial growers do is to assist nature a little in pro-ducing a better yield. The bushes are dusted or sprayed at inter-vals during ripening to discourage pests and disease, and the barrens are burned over in rotation every two or three years, a proceeding that prevents them from growing up to other vegetation and improves the berries.

The gulls and the curlews are the chief enemies of the grow-ers. They come far inland from the sea as soon as the berries are ripe in such huge flocks that often from a distance the ground seems to be covered with snow. It is a pretty sight, but not one to bring joy to the heart of the owner. Scarecrows are not very effective against them. Gulls are brash birds that do not scare easily. The only thing that upsets them is the sight of a dead member of their greedy tribe. So the blueberry grow-ers shoot a few gulls and hang the bodies on poles set at intervals across the barrens. This is by special dispensation. Gulls are protected by law in Maine. They are scavengers who keep the coast livable by cleaning up dead fish, waste thrown overboard from passing boats and other malodorous refuse. There are few garbage collectors in Maine coastal communities. They are not necessary. The gulls are natural garbage-disposal units.

The blueberry industry is seasonal. For over ten months of the year only the bushes are working in their quiet way, and the barrens stretch as far as the eye can see without any sign of human life or activity. Driving across one of the big barrens inland from Cherryfield or Columbia Falls is a strange and almost oppressive experience. You leave the highway along the coast, with its snug little villages and beautiful vistas of island-dotted bay and rocky headland, climb gradually for a mile or so, and find yourself in a landscape as bleak and featureless as that of the moon. On and on it extends, without sign of a house or even a grove of trees. The road unrolls toward the horizon, but nothing changes. It is as though you were wandering in a contaminated area devoid of life and meaning. It's an earthly limbo. Only in the late autumn do the barrens take on beauty. Then the low bushes turn red—every red from pale rose through a bright scarlet to a deep crimson that is almost purple—and the whole earth glows and throbs with a ruby fire. It is beautiful, but it is an uncomfortable, inhuman beauty.

During late July and August, however, the barrens come to life. Roadsides are barricaded with piles of empty crates, and everywhere the bent figures of the rakers move slowly over the land. Trucks carrying the berries to the nearest canning factory or freezing plant jounce and rattle over the roads at top speed, and company buses fly from hamlet to hamlet, picking up the women who pack and process the crop. In an area where money is hard come by, the blueberries save many families from the need to apply for relief during lean winters. School boys and girls on vacation clothe themselves for the coming year from their raking pay, which for a fast, ambitious worker runs as high as fourteen dollars a day—a lot of money by local standards. Women buy themselves the household appliances or new coats for which they have been longing, or put their wages by to help out their fisherman husbands when the lobsters are not crawling and the family still has to eat. Blueberry money is not easy money, but it is nevertheless a gift, not from Heaven, but from the generous earth.

The second of the original Maine industries, lumbering, is still of major importance. Millions and millions of feet of timber are cut annually, although the methods and purposes are very different from what they once were. The broadax is now almost a curiosity, and a good broadax man very hard indeed to find. The two-man cross-cut saw and more recently the power-driven chain saw are used instead. Teams of oxen are rare in the woods, and horses—except where the rough terrain makes them necessary—are giving way to tractors. Where logs were once driven down rivers on spring freshets, now much of the cut is transported to market on trucks. The day of the mast pines, the oak knees for ships, the twenty-three-inch floorboards and twelve-inch hand-hewn rafters, the split pine clapboards and cedar shingles—used as currency as late as 1840—is gone. Cardboard cartons and steel drums have taken the place of wooden boxes and barrels. Instead of putting up twenty or thirty cords of firewood each fall to see the family through the winter, the householder, except in truly remote districts, simply calls up the oil man. For what, then, is all this timber used?

A small part of it still goes into shipbuilding. The increasing use of steel in ship construction ruined many Maine shipyards, although some converted to the new material. Some of the others, after lying idle for years, are being reactivated. The growing popularity of small-boat sailing for sport or pleasure has given them a new lease on life, and they are turning out beautiful little sailing craft of all classes. Some carefully selected lumber is used, too, in the building of canoes, especially at Old Town, which is famous for its models based on old Indian designs. In interior Maine many small villages boast what are often called birch mills, because a large part, although not all, of the wood employed is birch. These mills make a variety of small objects—spools, toothpicks, dowels, chair rungs, toys, souvenirs and the like. A little firewood is still cut and sold, chiefly to summer people for their fireplaces.

By far the greatest consumers of Maine's timber are the pulp and paper industries, which are the most important of the state's present manufactures. Pulp was first made commercially at Topsham in 1868, and by 1914 Maine led the nation in its production. Out of pulp, of course, paper is made; not only rough newsprint and the even rougher pages of the so-called pulp magazines, but fine papers as well for expensive books, glossy magazines, gift wrappings and stationery. Almost any kind of wood can be used for pulp—fir, spruce, hemlock, poplar—and almost any size. Otherwise worthless timber, "not fit fer fencin' nor firewood," disappears into the maws of the giant mills at Rumford, Millinocket, Bucksport, Woodland and other cities to be digested and turned into paper.

The mills are models of modern efficiency and ingenuity, with huge machines that seem almost to possess intelligence in their ability to accomplish complicated series of tasks without human aid. I once spent the better part of an hour watching one receive wet pulp at one end and discharge dry paper bags, cut, pasted, folded and bundled at the other, while the operator, who was no more really than a watchdog and safety device in case of mechanical failure, stood by with his hands in his pockets. It was fascinating, but I had the uneasy feeling that I was in the presence of a monster smarter and defter than I, which might at any moment find voice and tell me to stop staring and go on about my business. When later I went to live in the heart of one of the great logging areas, it was a relief to find that this first phase of the pulp and paper industry was conducted on human and erratic terms that I could understand. The trees were felled, cut into pulp lengths and loaded on sledges with the aid of tools in the hands of men without whom they would be useless objects of metal and wood, men who could make mistakes and lose their tempers and catch cold and laugh at jokes. Here at least there was no danger of the machine's becoming the master.

For the lumber camps have changed very little in the past hundred years. They are still small, tight communities of tar-paper shacks set down in the forest which almost isolates them. They follow a traditional plan. There is a large bunkhouse which serves also as a recreation hall on stormy days and is called for reasons unknown the barroom. This has nothing to do with conviviality in the usual sense, since alcohol is strictly forbidden in the camps; a sensible precaution among men working with sharp and dangerous tools, who, moreover, consider a good no-holds-barred, knockdown-drag-out fight one of the delights of getting drunk.

Near the bunkhouse is a combined kitchen and dining room, ruled over by the cook, whose word is absolute law within his precinct. Some cooks are easygoing and some are martinets who insist that everyone wash his hands before sitting down to eat. I once went into a cookhouse at mealtime and found the cook brandishing a cleaver over three men who were sitting on the floor with their plates in their laps, eating beef stew with their fingers. Their crime was that they had gone to the table wearing their hats. "If they want to be heathens, I ain't got no objection," the cook announced broad-mindedly. "Live and let live, I always say. But heathens should be treated as such. Till they get civilized, they're goin' to eat heathenish, on the floor." There is one rule that all cooks, strict or indulgent, enforce— no conversation at mealtime beyond requesting in the fewest possible words that food be passed. Talk drags out a meal and puts the kitchen force behind in its work. Anyone with a long tale to tell can tell it later in the barroom.

The other buildings consist of a stable called the hovel, where the horses are bedded and usually pigs are kept to dispose of the vast amounts of garbage; and a small shack called the wangan, which is a store where candy, tobacco, snuff—still chewed widely in the woods—tools and clothing are sold. It is analogous to the slop chest on the old sailing ships, from which the crews were issued merchandise that was later deducted from their wages. A lumber camp, in fact, resembles in many respects a ship on a six months' voyage around the Horn in the days of the clippers. There is the same lack of communication with the outside world, the same self-containment, the same pressures and patterns peculiar to any society of men without women and without contacts outside their own occupation and circum-scribed physical range.

The same types of men go into the woods to work as once shipped before the mast; men who are misfits in the normal so-ciety of their times because of lack of education, opportunity or ability, or because of some character flaw; who may be at odds with the law, who are running away from responsibility or the stresses of the age, or who are drawn to the woods as a way of life as sailors are drawn to the sea. Like sailors, they do their work, obey orders, keep out of trouble and amuse themselves by reading—those who can—carving wood into intricate de-signs, mending their clothes, making pets of birds and small animals, and eternally talking about anything from the state of the nation to whether the cook put enough salt into his last batch of bread. At the end of the winter, they collect their accumulated wages and head downriver for the nearest metropolis, where, like sailors ashore after a long voyage, they go on homeric sprees. They're a tough bunch when they hit town, but when I lived among them, I found them to be good neighbors. They were helpful and considerate, simple men at home in simple surroundings with which they could cope, and which brought out the best in them.

Although the pulp industry is good for Maine's economy, making full use of one of her natural resources and giving employment to thousands, it has some undesirable side effects. In the past, concern over stream pollution was nonexistent. The waste from the mills poured into rivers like the Androscoggin, fouling the water and killing fish and plant life. Attempts are now being made to correct this condition, but there is still a long way to go. Selective cutting is unknown on a pulp operation. It is considered too costly. All the trees are cut, leaving wide slashes full of tangled tops and limbs. These become a bad fire hazard under the hot summer sun, and every fall Maine is plagued with extensive forest fires. In addition, the stripping of the forest cover leads to erosion and destructive floods. Formerly, when the forests seemed inexhaustible, no reforestation was practiced, and even now there is very little. The cut-over areas were expected to restore themselves; which, of course, in time they do.

A fairly recent offshoot of the lumbering industry is the Christmas tree business. Although this is strictly seasonal, it is large and growing larger. In November, the Christmas tree cutters—as often as not farmers and fishermen filling in the slack season of their chief livelihoods—go into abandoned back pastures and old pulp cuttings that are thick with second- and third-growth spruce and firs. Soon thereafter the sides of the roads are flanked with high piles of the evergreens, tied in bundles of eight or ten. They range in size from two-foot table trees, through family trees of six or eight feet, up to thirty- or forty-foot giants intended for hotel lobbies and municipal parks.

In early December, trucks start picking them up and heading south and west for Boston, New York, Philadelphia and even further. Almost everyone who owns a truck of any size deploys it from its normal use to haul Christmas trees, and soon the preponderance of commercial vehicles on the highways consists of these carriers, heaped high with their aromatic green loads and trailing the pungent scent of balsam. This traffic is so heavy, in fact, that the Maine State Turnpike Authority erects special signs each year: "Christmas Tree Trucks Use Outer Lane." The caravan seems endless, extending all the way from Nova Scotia to the bridge at Kittery, and the wonder is that there are any trees left in Maine for next year.

That there are is partly due to the fact that evergreen trees grow fast, and partly to the efforts of the Christmas Tree Growers Association. This forward-looking organization is devoted to the study and application of conservation methods, as well as to improving and marketing the trees. Cutting down healthy little trees for a brief moment of tinsel-and-light-decorated glory is not so wasteful and reprehensible as it sounds. The thinning of this undergrowth is actually beneficial to the forests. There's a certain poetry, too, in the idea of all these lovely trees scattered far and wide through cities and towns, bringing a breath of clean Maine air to homes hundreds of miles away from any forest.

Christmas wreaths are a business in Maine, too; a home business carried on by country women in farm and fishing-shack kitchens. Before the snow covers the ground, the children of back-country families go into the woods and gather sacks of trailing, princess and ground pine. This is heaped in barns and sheds where the cold will keep it green and fresh. A few weeks before Christmas, the girls and women of the family start making wreaths for export to the cities. The kitchens are pleasant places during wreath-making. The air is sharp with the clean, spicy incense of the evergreen, released by the warmth of the room, and everybody is busy and happy. Fingers and tongues fly. It is like an old-fashioned work bee, where sociability is as important as accomplishment. When the trucks pick up the finished, undecorated wreaths, the women receive about thirty cents apiece. A good worker can make three or four in an hour. Her pay therefore amounts to less than the minimum wage of the state, but to country women with no other way of earning actual cash for store-boughten Christmas presents that is not important. Wreath money is like money found loose on the forest floor. It's a godsend to people who do not expect God to send free help, but rather the opportunity to help oneself.

The third of Maine's original industries, fishing, has undergone radical changes since the Portuguese fleets anchored off Monhegan and the Pepperells spread their dunfish to dry on the bare ledges of the Isles of Shoals. The sail has disappeared from commercial vessels, which are now powered by gasoline or diesel engines and are no longer at the mercy of wind and tide. The catches need no longer be dried or pickled in brine to preserve them, but are rushed to market in enormous refrigerator trucks, arriving within hours of having been taken from the sea. "The lobster that you eat today slept last night in Casco Bay" is more accurate than many advertising slogans.

Not all fish is sold fresh. The perfection in the last century of the technique of preserving food in tin by Underwood and the more recent development by Birds Eye of the quick-freezing method of food preservation revolutionized the fishing industry as well as the eating habits of the nation. Nowadays almost every tiny fishing hamlet along the coast has easy access to a canning factory or a freezing plant. All kinds of sea food—clams, lobster meat, blue mussels, fish chowder—are canned, but the mainstay of the industry is the sardine.

Sardines are small herring, cleaned, packed in flat tins, steam-cooked and sealed. The process of changing a herring into a sardine is complicated and involves the services of a great many people in several capacities. Every sardine-packing company of any size owns and maintains a light seaplane and employs a pilot to fly it. From the air he is able to locate schools of herring shoaling in coves and inlets, and to transmit the information to the factory by radio. Seine boats are immediately dispatched to the scene to string nets—always referred to as "the twine"— across the mouth of the cove to trap the fish. Then the sardine boats, the carriers, arrive, and the seine is gathered into a pocket, concentrating the herring in a small, densely packed area. They are pumped through a large hose into the holds of the carrier, the sea water being sluiced overboard through sieves which catch the scales scraped loose in the process. These scales, which used to be a waste material, are now almost as valuable as the fish. They are used in the manufacture of imitation pearls, nail polish, commercial paints and lacquers, and various synthetics. The proceeds of the sale of the scales, which may be as much as ninety or a hundred dollars a trip, go customarily to the three or four members of the carrier crew, a nice bonus.

Now the captain of the sardiner informs the factory by short-wave radio of the number of hogsheads of fish he has aboard and the estimated time of his arrival. It is important that the herring be processed as soon as possible to prevent spoilage. A spoiled catch—and there are inspectors on hand to see that none gets by—can still be sold to cat food or fertilizer factories, but at much less profit. The factory whistle sounds several short, piercing screeches that can be heard for miles, and women and girls all over the area drop whatever they are doing—making a pie or washing their hair—to get ready for work before the factory bus arrives to transport them. They are the packers, almost incredibly quick and deft at putting the tiny fish neatly into the small cans. In their clean cotton dresses and the hairnets required by law, they gather at the corner, laughing and joking and full of good humor.

This is understandable. The whole economy of some of the far Down East hamlets depends on the herring. Although they furnish seasonal employment which must be exploited during the few short summer months, the money earned more often than not makes all the difference between comfort through the bitter winter to come and actual deprivation. The summer of 1961 was almost catastrophic along the Maine coast, putting it into the disaster area class. The herring—why, no one could figure out—disappeared and a prolonged drought ruined the blueberry crop. There simply was no work at all for the women by which they could augment their husbands' earnings and provide a narrow margin of economic safety. Tempers grew short, faces grew long, and it was almost impossible to get a pleasant word out of anybody.

The following summer—and nobody could figure out the why of this either—the herring came back more abundantly than ever, and every day the wonderful words "We got fish!" went out. Then the barrens were discovered to be literally blue with berries. It was a wonderful summer. Old debts were paid up, houses blossomed with new paint, and everyone on the whole coast was merry as a grig. The herring were shoaling, the berries were thick as spatter, and all was right with the world.

Probably the best-known and certainly the most highly publicized of the Maine sea foods is the lobster. It has become almost a symbol of the Down East coastal area, appearing on postcards, barbecue caps and aprons, dinner plates, ceramic tiles, paperweights, junk jewelry, sofa pillows, dish towels and any number of other items of tourist merchandise. These representations are invariably of a brilliant scarlet, although until cooked a lobster is dark green, a protective coloration that blends with his underseas habitat. An embittered lobstering acquaintance of mine insists that the gift shop owners make more money in a year off lobsters than the lobstermen do, with a lot less effort. He was looking into a shop window at a lamp made from a lobster trap, topped by a lobster-stenciled shade, and priced at fifty dollars when he made the pronouncement. "More'n I make in a week," he stated, then asked in honest wonder, "Who's goin' to buy the thing? Wouldn't give it shed room myself. Tourists must leave their wits t'home."

Maine publicity labels Maine lobsters the best in the world, and gourmets in general agree. The flesh is unusually firm and succulent, because of the extreme coldness of the water in which they live and breed. The same is true of Nova Scotian lobsters, although this is not often mentioned in Maine. Lobsters can be kept alive for some time after capture either in submerged crates, in pounds or in refrigerator trucks, but they lose weight—"gant up"—and flavor in confinement. The place to sample them at their best is along the coast itself, when they are fresh out of the ocean. The city of Rockland capitalizes on this by promoting a three-day Lobster Festival each August. There is a parade with floats and bands, a Lobster Queen and similar frills; but the chief attraction is the food. Lobster dinners are served to thousands each day as both natives and vacationers flock to Rockland. For the benefit of those from the hinterland who have never before been faced with the engineering problem of extracting the meat

from the shell, printed instructions on how to eat a lobster are distributed. It is a very gala affair.

Lobstering is hard, speculative and sometimes dangerous work, but few who are employed in it would change to any other means of livelihood. Most of the lobstermen were hauling their own dozen or so traps before they were ten years old, working alongshore in rowboats, selling their catches to the local dealer and saving their money toward a real lobster boat. They know all about getting up before dawn and working until dark, about losing all their gear in a bad storm, about summer's pitiless sun and the bone-biting gales of winter. They know that the bottom may drop out of the market, lowering prices to a level that will hardly pay for gasoline for their boats. They know about long hours alone in a small boat on the pathless prairies of the sea, when a clumsy move can mean death by drowning, with no one near to help or even see.

None of this counts with the lobstermen. They are in love with their way of life. Nobody tells them what to do; they go out to haul or not as they please, and return when they see fit. They are masters of their environment, handling their boats almost absent-mindedly, with a skill as natural and thoughtless as breathing. They are entirely at home in their world, doing exactly what they want to do most, and doing it well. That's all they ask of life, without even realizing that it is a great deal more than most people get.

As Maine developed, other industries were added to the basic three. One of these was the ice-cutting and exporting business, inaugurated almost by accident. During the depression following the Civil War, when cargoes were frequently difficult to secure, shipowners started using ice, which was plentiful and free, as ballast. They found to their delighted surprise that what was an almost worthless commodity at home could be sold at substantial profit in the tropics and semitropics, and in the South. This was a bonanza that could not be overlooked. Almost everyone within reasonable distance of a body of fresh water promptly became an iceman.

The heart of this industry was the Kennebec Valley. Kennebec ice was supposed to be the cream of the crop, purer, clearer, longer-lasting, better in every way. There was no really sound basis for this claim. The Kennebec was unpolluted, it was true; but in those days so were most other streams, and their ice equally safe and clean. Through ingenious promotion, however,

Kennebec ice became status ice and commanded a higher price than any other. As would be anticipated, unscrupulous persons took advantage of this preference. In Baltimore and London, in Cairo and Manila, in Cuba and Kansas, ice wagons bore the legend "Kennebec Ice" painted conspicuously on their sides. Much of this ice never saw the Kennebec or even Maine. A great deal of it actually came from the Hudson. The Knicker-bocker Ice Company of New York, which eventually handled most of the Kennebec crop, depended also on the Hudson as a source of supply. It is not too surprising that, in the interests of profit, they conveniently lost track of which ice came from where.

Along the Kennebec, from New Year's on, everyone watched their thermometers like hawks. A prolonged mild spell threw the entire population into deepest gloom, while a plunge to below zero on a clear and windless night sent spirits soaring. All preparations had long since been completed, the cutting tools honed, the horses sharp-shod with calks of steel, the great ice-houses along the river cleaned of last year's musty sawdust. All that was needed now was a good cold snap to start things moving.

Usually the cold came. The Maine climate, perverse though it often is, could be depended on for that, give it time. Then an almost carnival atmosphere prevailed. Every able-bodied man in the whole valley was out harvesting ice, and the women and children, freed from school for the occasion, were there, too, skating, watching, tending big bonfires along the shore, keeping kettles of soup and pots of coffee hot for the workers, exchanging gossip and recipes. Cutting ice was a business, but it was also a social event. It broke up the monotony of the winter and lent it gaiety and charm.

The ice-exporting business flourished up to the beginning of the twentieth century, and then it declined in the face of modern methods of refrigeration. Now very little ice is cut in Maine, except by private persons for their own use. Children on hot city streets no longer run after the red wagon of the iceman to beg a sliver of Kennebec ice that was more blissful to suck than the biggest lollipop. Accustomed to the cloudy cubes of artificial freezing, people have forgotten the crystal clarity of pond or river ice. Somehow the irregular splinters seemed colder than ice does today and chimed more musically against the sides of a pitcher of lemonade. Be that as it may—and it may be only nostalgic nonsense—ice helped Maine over a difficult period of her finances.

Another heretofore unexploited resource aided Maine in the postwar days. This was granite, as durable as ice is perishable. All Maine rests on granite, beneath the forest and the farmlands, and along the coast and on the off-shore islands the rock is near the surface or actually exposed. To this advantage of easy quarrying was added that of convenient transportation by boat to destination. There were two distinct types of granite—the beautiful blue-gray found on Vinalhaven, and the soft pink from Deer Isle and Hurricane Island. The latter is often called Cadillac granite, because Cadillac Mountain on Mount Desert Island is composed of it. Both kinds are of finest quality.

Granite was quarried on Vinalhaven as early as 1829, when a man named Tuck shipped a load to Massachusetts for the walls of a state prison. It wasn't until after the Civil War, however, that the industry really boomed. Suddenly there was a tremendous demand for granite, and the quiet little islands exploded into activity. The working of granite is a highly specialized trade, some phases of which require a long apprenticeship. To supply the necessary skill, expert craftsmen were brought in from Norway, Sweden, Wales, Scotland, and especially from Italy. These were the cutters, polishers and carvers. The sawyers, dynamite boys and quarrymen, who worked on the face of the rock and whose jobs required less skill, came from the native Yankee population; at least until they had learned enough from the masters to graduate from their relatively lowly positions.

The immigrants knew their business, and they also knew how to enjoy life. They laughed and sang a lot, drank with enthusiasm at times, delighted in athletic contests, organized bands and choral groups, and entered wholeheartedly into the celebration of any event, great or small. They opened the eyes of the more restrained Down-easters to the possibility of having a thoroughly good time just by being alive. Folks still talk about the Fourth of July parade of 1872 of Vinalhaven, when the local bands were carried in long granite wagons drawn by seventy-two yoke of oxen.

These lusty newcomers were among the best granite men in the world. They brought the largest monolith of modern times out of the Vinalhaven quarries. It is a sixty-foot shaft, comparable to the obelisks of antiquity, that stands in Troy, New York, as a monument to General John Ellis Wood, a hero of the Mexican War. Four blocks had to be quarried before the perfect one was achieved. Vinalhaven stone was used in the War and Navy Department Building in Washington, in the Pilgrims' Monument at Plymouth, Massachusetts, in Grant's Tomb and the Brooklyn Bridge in New York, and in more post offices and public libraries throughout the United States than it is possible to count. Whether they know it or not, most people in this country have at some time come in contact with granite from Maine.

The last big job of the Bodwell Granite Company of Vinal-haven was the supplying of the four 120-ton columns at the sides of the choir altar in the Cathedral of St. John the Divine in New York City. These came from the quarry in the form of gigantic slabs of rock sixty-four feet long, with cross dimensions of seven by eight feet—the largest stones quarried anywhere in the world since before the birth of Christ. Finished, they were to be simple, highly polished columns sixty feet in length. Unfortunately, the first three broke on the lathe during the early stages of polishing. It was then decided to make the columns in two sections of forty-five and fifteen feet, more manageable lengths. The seam is near the top of each and impossible to detect by casual observation, but they were a source of chagrin to the craftsmen of Vinalhaven, who took great pride in their work. For the $20,000 being paid for each shaft, they felt that the buyers were entitled to perfection.

Vinalhaven was named for a Boston merchant, John Vinal, who became interested in the island's affairs and arranged various legal services for the islanders. His son William made the island his permanent home, and from him is descended the modern poet, Harold Vinal. In 1870, William sold an off-shore islet called Hurricane to General Davis Tillson for fifty dollars. Hurricane was not much more than a huge granite boulder rising out of the sea, covered sparsely with meager grass and wind-tortured scrub spruce, and inhabited only by gulls and terns.

General Tillson, though, had ideas for this Godforsaken rock. In almost no time, there was a village of 850 people on Hurricane, granite workers from far parts of the world and their families. Roads were built of rejected granite slabs, there was a store, a church and a school, boardinghouses for bachelors, a bandstand and a bowling green, and Anarchy Hall where the Finns and Swedes played checkers and discussed trade unions and socialism. It was only talk. If ever there was a company town, it was Hurricane. General Tillson owned everything and controlled everything. The possible exception was the brilliant flower gardens frothing out of what seemed solid rock, where garden lovers had carefully collected, almost spoonful by spoonful, precious loam to fill small crevices in their granite dooryards and planted and tended seeds brought from home.

Granite was not the only industry. General Tillson built a canning factory on the island where great quantities of clams, mackerel, herring and lobsters were packed. There was work for everyone, women as well as men, and everyone prospered. At one time over two thousand people made a living on Hurricane, and it seemed as though the good times would last forever.

Then granite was replaced by concrete, artificial stone, steel and glass in construction, and the rosy stone of Hurricane became a drug on the market. New conservation laws governing the taking of lobsters and shellfish hampered the profitable operating of the canning factory. Suddenly there was no way of earning a living on the island, and the people, first in driblets, then in a final mass exodus, left. They had no choice, even though to many of them the leaving of this place that had become home was heartbreaking. Today no one lives there at all, except the returned sea birds. The roads and fallen buildings are overrun with bindweed and bearberry vines, and where once rang the sounds of human activity and human voices are now only the pounding of the surf, the sigh of the wind and the mewing of the gulls.

At one time there was in Maine a lively and profitable business based on cobblestones. These could be gathered free by the shipload on any exposed stretch of coast east of the Penobscot, where the heavy surf polished them smooth and graded them according to size. There were very few cities in the Eastern half of the nation that did not contain streets and marketplaces paved with Maine cobblestones, over which the iron-rimmed wheels of drays and carriages rumbled and rattled, and citizens picked their cautious way. The development of new surfacing materials put an end to the cobblestone trade, and the requirements of the automobile caused the replacing of most of the old cobblestoning. Some communities that place a high value on the old and traditional, however—such as Alexandria, Virginia, and Boston—still cherish sections of the outdated pavement in their older, historical streets.

Over the years, Maine has exported some rather odd articles. From 1675 to 1750, during the period of the French and Indian Wars, for example, genuine, guaranteed French or Indian scalps brought as high as a hundred pounds apiece in Europe. The price depended on the condition of the merchandise and the degree of eminence or notoriety of the original owner. Today, driftwood picked up along the old cobblestone beaches enjoys a vogue. These beautifully weathered, fantastically shaped pieces of satiny gray wood are used by decorators in the making of lamps and furniture, for the trimming of department store windows, and just as objects of art—which they are—in modern homes, offices and hotel lobbies. Commercial driftwood collectors have been known to run this article of trade, which costs them only the effort of finding it and picking it up plus a slight transportation and sales overhead, into $20,000-a-year businesses. This is a high reward for walking along the shore in the sun and salt breeze, picking up sticks.

Another beachcombing activity is the collecting of sea-smoothed pebbles of granite, jasper, agate, chalcedony and the like. These are polished highly and fashioned into jewelry. Some of these pieces of handicraft are very beautiful. The shapes of the stones are odd and irregular, and the polishing brings out deep, strange, glowing colors. They range in price from about two dollars for a key ring set in silver to seventy-five or more dollars for a bracelet or necklace with a gold or platinum setting. Both this and the driftwood business fall within the good old Maine tradition of ingeniously and shrewdly making a profit out of something that you have acquired for nothing.

Although Maine is still largely an agrarian state, certain areas do produce manufactured goods aside from pulp and paper. Chief among these are footwear and textiles. The city of Auburn is the shoe center and employs about half the shoe workers in the state. A Maine specialty is moccasins and hunting boots. Wilton is famous for the Bass moccasin, and L. L. Bean of Freeport for his unique gum boots, so called, which have a rubber foot and a one-piece leather upper. Sportsmen from all over the world send to this little store for these woods boots, by which they swear. The first textile mills of Maine made woolen goods, but after William King introduced the idea of importing raw cotton from the South, cotton mills sprang up everywhere. The modern trend of the mills to the South, nearer the source of supply, has curtailed cotton manufacture somewhat, although mills still operate in Lewiston, Waterville, Sanford and especially Biddeford-Saco.

The twentieth century has seen the evolution of the type known as the organization man, the man who is a part of a huge, efficient machine, a functioning unit in a complicated anatomy. The climate of the organization is the one to which he has adapted and in which he feels secure. While there are no statistics available to prove the point, it is probable that there is as low a percent of organization men in Maine as in any other state in the Union. Here a very large number earn their livings rather by individual effort, competing not against others for a higher place in the pecking order, but against man's original and implacable foes, the wind, the weather, the seasons and their own limitations for survival. All the lobstermen and fishermen, all the farmers and woodsmen, belong to this category. They work for themselves, at their own pace, and with a minimum of outside aid, supervision or interference; and they hope to receive for their labors enough to allow for a few luxuries, most of which—television sets, hot running water, deep-freeze units —are considered necessities in the average modern community.

Others besides these follow livelihoods in which they have wide jurisdiction over their own comings and goings, their own working hours and conditions, and a great deal of latitude of choice as to their hour-to-hour and day-to-day activities. There are hundreds of registered Maine guides who accompany hunters, fishermen and campers through the forests and along the streams of the state. These are men who know the wilderness well and love it, who are almost throwbacks to the days of the Indian scouts and the *coureurs de bois*. Although technically in the employ of their "sports," as they call them, they are actually in complete charge. They decide where to go, when to eat and what, when to sleep and where. If for any reason they dislike the looks or the manner of prospective clients, it is always their privilege—which they exercise freely—to refuse the job and go fishing by themselves instead. They are at the beck and call of nobody. No time clocks or factory whistles regulate their days. They are as much their own men as it is possible to be in any society.

The same thing is largely true of the many game and fire wardens. These men are employed by the state and given definite areas to patrol in the line of duty, which is to prevent or fight forest fires and to enforce the game laws, respectively. The wardens are required to make reports to their distant superiors at intervals; but aside from that, they are practically free agents with a great deal of leeway. They make their own decisions as to where their day will take them and how it will be spent. Much of the time they are alone, and that is the way they like it. "Me lonely?" one of them once said to me. "Isn't everybody? At least I can be lonely in good company—my own." So much of Maine is so sparsely settled that solitude or semisolitude is for many a normal condition that holds no terrors.

All the solitaries are not engaged in physical labor. In Maine there are a surprising number of artists, writers, sculptors, musicians and craftsmen, the nature of whose work cuts them off from normal contacts with their neighbors. Though they may live in busy villages and participate in community projects, a large part of their time must be spent in a mental isolation as complete as that of a lobsterman alone far at sea in his small boat, or a fire warden alone in his tower on a wilderness mountain. Nobody can paint a man's picture for him, or write his book, or compose his symphony, or carve his statue. Nobody can even help him. The creative part of his life must be lived hermetically, in a cell—actual or figurative—where he fights his own battles apart from the world.

The dedicated artist can do this anywhere, but it is easier in Maine than in most places. There is less hurry and confusion, fewer demands and distractions. In addition, nobody cares what you do for a living, whether you are famous or not, so long as you speak civilly and pay your bills. Nobody bothers you.

There is, and always has been, a streak of eccentricity in most Down-easters. Therefore they understand and accept what might elsewhere be considered eccentricity in others. If a man wants to fritter his time away putting paint on canvas or words on paper, that's his business.

As a result, many illustrious names are identified with Maine. Some belong to native sons and daughters, some to the adopted who found there something they had been seeking. There are Longfellow and Artemus Ward, Sarah Orne Jewett, Nordica and Edna St. Vincent Millay, Robert Coffin and Kenneth Roberts. Hawthorne, while a student at Bowdoin, wrote and had published in Brunswick his first novel, *Fanshawe;* and Harriet Beecher Stowe, during her Maine residence, wrote *Uncle Tom's Cabin.* Benjamin Paul Akers and Franklin Simmons found inspiration for their marbles in Maine; and John Marin, Winslow Homer, Marsden Hartley, Andrew Wyeth and Waldo Pierce for their paintings. The list is long and growing longer. All along Maine's coast and in her sheltered valleys, men and women who are or may well become famous work quietly and undisturbed with their wood and stone, their oils and water colors, their tones and harmonies, their words and phrases. Ideas are as much a product of the state as are potatoes and sardines, and as important.

10. HARASSED BY ANGELS

The typical Down-easter is generally accepted as being shrewd, cautious, industrious, hard-headed, tight-fisted, strait-laced and well endowed with common sense. He is nobody's fool. He knows on which side his bread is buttered and when to come in out of the rain. Admittedly, it is dangerous to generalize about group characteristics. There are bound to be exceptions that make nonsense out of such sweeping statements. All Scots are not penurious, all Westerners not breezy and open-handed, and all Southerners not indolent and charming; nor are all Yankees the prototype of the coldly canny horse trader. Nevertheless, the type is very clearly and sharply defined, and remarkably coherent. There is such a thing as the Yankee character, and it does dominate in Maine.

It always has. Down-easters are a peculiar breed, tough, independent, self-sufficient and generous neither with words, emotions nor worldly goods. The demands of the harsh land and bitter climate have encouraged these traits, but they did not engender them. These people were Down East Yankees long before they ever came here. The country did not change them. All the country did was to eliminate the incapable ones, to dismiss the soft ones to easier-living places. Those left were of the pure, obdurate strain, hard-shelled as butternuts and as difficult to crack, who admitted to no superiors on earth. Take them or leave them, they did not care. They were as they were, and proud of it. Their descendants of today are exactly like them.

There is one aspect of their character, however, that is often overlooked by those who do not know them well. It could be called Conscience, but it is more than that. It is not a still, small, admonitory voice within, although that is part of it, but more a gnawing passion to be better than it is humanly possible to be. The Down-easter broods overlong on angels, not realizing that to be concerned with angels in a practical world is dangerous. It obscures the course of self-interest, commits the individual to unlikely and unworldly causes, leads the sensible man into conflict with his own inner idealist. This contradictory quality has been responsible for some strange and unrealistic behavior on the part of a people who pride themselves on their down-to-earth realism. Unsympathetic to half-measures in all things, Down-easters have never been content to toss the bonnet of common sense over a mere mill. When they decide to divest themselves of it, they fling it with abandon over the far horizon.

This clean-sweeping attitude manifested itself early in regard to the consumption of alcoholic beverages. It would be inaccurate to say that the State of Maine was founded on alcohol, but alcohol nevertheless played an important part in many phases of its development. Although it is not often mentioned in history books, one of the more severe hardships that the very early settlers had to undergo—in addition to cold, hunger and Indian attacks—was being obliged to drink water. The English yeomen who established the first colonies had been accustomed all their lives to drinking ale and beer with their meals, between meals and at any time they felt in the mood. They were not sots. They were ale drinkers as people today may be coffee drinkers, and being deprived of their habitual brew aggravated an already difficult situation. It was another, and weighty, straw to the load.

This lamentable state did not last long. Sources of supply were soon established, and thereafter the first two buildings in any new community were almost invariably the church and the tavern. These usually stood side by side and were equally patronized by the most worthy and respectable citizens. Drunkenness was not a problem. Those who abused the privilege of imbibing were exposed in the stocks to public ridicule and contumely with chastening effect. As foreign trade developed and expanded, rum made from West Indian molasses became the common man's drink, being plentiful and cheap; and the wealthier shipowners and merchants drank fine imported wines and whiskeys and rare liqueurs brought home in the tall sailing ships that spun a web of commerce between Maine ports and the far corners of the globe. Unimpeachable ladies sipped a glass of sherry or Madeira before dinner or when feeling faint, and pillars of the church aided digestion or sealed bargains with snifters of old brandy. Laborers had their tots of rum or mugs of ale, and farmers relied on hard cider to see them through difficult foalings or neighborhood barn-raisings. Everybody drank, reasonably and temperately.

The building of a ship required almost enough rum to float her between the laying of her keel and her launching. Contractors and builders included in their costs this necessary commodity. The laboring day of shipyard workers was from sunrise until sunset, which in summer amounted to sixteen hours or more. In winter, the day was shorter, but it was made miserable by raw winds blowing in from the sea to stiffen joints and chill marrow. In any season, each man was issued a tumbler of rum and water—more rum than water—as soon as he arrived on the job, to get him well started on his day. This was repeated at eleven in the morning and again at four in the afternoon, in what might be considered the equivalents of today's coffee breaks. Unusually foul weather called for additional refueling, and significant points in the progress of the ship's construction, such as the raising of the stern post, the stepping of a mast or the hanging of the anchor, were celebrated by libations all around.

The launching of a ship was an event of community interest and importance. Even those who had taken no active part in her construction had watched her grow with civic pride. Very often, therefore, a local holiday was declared for the launching, and everyone dressed up and attended. After appropriate speeches, a bottle of rum or champagne was smashed over her bow to bring her luck, the wedges were knocked out from under her ribs, and she glided down the smoking ways to the cheers of the populace. Then everyone partook of a banquet provided by the owners. The workmen and their families and friends ate from trestle tables made of horses and planks set up in the yard, and the more illustrious guests ate at more elaborate boards spread in the mold loft or sail loft. Ale and rum were served in the yard, champagne and whiskey in the lofts, but in either place the flow was unstinted. Building a ship without the aid of alcohol from start to finish was unthinkable.

Nevertheless, the harried angel that lurks beneath the cynic Yankee outer man finally turned a disapproving eye on a time-honored usage that was part and parcel of the social fabric. What had been a solace and a very present help in extremity became a demon to be cast out. To this end, the first total abstinence society in the world was founded in Portland in 1815. Slowly it gained converts, until in 1834 it launched at a convention held for the purpose the first state prohibition movement. This was an unheard-of notion—that drinking should and could be regulated by law. Some religions in various parts of the world had heretofore forbidden the use of intoxicants by their adherents, and some groups had tried to discourage their use by moral suasion. But to advocate a *law*—that was asking the impossible.

Twelve years later, in 1846, such a law was written into the Maine statutes. In Maine, the impossible always takes a little longer than the merely difficult. The man chiefly responsible for this triumph was General Neal Dow of Portland, known as the Father of Prohibition. As such he has been both widely praised as an intrepid crusader and damned as an interfering old busybody. Those who knew him, even the ones who thoroughly disagreed with his viewpoint and deplored his zeal, agree that he was a kindly and rather lovable man, with a cold and narrow streak of fanaticism on this one subject alone. His zeal extended beyond the borders of his own state. He worked tirelessly and unceasingly to spread his doctrine all over the world, with the result that for a long time a prohibition law anywhere was known as a Maine law. The original manuscript of the precedent-breaking statute as he drafted it still lies on the desk in the library of his old home in Portland, and the house itself, which will eventually become a museum, is already a shrine to the members of the Women's Christian Temperance Union.

That original prohibition law was not very successful. It did not appreciably lessen the amount of alcohol consumed, only the circumstances under which it was bought and sold, the conditions under which it was consumed and the price it commanded. It was subsequently amended in a futile effort to make it more enforceable, then replaced by a long series of similar laws, some of which were lenient enough to permit the making of hard cider, and some so stringent that it almost became a crime even to mention the Demon Rum, a generic term applied by prohibitionists to any beverage with an alcoholic content. During this period, ships were of necessity christened with bottles of Poland Springs water, a sad emasculation of a robust tradition. Very few of these vessels distinguished themselves on the seas, interestingly enough. When national Prohibition became a fact in 1934, Maine had already had nearly a century of experience in which to find out that it would not work.

This disillusionment, combined with an ideal location next door to Canada and the Yankee opportunism in money matters, produced a large population of bootleggers. Smuggling contraband had always been a Maine specialty. Now great-grandsons of the men who had slipped cargoes of British wool from Nova Scotia through the blockade during the Revolution made almost a game of evading the revenue cutters with their lobster boatloads of good Canadian liquor. The Down East coast is broken and ragged, with dangerous reefs, narrow guts between islands,

and deep coves and estuaries in which to hide. The lobstermen and fishermen knew the area like the backs of their hands,
and their small boats could thread through channels impossible
for the government watchdogs. They would land their cargoes
at the dark of the moon, store it in the barn of a friend or in their
own fish houses, and next day transport it inland under a load
of hay or herring seines.

Very few were ever caught. This was at least partly due to
a local solidarity that precluded informing. Down-easters are a
close-knit clan who stick together, right or wrong; and besides,
the illegal traffic benefited everybody. Occasionally a close-
pressed smuggler jettisoned his cargo rather than be caught
red-handed, and a few days later the shore would be littered
with bottles. Then everyone went beachcombing, even rampant
teetotalers who would rather die than let liquor pass their lips.
Through an intricate form of rationalization they managed
without much difficulty to convince themselves that drinking
liquor was one thing and selling liquor sent by Providence was

quite another. The folly of looking gift horses in the mouth entered into it somehow, as did the sinfulness of waste. And any-how—and this is a typical Down East reaction—choosing Prohi-bition for themselves was a very different matter from having it imposed on them by Washington. No outsiders were going to dictate to *them.*

So there was no stigma attached to running rum, nor was it particularly a matter of pride. It was simply an opportunity that was taken. Not long ago I remarked to a sweet and innocent old lady on the beauty and convenience of her home, far out of keeping with what I was sure were her rather straitened circum-stances. " 'Tis nice," she granted. "Harvey—he was my husband —built it durin' his bootleggin', when the money was rollin' in." She neither blushed, stammered nor apologized, in spite of the fact that she was staunch in the WCTU and currently en-gaged in a hot campaign to prevent the local general store from obtaining a beer license.

Sometimes, though, principle was upheld, and on rather un-promising fronts. During the year following Pearl Harbor, I lived in a very tiny town indeed, where the keeper of the general store augmented his slim living by farming on the side. I had learned early in my residency that when dealing with him it paid to be alert. He operated on the principle of *caveat emptor,* hav-ing a tendency to rest a finger on the scales when weighing a pound of cheese and to slip a soft orange into the bag when counting out fruit. I would have said unhesitatingly that where money was involved, his conscience was as dead as the dodo.

That fall a buyer came around the countryside purchasing potatoes for the government. The crop was good that year, and the price offered well above what could be expected on the open market. Everybody sold. It then developed that the potatoes were to be used not to feed the troops, as had been assumed, but in the manufacture of medicinal and industrial alcohol to further the war effort. This made no difference to anybody except my penny-pinching friend, who promptly withdrew his considerable crop from the deal. Alcohol was a curse to mankind and he would not be associated in any way with the hellish traffic. Let others sell their immortal souls if they wished, but he was too wise to Satan's guiles to be fooled by words like industrial and medicinal. Rather than pander for the forces of Evil, he would feed his potatoes to the pigs or let them rot in the ground. And that is just exactly what he did.

Since national repeal, Maine has adopted the middle course of controlled sales of alcohol through state stores under the supervision of a State Liquor Commission. These stores are located in the cities and larger towns, and are uniformly painted green, for some reason to which I am not privy. So strong a hold did the old Abolitionists have on the Yankee spirit that the mark is still visible. Very seldom does a Down-easter come right out and say that he is going to the liquor store, and he flinches if an outlander makes such a blunt statement. The liquor store is known universally and euphemistically as the Green Front, or even more delicately as Doctor Green's. Furthermore, its presence is sometimes ascribed to the tourists and vacationists, who have to be encouraged by all means. If it were not for this necessity, the Green Front would presumably wither and die. This seems to me a very neat little exercise in ignoring the facts of life and history and in establishing an armistice between the purse and the conscience.

Down-easters are usually characterized as being rigidly orthodox in their religious observances, and so they are, in general. For example, one of the two churches in the small community where I spend much of my time is the Baptist. (The other is the Mormon, or Latter-day Saints.) The Baptist church is a small, plain edifice that does not contain a baptismal tank. The tenets of the church require complete immersion for the washing away of sins before membership can be granted, and for this purpose a nearby pond is used. The ceremony takes place in June, before the advent of the summer people disrupts the church schedule. The congregation gathers on the shore, hymns are sung, and the minister reads the appropriate service. Then the aspirants to membership, clad in flowing white, are led into the water by two lobstermen in the hip boots of their livelihood, who, supporting them strongly, plunge them beneath the surface. It is a simple, rather primitive affair, and strangely touching, carried on as it is against the background of spring's tender leafing and flowering in the fresh golden light of June's sun.

Two or three years ago, an elderly woman of my acquaintance decided that it was high time she made her peace with God by joining the church. She was going on eighty-seven, her heart was not so good as it used to be, and she'd abandoned any notion of living forever. She made the necessary arrangements with the minister, stitched up the required white robe on her sewing machine and spread the glad tidings among her friends. At this point her family intervened. They were worried. The water of the pond, only a short time free of ice, was still almost paralyzingly cold, and they doubted that her heart would stand what would be a shock to much younger and more robust systems. The family doctor agreed with them. He suggested that in view of the circumstances some dispensation might be allowed whereby sprinkling would serve as well as total immersion. Otherwise he would not be responsible for the consequences.

She would have none of this namby-pamby compromise. A

lot of good sprinkling would do! She'd lived well over eighty years. In that length of time even a saint would be bound to make a few mistakes, and she had never pretended or attempted to be a saint. It would take more than sprinkling to wash her slate clean. And everybody could just stop worrying about her heart. Let them worry instead about their own lack of faith. If they had no confidence in the Lord, she had plenty. Not that she wished to be blasphemous, but she was bound to say that He would be very foolish indeed—and He was no fool—if He chose this occasion to strike her dead. It would be against His own interests, quite aside from the tender mercy she trusted Him to show. She was going to be baptized properly, no two ways about it, and they could put that in their pipes and smoke it.

And she was; and lives, intractable still as an aged eagle, to this day the flower of orthodoxy, which is defined as conformation to the Christian faith as represented in the fundamental, ecumenical creeds.

But when the orthodox Yankee broods too long on angels, some curious things occur. He withdraws from the world of practicality and expediency and becomes obsessed with Heaven on earth, which seems entirely possible if only the way could be shown. He is therefore heedful of voices crying in the wilderness, receptive to the words of prophets, susceptible to visions. Reared in belief, he is prepared to expand his belief; familiar with the letter of the Word, he is ready to embrace its spirit. Such a thing occurred when a group of members of the United Believers in Christ's Second Appearing, more commonly known as the Shakers, toured Maine in 1793 in search of converts.

The Shakers—so called because in the religious frenzy of their meetings they often trembled and writhed—became a uniquely American phenomenon, but the sect had its origins in England.

Ann Lee of Manchester is considered the founder, although Jane Wardlaw, a Quaker, contributed a great deal to the Covenant. The Shakers, basing their view on a chapter of the Psalms, believed that Christ would be reincarnated in the form of a woman; and Ann Lee believed and convinced others that she was that woman. She preached her doctrine in the streets of Manchester and was consequently thrown into jail for obstructing traffic. There it was revealed to her in a vision that she should go to America; so upon her release in 1775 she sailed for New York with seven proselytes, five men and two women. Her husband, Abraham Stanley, whose patience had been sorely tried by Ann's activities, refused to go and disappears from the picture. It is possible that his defalcation is responsible for the inclusion of celibacy as a tenet of the faith.

The Shakers, like the Quakers, advocated peace and the turning of the other cheek. They refused to fight in the Revolution, which was in progress at the time, thereby making themselves extremely unpopular; so unpopular, in fact, that they were imprisoned as spies at Poughkeepsie, where they had gone on a missionary tour. In spite of this, and the ridicule that was heaped upon them, and the slanderous whispers of immorality that seem inevitably to be directed against any cult practicing celibacy, they managed to convert a large number of people to their beliefs. Ann Lee died in 1784—"was withdrawn from sight" in the term of the Shakers, who did not accept death—and her place was taken by Joseph Meacham and Lucy Wright.

Under the new leadership the practice of a community of goods was introduced, and the Covenant was rewritten. Briefly, it was this: that the Kingdom of Heaven had come to earth and the personal rule of God had been restored; that Christ had reappeared in the person of Ann Lee; that the old dispensation had been ended and a new begun wherein Adam's sin had been atoned and man freed of all error but his own; that the curse had been lifted from labor; that believers die to the world and enter a new Heavenly life on earth, where there is no marriage and where death is but a transfiguration.

Although some of the articles of this covenant might be difficult for the average person to accept, they offered no particular obstacle to those Maine Yankees who were at war with themselves. The Shakers themselves proved on acquaintance to be not dim-witted crackpots, but honest, intelligent, industrious men and women who were simply trying their level best to be good. This was something that the Down-easters could understand and with which they could sympathize. They wanted to be good, too; much better than was possible under the conflicting demands of their own orthodoxy and their competitive way of life. The Shakers' indifference to personal gain and worldly trappings and their attitude toward labor as a manifestation of faith, not as a necessary evil, appealed to them. Whatever their other shortcomings, the people of Maine had never been afraid of hard work. So when the Shakers came proselyting in 1793, many of them were ready for conversion to this new and sensible way of thinking and living. Two communities were established almost immediately, one at Alfred and one at Sabbathday Lake. Shaker Village at Sabbathday is still in existence and operation, one of three surviving today of the eighteen scattered throughout the Northeast and housing over nine thousand members at the height of the movement, in 1870 or thereabouts.

By this time, so sincere and true to their principles had the Shakers demonstrated themselves to be that the old prejudice against them had been replaced by a deep respect among all who came in contact with them. Nonbelieving neighbors who helped build the Shaker church at Sabbathday in 1794 were so impressed with Shaker reverence that they spoke only in whispers while at work, and many of them subsequently joined the community.

A prospective member was scrutinized carefully before being admitted on probation. Not only his morals and seriousness of purpose were examined, but his health as well. At the end of a year, if he still wished to belong, he turned over all his property to the society, but he was still free to change his mind at any time. As a result of their selectivity and of their very advanced standards of community hygiene, illness was almost unknown in the Shaker villages. They were happy, busy places, where people lived to serene old age. When a member was finally "withdrawn from sight," his funeral sermon consisted of just seven words: "He is not here. He is risen." Then he was buried, with quiet respect and without any open demonstrations of grief, beneath a plain slate slab.

Since this was a celibate society, the future of the community was assured by the adopting of orphaned or unwanted children, who were at liberty to leave when they became of age, if they wished. Most of them stayed, and of those who left, most returned. Nowhere else could they find an atmosphere of such serenity and loving-kindness in which to work out their destinies. They were spoiled for the world.

The Shaker population was largely made up of country people who loved plants and animals and were accustomed to farm work. Under their united efforts, the fields and orchards of the community flourished abundantly, producing much more than was required to meet the needs of the village. The surplus was sold about the countryside to provide a backlog of cash for unusual expenses and expansion. Very early the Shaker farmers conducted controlled agricultural experiments and produced many good hybrids. The best seeds of these selected strains were packaged and sold, delivery being made by a dignified Shaker driving a horse and buggy about the back roads of the region. These were the first packaged, labeled and guaranteed seeds in the history of agriculture.

The Maine Yankee has always been of an inventive turn of mind, and the placid, pressure-free Shaker way of life encouraged this bent. Altogether, the Shakers are credited with almost a hundred inventions, from which others have profited. They did not believe in patents, as being too grasping. These include the circular saw, the rotary harrow, Babbitt metal, horse collars, metal pens, flat brooms, condensed milk and wrinkle-proof and water-repellent cloth, to mention only a few. They also made and sold beautiful, simple furniture, designed to be "strong as truth, light as laughter." There were poets among the Shakers, too.

This furniture is still made at Sabbathday Lake and sold in the little store, all whitewash and Shaker-blue paint, that was once a chapel. Other Shaker-made products are sold there, too: hand-woven linen and woolen fabrics, hand-knit sweaters, garments —the infants' and children's clothing is especially fine—candles, cookies, candy, honey and maple syrup, churns that adapt well to lamps, wooden boxes of a variety of sizes and uses, and very nice poplar splint baskets. The prices are fair to both the buyer and the craftsmen. This comes as a pleasant shock to one fresh from the usual gift shoppes of Vacationland with their collections of high-priced junk. Here each article bears the Shaker mark of honest and painstaking workmanship, of as near-as-possible perfection. Even the packing cases that the village manufactures for the Poland Springs Bottling Works are stamped with the Shaker belief that good work is a manifestation of faith.

The Sabbathday colony is small now and growing smaller. There seems to be little place today, even among the conscience-driven Down-easters, for their calm, joyful and selfless philosophy. In addition, state welfare agencies now assume responsibility for the waifs and strays who once found security among the Shakers and grew up to carry on the community. So, slowly, it dwindles; and the massive old stone buildings on their high ridge overlooking miles and miles of lovely, rolling country-side come nearer and nearer to the day when they will be only monuments to something good that is gone.

The Maine Yankee has not always been so fortunate in the angel he chose to follow. Sometimes it has been a dark angel of destruction. Such a one arrived in Jonesport in 1866. Jonesport, in this year following the Civil War, was a small, isolated, back-ward community of naïve, trusting and devout fishermen and farmers. They had almost no contact with the outside world and very little to think about at home aside from their liveli-hoods and their religion. They were good churchgoers, deeply concerned with the state of their souls. Being unworldly and in-genuous, they were easy prey to the blandishments of George Adams, who arrived more or less out of the blue.

Adams was an apostate of the Mormon Church who had originally been an English actor. He was eloquent and practiced, trained on the stage to hold and sway audiences. He had been an effective missionary for the Mormons until he ran into trouble with Brigham Young, in Illinois. This was serious enough so that he fled east, dreaming up a religion of his own as he went. By the time he reached Jonesport, this had crystallized into the Church of the Messiah, of which he was of course the founder. He preached the Second Advent of Christ, to take place almost immediately in Palestine, and urged his hearers to give up all their worldly goods to finance a pilgrimage, so that they could be on the spot when this event took place. He bolstered his arguments with chapter and verse from the Bible so effectively that a large group of the citizens of Jonesport and neighboring hamlets was convinced. They sold their possessions to more skeptical neighbors and turned the money over to Adams.

Perhaps by this time Adams had convinced himself of his message; or just possibly he had been sincere all along, although in view of future developments this seems a little unlikely. At any rate, he did not abscond with the funds, as might have been expected. He arranged for the lease from the Sultan of Turkey of some land near Jaffa, and chartered the barkentine *Nellie Chapin*, built in Columbia Falls. She was loaded with lumber for the homes that the pilgrims would build in the Holy Land, seeds for gardens, necessary implements and tools, and supplies. Then the party went aboard—150 of them, including women and children—and the ship set sail under Captain Warren Wass of Addison. Among the group was Arthur Rogers, aged eight at the time, to whom we are indebted for some of the facts of the affair.

At first the trip went very well. The *Nellie Chapin* was a good steady vessel, the winds and weather were favorable, and everyone was full of faith, hope and optimism. Even when Adams began to drink heavily, the pilgrims were inclined to excuse him on the grounds that he had been working very hard and was under a strain—a singularly broad-minded attitude in view of the religious nature of the enterprise, and a tribute to Adams' ability to ingratiate himself.

Jaffa, however, was a disappointment from the first. The countryside was dry and barren, very unlike Maine with its soft fogs and green forests. There was no wood available for fuel or building, and—to the amazement of the Yankees, to whom such a thing was unbelievable—no wheeled vehicles. The water supply was scant, polluted and full of goat's hair; and lice, maggots and fleas abounded. This appalled the Jonesporters, who had been brought up in the Down East belief that there was no disgrace attached to being poor, but that there was no excuse at all for being dirty. However, they unloaded their cargo, saw the *Nellie Chapin* off and set about establishing their colony. Everyone was baptized first in the River Jordan, of Biblical story and sacred significance, as confirmation of their dedication. Then they got busy building their sturdy Down East houses and planting their tidy Yankee gardens in the desert.

They worked hard, but from the beginning everything was against them. The food they had brought with them soon gave out, and the gardens were a failure. The soil was too poor and water too scarce to make more than a token crop. Sickness began to take a frightening toll. Unused to the climate and the filth, the half-starved pilgrims were easy victims to germs against which they had never had a chance to build up an immunity. In a short time, half of them were dead of smallpox and other unidentified diseases. The plight of the survivors was pitiful, and it was about to become even worse.

Adams, who was seldom sober, buoyed his followers up for a time with promises of relief forthcoming when a loan that he was negotiating came through; but when it actualy did materialize, he vanished with all the money. This was the final demoralizing straw. The colony began a rapid disintegration. Some settlers left to make their way home as best they could, some disappeared entirely and forever, and the small remainder of forty persons who had no means of escape resigned themselves to death by starvation and disease.

At this crucial juncture there arrived on the scene by fortuitous chance a reporter from the New York *Sun*, Moses S. Beach, who was on a semiprofessional tour. Mr. Beach was horrified at the conditions he found in Jaffa and the hopeless situation of his fellow countrymen. He personally donated fifteen hundred dollars to evacuate the survivors and arranged passage for them on the *Quaker City* to Alexandria, thence on the *Isis* to Liverpool, and finally on the *Chicago* to New York. Aboard the *Quaker City* was Mark Twain, who gives an account of the Jaffa affair in *Innocents Abroad*. According to the pilgrims, the only part of this report that is accurate is the description of the miserable environs of Jaffa. However, something may be said in defense of Mr. Clemens' reportorial talents. He prefaces his remarks by admitting that it was almost impossible to get any information out of the disillusioned colonists. This is undoubtedly true. Nothing irks a Down-easter more than to be proved wrong, and he will go to great lengths to avoid granting such a possibility in so many words.

Not all the pilgrims took advantage of Mr. Beach's generosity. At least three stayed behind in the Holy Land. One woman married a Bedouin and settled down in Palestine. She lived for twenty-five years among her husband's people in apparent felicity, the only complaint that she was known to have registered being that the country was poor potato land. The second was an enterprising young man who decided that what the Holy Land needed was a stage line between Jaffa and Jerusalem, which he would attend to. His project was successful, and he died a well-fixed man, as they would say in Jonesport. The third, an elderly woman, stayed—in her own words—to spite herself for having been a big enough fool to come in the first place. This is a typical Yankee reason for performing any self-punishing act. Maine is full of people going around all winter with bare, half-frozen hands to get even with themselves for having lost their mittens.

Of the rest, only the Rogers family returned to Jonesport.

The others scattered from New York to various parts of the country rather than go home and face the I-told-you-so's of the neighbors. Most of them prospered in their new lives, bringing to them their Yankee drive and the bitter experience gained in Jaffa. They felt obliged to make good. Someday they might want to go back to the Maine coast, and when they did, they wanted to go in style or not at all.

As for George Adams, he reappeared a few years later in California, but only briefly. He soon vanished again with the funds of some people who had been seduced by his golden tongue and persuasive personality. Still later he was reported to be preaching in Philadelphia, although this is a little uncertain. Confronted, the man who looked and talked just like Adams stoutly denied that identity, and nobody had the time or interest to press the matter.

In Jaffa, after almost a hundred years, the well-constructed buildings of the pilgrims still stand, testimony of Yankee workmanship, and the wheeled vehicles and agricultural methods that they introduced are still used to cultivate crops of the beans, peas, corn, potatoes and pumpkins that were unknown before the Down-easters came. So perhaps the pilgrimage was not an entirely wasted effort.

The search down twisted corridors for salvation of the soul has not been confined to other, less enlightened days; nor have the prophets crying in the wilderness necessarily been sent to Maine from strange, far places. In the early days of this present century a new cult was founded by a native son, Frank W. Sandford. This was officially called The Kingdom, Incorporated, but was better known as the Holy Ghost and Us Society, or sometimes simply as Sandfordism.

Sandford was born in Bowdoinham, graduated from Bates

College, and traveled about the state as a semiprofessional baseball player for a time. He then entered the Baptist ministry, where his powers as a truly hypnotic preacher were revealed. Of imposing presence, he found that he was able to move congregations to highly emotional extravagances; and it was not long before he began thinking about a wider field in which to exercise his undoubted and considerable talents to his own benefit and glorification. The result was the Holy Ghost and Us Society, based on following the teachings of the Bible to the exact letter, and on absolute belief in the efficacy of prayer. Conditions of membership included the turning over of all material possessions to Sandford, who now insisted on being addressed as Elijah, and unquestioning obedience to his direction, the course of which was determined by visions and revelations with which he was favored. Or so he said, very convincingly.

He was convincing enough, in fact, to accumulate a more than respectable bank account in a relatively short time, and then he expanded his plans. He told his converts that he had been instructed in a vision to build a temple for his sect, where they could all live together and work for the common cause. With superb showmanship he displayed the means he had been given to make a start—a shovel, a wheelbarrow and a copper penny he had found in the road. From this small beginning, he said, a great structure would grow, brought about through miracles founded on complete faith. If everybody would work, and pray, and trust, funds would appear when they were needed. And so they did, in the form of checks against his account.

Thus Shiloh came into being, a huge establishment on a high, wind-swept hill near Freeport. It contained five hundred rooms in several buildings, including dormitories, a hospital, a playhouse for children and various communal halls. The main

building was topped by a five-story tower known as the Eye of
the Needle, supporting a domed and gilded cupola on slender
columns. It was an unusual and imposing edifice, and it was
used as a place of constant prayer.

Life at Shiloh was not all prayer, however. The converts—
and there were hundreds of them, not only from the vicinity, but
eventually from all over the world, including a Japanese lady,
an African prince and a wealthy Texan—worked like coolies.
They labored with pick and shovel, with garden hoe and spade,
with hammer and saw and needle and paintbrush, each according
to his utmost ability. For this they received their keep, and a
very restricted keep it was. Two meals a day were served, consisting chiefly of bread, cereal and pea soup. Plain living was the
rule at Shiloh. No worldly vanities were allowed—not even
haircuts, and certainly not makeup, smoking, drinking or dancing. The wearing of jewelry was forbidden, and all such fripper-
ies, even wedding rings, were turned over to the common
treasury upon entrance into the colony. It has been charged by
disaffected members that the residents of Shiloh were nothing
more than slaves who, stripped of cash and assets, had no means
of escape; and who, when they had worked themselves into illness, were cast out with not even the carfare home. While this is
prejudiced testimony, there seem to be grounds for it. Charlatan
or fanatic, Sandford certainly got the most for the least out of
his following.

In 1911 it was revealed to Sandford in another vision that the
end of the world was at hand, and the day and the hour thereof.
The Day of Doom was given over to continuous prayer, not
only on the part of the members of the colony, but throughout
the entire area and beyond, by people to whom the word had
spread and who were sufficiently convinced at least to play it

safe. When the sun set and the world still swung unfaltering in its orbit, Sandford had lost a great deal of prestige, particularly among nonbelievers who had hastily disposed of all their belongings in the hope that this last-minute change of heart would insure their salvation.

This was a serious blow, and some quick thinking and fast talking were required to recover from it. Sandford was equal to the occasion. He speedily announced still another vision in which it was disclosed that God had been touched by the prayers of the faithful and decided to spare the sinful world on condition that the doctrine of The Kingdom be spread over the entire earth. To make this possible, another miracle had occurred in the form of a check for ten thousand dollars from some divine source, easily traceable to Sandford's account by anyone skeptical enough to investigate. But when Yankees start chasing angels, they throw their inbred skepticism overboard as hindrance.

With this miraculous windfall, Sandford purchased the 150-ton sailing vessel *Coronet* and set forth from Portland with a crew of forty-five members of the cult. As the ship moved majestically out to sea, he stood on the bridge in a flowing purple robe and a sailor hat, his great Bible under his arm, his luxuriant long beard streaming in the breeze. Business in the harbor came to a temporary halt through sheer amazement while this apparition passed. The party proceeded to Jerusalem, where there was already a branch of the Society, there took aboard an ailing and enfeebled woman who had had enough of Sandfordism, and continued to Africa, presumably a fertile field for conversion.

But the native Africans were not impressed. They found Sandford's eloquence just so much meaningless ranting and his robe, hat, beard and Bible extremely funny, so funny that they chased him back to his ship with hoots and scoffing. The woman from Jerusalem then decided that she wanted to be put ashore to make her own way home, but Sandford refused her request. She managed to get word to the United States consulate that she was being detained by force and against her will, but before action could be taken, the *Coronet* had set sail for home. The woman was released in Portland, her original discontent now grown to be a full-scale, deep-seated grudge.

Before she could take any legal action, however, the *Coronet* was again at sea. After this first wholesale failure to convert the heathen, Sandford evidently decided not to return to Shiloh until he had more favorable news to report to followers whose faith was already shaken by the false Doomsday prediction. Whether because of this hasty departure or because funds were now running low, this was an ill-prepared voyage. The ship was inadequately provisioned, she had not undergone the necessary overhauling, and she did not carry a qualified captain. Sandford assumed this office himself, although unlike many Maine sons he had had no experience in navigation. Under these inauspicious circumstances, the *Coronet* wandered about the Atlantic, first back to Africa, then north toward Greenland, until she became a virtual hobo of the seas. She leaked badly, her food supply was so depleted that rations were reduced to two biscuits a day per man, and finally scurvy developed among her crew.

In spite of the sorry conditions and the frenzied pleas of his company, Sandford stubbornly refused to put ashore. At last, when eight men died of scurvy and malnutrition and were buried at sea, he was forced to give in and return to Portland. Here he was greeted by charges of detaining the woman from Jerusalem against her will for two years, to which were added, when the *Coronet's* story became known, eight charges of manslaughter through criminal neglect. He was found guilty and sentenced to ten years in the Federal penitentiary at Atlanta. Actually, he served only two before being released for good behavior. The First World War was in progress at the time, claiming public attention, so he was able to slip quietly back to Shiloh, which was still operating under a reduced staff of the truly faithful. He was now widely discredited, naturally enough, and the days of his power and glory were over. And that should be the end of the tale.

Oddly enough, it isn't, although details of further developments are hard to verify. Understandably, the members of The Kingdom, Incorporated, have been extremely reticent about their activities since the scandal, and the premises of Shiloh are conspicuously posted against trespassers. This restriction is enforced. In 1946 the guard went so far as to shoot down a mentally unbalanced veteran of World War II who was attempting to enter, and there have been other reports of violent defense of the place. This veil of secrecy inevitably gives rise to all sorts of rumors, most persistent of which is that Frank Sandford is still alive in Shiloh and planning a revival of his cult. An alternate version is that the revival is planned, but by Frank's son.

This is pure speculation, but it is supported by a certain amount of evidence. After years of neglect, those buildings of the colony that had not been demolished were observed to be under repair, and the cupola of the Eye of the Needle was regilded in 1932 and again in 1962. Twice, in 1936 and in 1952, the *Coronet*, still moored in Portland Harbor, was reconditioned and made ready to sail. For several years services have been held in a large, well-carpeted room of the main building, which has recently been open to the public. Currently as many as 250 worshipers from outside attend, although whether from conviction or out of curiosity it is impossible to determine. These visitors may not under any circumstances inspect the other buildings or the grounds at any time, and the permanent residents will answer no questions whatsoever.

So mystery surrounds the Holy Ghost and Us Society. Is Frank Sandford still alive within the walls of Shiloh? Why was the *Coronet* prepared for voyages that she never took? Is a revival of The Kingdom at hand? No one outside the Holy Ghost and Us Society really knows.

It is about time for the rise of a new cult, or the rejuvenation of an old. The practical Down-easter, busy with his plow, his lobster traps, his chain saw and his tourist cabins, has not forgotten the angels in their ancient places. Preoccupied though he may be with the price of bait or the painting of the barn, he is still aware in his innermost being of their shadowy presence. It would not surprise him at all to hear, beneath the supersonic booms of the jets flying out of Dow Air Base, the deep tones of prophetic voices nor, turning a stone, to start a wing. Then, as he has done so many times before, he will turn his back on the world and his face toward the light that has been shown.

II. A FEW TO BE REMEMBERED

Maine, in spite of her relatively small and scattered population, probably produces a greater crop of individualists than any other state in the Union. The very fact that each man has plenty of space around him, both physical and figurative, contributes to the evolution of what the summer visitors call "characters." The original pioneers were largely square pegs escaping the round holes of more thickly settled areas, and their descendants still cling to the view that what a man does and what he thinks are his own affair, so long as he pays his bills and refrains from stepping on his neighbors' toes. There is little pressure of public opinion exerted to force the eccentric to conform, and little social friction applied to rub off the odd corners. The individual is like a tree growing in an open pasture, with room to expand and develop strange offshoots; unlike a forest tree, which is crowded into uniformity with its kind.

Up until a few years ago, the educational system of the state fostered this self-direction. Every tiny hamlet had its own one- or two-room school where the child stood out as an individual; and those families—and there are many in Maine—who lived in true isolation on off-shore islands or deep in the backwoods were provided by the state with teachers who took up residence as members of the household. This had both the advantages and the disadvantages of private tutoring. The teachers were usually young, just out of normal school and full of enthusiasm for their jobs, and they were able to give their pupils a great deal of individual attention. These backwoods boys and girls could read, write and figure on a level far beyond the average children of their ages. They failed to learn, through lack of opportunity, how to get along with strangers from different backgrounds. This, when times were different and few were going to venture far from home, was no particular handicap.

When the world started shrinking and modern means of transportation and communication put Out-of-State in Maine's back yard, the authorities decided that it was time Maine children had included in their educations some experience in functioning as members of large and not necessarily compatible groups. So the little red schoolhouses were closed and their pupils are now transported daily to big, new, consolidated schools where they have to learn some degree of conformity. Those from the islands and backwoods beyond the range of school buses are boarded at state expense in school districts. Undoubtedly this is a good thing and not very likely to reduce the Maine personality to any rigidly standardized pattern. The old traits of independence and originality of thought and action are too deeply ingrained for that.

While in some parts of the country a man has to be rich or famous or both before he can afford to be eccentric, in Maine eccentricity is a fundamental right of everyone, along with life, liberty and the pursuit of happiness. A friend of mine, the owner of an impoverished farm in the hill country, one winter attended faithfully the weekly courses given by the Farm Bureau, with the idea of increasing the income of his tip-tilted acres to above the bare subsistence level. He and his neighbors learned all about crop rotation, contour plowing, the use of mulches and the rest; and come spring, they all set out to put their new knowledge into practice. That year, the agents of the canning factory wanted string beans planted. Since they provided the seed and agreed to purchase the crops at a prearranged rate, everyone diligently sowed beans according to the wise precepts of the Farm Bureau.

Everyone, that is, except my friend. The thought of the whole township given over to orderly acres of scientifically tilled bean fields was suddenly too much for him. He was oppressed with a feeling of being regimented, of being told what to do on his own property. He wished he were free to plant broccoli or dahlias or any other impractical thing; or nothing at all, for that matter. He had already signed a contract with the factory and accepted the seed, however, so he was committed to bean culture.

But nothing had been said about ways and means, so he decided that since he had to go through with the boring business, at least he would have the distinction of owning the longest row of string beans in Maine. He started in the exact center of a twelve-acre pasture and plowed one long, expanding spiral of a furrow to the very edges. This he planted to the obnoxious beans. His patch was harder to sow, cultivate and reap than the orthodox fields of his neighbors, it looked pretty peculiar, and the yield was considerably less than normal. All this bothered him not a bit. He was still able to pay his taxes by working out a part of them on the roads and cutting a few corners here and there; nobody in the state and possibly in all New England had a longer row of beans than he did; and he'd escaped by the skin of his teeth the galling experience of knuckling under to the regional facsimile of an overlord. He was the happiest, albeit the poorest, farmer in Oxford County.

This tendency to take decided and often self-punishing action for the sake of a principle has always been evident in Maine. At the time of the Civil War, the entire population of Louds Island in Muscongus Bay put themselves to considerable trouble and expense to defend a right. The islanders were in a peculiar position. Louds Island lies a mile and a half off Round Pond village in the town of Bristol, and is of fair size—four miles long and over a mile wide. People lived there as early as 1650, and by 1745 it was pretty well settled. In spite of this, through some oversight no map or chart of the area showed it, so it was officially under no jurisdiction, a fact disregarded by everyone concerned. The islanders considered themselves citizens of Bristol, where they went to vote, and Bristol agreed. Every year the tax collector rowed himself over to Louds, chalked on the door of each house the amount of the taxes due Bristol from the owner, and when it had been paid, erased his chalk marks. A general feeling of understanding and goodwill existed between island and mainland.

This was shattered in 1860, when Lincoln ran for the Presidency. Maine was at the time an almost solidly Republican state, but the inhabitants of Louds Island, exercising insular contrary-mindedness, were all Democrats. Their vote was large enough to carry the day at the Bristol polls. This was a shocking and disgraceful thing to the town fathers, and a blot on the fair name of Bristol. In the nick of time, just before the results had to be made public, it was recalled that Louds Island was not on the map and had no official existence. Therefore, the authorities reasoned, the island votes could be considered invalid. So they were all torn up and thrown away, and Bristol was able to report itself respectably Republican.

When the islanders learned this, they were consumed with fury, as well they might be. They formally notified Bristol that they were seceding from the town and would thereafter conduct their own affairs. When the tax collector showed up on his annual round, they quoted "taxation without representation," rubbed his marks off all the doors and ran him off the island. They then set up their own independent republic, with excellent results. They were determined to prove that they could get along very well without Bristol; and for a while, Bristol was very glad to get along without them.

Then came the drawings for conscripts into the Union Army. The names of nine Louds Islanders appeared on the Bristol list, and recruiting officers went over to notify and enroll the men. Every man on the island, armed to the teeth, went down to the shore to prevent the boats from landing, and a state of open warfare between the Republic of Muscongus and the Town of Bristol was declared. One conscientious recruiter came back later, but he was bombarded so heavily with potatoes thrown by the island women that he retreated in disorder. When he got back to Bristol, he swore that nothing under the sun would induce him to return to Louds Island, adding that if only he could have a single regiment of Louds Island women under his command, he'd undertake with confidence to capture Richmond and bring the Confederacy to its knees.

Having made their point, asserted their independence and protected their rights, the islanders then conducted their own draft of the required nine men. Then, to show that they held no hard feelings against the United States, but only against Bristol, they raised nine hundred dollars among themselves—a really impressive sum for the time and place—which they sent to the U.S. Treasury to be used in furthering the war effort. This last gesture was unnecessary and must have strained the resources of the hard-working islanders, who depended largely on a barter system and seldom had much cash in pocket. But it was the stiff price they voluntarily paid for their self-respect.

Out of the great company of nameless individualists who have shaped Maine's history and in their various strong-headed and singular ways made her what she is, a few stand out to be remembered especially. This is not because they are any different from the majority of their fellow Mainiacs. They're the same, only perhaps more so; or else circumstances happened to call attention to their activities. One of these was Samuel Clough, the sea captain who is given the credit for bringing the coon cat to Maine.

At the time of the French Revolution, Captain Clough was master of the *Sally*, a merchantman engaged in trade with France. In 1793 he and his ship became involved in a plot to save Marie Antoinette from the guillotine and spirit her away to the coast of Maine, where she would find sanctuary in the Clough home near Wiscasset. There are two opinions as to why

Samuel Clough lent himself to this enterprise. The romantic view is that his heart was touched by the plight of the hapless Queen and that this attempt to rescue her was an act of pure chivalry. Others believe that he was simply hired by the Royalists to carry the Queen to America. They say that no level-headed Yankee skipper would endanger his ship and his person in such a risky venture unless the stakes were high enough to make the chance worth taking. On the other hand, since he was making himself personally responsible for her well-being in exile, the matter must have had more meaning to him than just a business arrangement for transportation.

So that the Queen would not be too unhappy and uncomfortable in the plain home of a Maine seafarer, many of her personal belongings and furnishings were smuggled aboard the *Sally* as she lay waiting in the French port. There were dresses and cloaks and toilet articles, and even rolls of lovely French wallpaper, heavy damask hangings and priceless bric-a-brac to furbish the austere Down East quarters intended for her. Marie Antoinette was under house arrest at the time, so the collecting of this cargo of luxury items of an extremely incriminating nature had to be carried on under the noses of guards. It was doubtless accomplished by the lavish use of bribes, in itself a dangerous business since any one of them might turn informer and bring about the imprisonment of the captain and the impounding of his vessel. Even if he was being well paid for his activities, Captain Clough was taking some very long chances of never seeing Wiscasset again.

What seemed to worry him more—and with reason—was his wife's attitude when he came bringing home a royal guest who would undoubtedly disorganize the entire household. He wrote Mrs. Clough several letters trying to reconcile her to the dismaying prospect of sheltering this pampered and aristocratic Frenchwoman, so different in background, tastes and experience from the Maine seacoast women. "Do not prepare to receive a queen," he begged, "but only a very sad and broken-hearted lady."

If Mrs. Clough was a little apprehensive and resentful, it is hard to see how she can be blamed. Here her husband was risking life and limb for another woman, and in addition he expected her to turn her whole house upside down to accommodate this foreigner. He did not think the plain old furniture that had been good enough for his own wife all these years was fit for the visitor. Everything had to be done over new. And what did one feed a queen? Would she be satisfied with fish chowder and johnnycake? How did one treat a queen? It was all very well for Samuel to say that she was just a sad lady, but could you expect a Queen of France to make her own bed and help with the dishes like one of the neighbors? Mrs. Clough had her problems.

She never had to find out the answers to them. Before the *Sally* could sail from France, there was a sudden outbreak of violence during which Marie Antoinette was seized and eventually beheaded. Captain Clough slipped anchor and fled to avoid being arrested for his participation in the plot. There was no time to unload the Queen's belongings. They, at least, were transported safely to Wiscasset; and there is a legend that Talleyrand and Marie Antoinette's son, the Dauphin of France, boarded the *Sally* at the last moment and were guests of the Cloughs' for some time.

For a long while the Cloughs stored the Queen's possessions, unused, in a spare room of their house. The romantics insist that this was a sentimental gesture on the part of the Captain, arising from his personal devotion to the unfortunate Queen. It seems more likely that his strict Yankee conscience would not allow him to use or dispose of property that did not belong to him and that he had acquired in a rather irregular manner; or that Mrs. Clough refused to have any part of these reminders of what she was bound to consider a foolish and dangerous episode in her husband's career.

Gradually, however, as events faded into the past and no one came to claim the cargo, the articles were put into use in the big, plain colonial house. An elaborate satin robe worn by the King of France on state occasions was made into a Sunday-go-to-meeting dress by Mrs. Clough, and a beautiful clock presented to Marie Antoinette by the maker on the Dauphin's birthday told off the brisk and busy Maine hours in the Clough kitchen. After the death of the Cloughs, everything was auctioned off. Some pieces found their way to the Metropolitan Museum of Art in New York, and a few remain in the Clough house, which has been moved to Edgecomb. Most of them are scattered around among the homes of the countryside about Wiscasset and Edgecomb. The fragile gilded chairs, ornate mirrors and bright cloisonné snuffboxes seem as improbable on that bleak coast as the fantastic adventure of which they are sole survivors.

It has never been necessary, however, for Maine Yankees to chase off to the ends of the earth in support of glamorous lost causes in order to express their individuality. One quiet little woman never in her life went very far from her birthplace in South Berwick, yet simply by following her bent and being herself she achieved lasting fame. She was Sarah Orne Jewett, of one of whose works Willa Cather said, "If I were asked to name three American books which have the possibility of a long, long life, I would say at once, *The Scarlet Letter*, *Huckleberry Finn*, and *The Country of the Pointed Firs*." It is generally agreed that Miss Jewett's writings provide a landmark in American literature. In a day when most writers of fiction were busy with matters far outside the average reader's ken—belted earls, haunted castles and poor but virtuous heroines of unearthly beauty—she concerned herself with the things of which she knew through her own rather circumscribed experience. She wrote about ordinary people and everyday events against the background of the Maine coast with such insight that her stories struck a responsive chord in the hearts of everyday people everywhere. She was the first of the good genre writers and still remains one of the best.

Sarah Orne Jewett was born in 1849 in a beautiful house that is today owned by the Society for the Preservation of New England Antiquities. Her father was a country doctor, and when she was still a very little girl, she went with him on his rounds to remote farms and the cottages of fishermen and sea-farers. She waited in country kitchens with members of a family while her father brought a baby into the world or regretfully closed the eyes of an old man he had been unable to save. Young as she was, she understood about birth and death and joy and sorrow, about life with its tragedies and its comedies, too. People opened up to her as they awaited the doctor's verdicts, telling her stories of the past, pouring out their hopes for the future.

On the long, slow drives over rural roads behind the jogging horse, her father talked constantly, passing on to her all that he had learned in schools and through a doctor's intimacy with the problems of his patients, informing her, philosophizing to her about life and its meaning. She had an unerring eye and ear and a retentive memory, and almost without volition she began putting down on paper the things she saw and heard. Her first story was published in the *Atlantic Monthly* when she was twenty years old, a true distinction for a country girl of little formal education. Years later, in 1901, she was to be awarded the degree of Doctor of Letters by Bowdoin College and to become the first woman so honored by that institution.

Once she ventured from home to Martinsville, a tiny hamlet near Port Clyde at the entrance of Penobscot Bay, where she taught for a season in the little one-room school. Here she wrote *The Country of the Pointed Firs*, working in the schoolhouse after hours, because her landlady was so very sociable that it was impossible to concentrate under her roof. It is a simple book, dealing with unimportant happenings of the vicinity of Martins-ville, but, although it was written in the 1890's, the descriptions are accurate today. "I watched the gulls turn and agree," she wrote, "and sway together down the long slopes of air"; and of coastal houses, "the small-paned high windows in the peaks of their steep gables were like knowing eyes that watched the harbor and the far sea-line beyond." From Kittery to Eastport, the gulls still coast down the airy hills, and the cottage windows still peer suspiciously at the sea, exactly as they did then.

Some of the conversations recorded could have taken place this morning anywhere in Maine.

"I wonder who she was before she was married?" said Mrs. Todd, who was usually unerring in matters of genealogy. "She must have been one of that remote branch that lived down beyond Thomaston. We can find out this afternoon. I expect the families'll march together or be sorted out some way."

"I seem to see the family looks," said Mrs. Blackett. "I wish we'd asked her name."

"She resembles Cousin Pa'lina Bowden about the forehead," said Mrs. Todd with decision.

Just so do women still track down family connections.

Miss Jewett's characters could step off her pages into the contemporary Maine scene without causing a head to turn. There are the two families who shared an island for three generations without speaking a word to each other even at times of death. They liked it that way. They enjoyed it. It gave them an interest. I know two women living side by side in a very small hamlet who have not exchanged words for over seven years, as the result of a trivial disagreement. This feud, too, gives an interest; and it, too, shows every indication of lasting for at least three generations.

There is Captain Littlepage, a sweet and vague old man who had overset his mind with too much reading; and his housekeeper Maria Harris, who should, according to local opinion, let the old gentleman think he was having his own way, 'stead of arguing everything down to the bare bones; and gentle William Blackett, whose sister suspects him sometimes of being kind of poetical, though, she adds, "You'd think if anything would cure him of it, 'twould be the fish business"; and many, many more whose spit'n' images today walk the streets of the tiny coastal towns. A person planning a first visit to Maine could do worse than read Sarah Orne Jewett in preparation.

Miss Jewett was not by any means the only Maine writer to find in her immediate environment an inexhaustible source of material. The first to recognize the great wealth lying all about her was Sally Sayward Barrel, born in York in 1759. By 1790, under the name of Madam Wood, she had become one of America's first popular novelists and was supporting her three children on the proceeds of her books. The nature of her subject matter is explained in the introduction to one of her novels: "The following pages are wholly American; the characters are those of our country. The author has endeavored to catch the manners of her native land; and it is hoped that no one will find, upon perusal, a lesson, or even a sentence, that authorizes vice or sanctions immorality." By today's standards, Madam Wood's works seem naïve, stilted and slightly unrealistic; but she was nevertheless the trail-blazer for a distinguished company.

One of the best loved of these was Henry Wadsworth Long-fellow, whose *Evangeline* is integral to the body of American literature. Longfellow was born in Portland and grew up in the home of his grandparents, now a literary shrine. This beautiful house and garden, an oasis of peace and serenity in the middle of the noise and confusion of downtown Portland, do much to explain the happy, sunny personality of the man. Although much of his work was done after Longfellow left Maine to become pro-fessor of modern languages at Harvard, he harks back constantly to the scenes of his childhood. His best poem, *My Lost Youth*, is a nostalgic and moving recollection of the days when he was a boy and thought the long thoughts of youth. It is full of lovely, evocative images:- "a sabbath sound, as of doves in quiet neighborhoods"; "the Spanish sailors with bearded lips"; "the breezy dome of groves." Nowadays Longfellow is often dis-missed rather lightly, and it is true that some of his poems are mechanical and some are almost doggerel, but no one except a true poet could have written *My Lost Youth*. For that alone he deserves to be remembered.

It is impossible to list all the Maine writers who have achieved fame far beyond the borders of the state. There are Edna St. Vincent Millay, Artemus Ward, Mary Ellen Chase, Gladys Hasty Carroll, Ben Ames Williams, Robert P. Tristram Coffin, who won the 1936 Pulitzer Prize, and a host of others. Kenneth Roberts, however, deserves special mention for his novels, which bring to vivid life the events of Maine's past without ever sacrificing historical accuracy. They are all of them—*Arundel*,

The Lively Lady, *Northwest Passage*, *Rabble in Arms*—thoroughly absorbing tales in the best tradition of the American historical romance. It is perhaps not by accident that Roberts achieved distinction in this particular field. He was born in Kennebunk, in the Storer house, which was the home of General Joseph Storer, a Revolutionary soldier and a personal friend of Lafayette. Roberts could not very well help being aware of the past from earliest childhood.

But this may be true of all Maine writers in somewhat less obvious case. In Maine, things change slowly. Old customs, old speechways, old standards and old memories remain current and significant long after they have been abandoned by the rest of the world; and so the past is not something to be reconstructed with difficulty, but something that is lived every day. This may at least partly account for the special flavor and style of most Maine writing.

Maine has contributed extensively to American art as well as to American literature, and in typical fashion. There has never been a Maine school or movement in painting, and it is unlikely that there ever will be. It would go against the Down East grain. Let others have their schools and movements, running the risk of being copycats. In Maine, everyone paints the way he wants to paint, and if the result turns out to be a poor thing, at least it is the artist's own. This prickly and independent attitude has produced some truly great and original work.

It is impossible to say who is the "best" Maine painter. Being "best" in any line of creative work depends on too many elusive and imponderable factors. It must necessarily mean coming closest to the artist's own intention, and only he can judge how successful he has been in translating his preconception into reality. Furthermore, any form of communication—whether it be by paint on canvas, shapes carved from wood or stone, sounds from the lips or from instruments, or printed words on a page— is a two-way affair. Being best must therefore depend partly on the taste, responsiveness and personal bias of the individual critic. So we will not attempt to decide who is the "best" Maine artist.

We can say, however, that Winslow Homer is probably the best known. He has been called, by those who know, the most powerful representative of open-air painting in America, and his dramatic and brilliant canvases are familiar at least in reproduction to almost everyone. Although he was born in Boston, Homer was of Maine parentage, and his family spent their summers at Prout's Neck, near Portland. In 1884, Winslow built a studio there on a rocky point overlooking the sea, and thereafter made it his permanent home. A natural solitary, he lived there alone the year round, except for a few winter trips to Florida or the Bahamas. "The life I have chosen," he once wrote a friend, "gives me my full hours of enjoyment for the rest of my life. The Sun will not rise or set without my notice and thanks."

Out of this absorption grew a familiarity with the countless aspects of the natural world and an understanding of man's relation to it. These things come through clearly in his strong, uncluttered paintings. Homer has been called an illustrator, and that he is. But he is more than that. He is a master of design as well. "Never put more than two waves in a picture; it's fussy," he once advised a young artist. Even his detractors could never accuse Winslow Homer of being fussy.

The roster of artists from other areas who have spent considerable time in Maine and made her scenes familiar far beyond her boundaries is long and distinguished. It includes among many others John Singer Sargent, Rockwell Kent, George Bellows, Robert Henri, Andrew Wyeth and Georgia O'Keeffe. The

Maine coast as much as any region in the world has had a persistent impact and influence on successive generations of artists,
and at least one native artist has had his effect on modern painting.

He was Marsden Hartley, born in Maine but self-exiled for
most of his adult life. Like the Maine farm boys of an earlier
day who ran away to sea, putting behind them the known land
routine, Hartley ran away to Europe, deliberately turning his
back on the artistic traditions of his homeland. He experimented
with abstractions in Berlin, studied Cézanne's techniques and
ideas, identified himself with the most advanced and revolutionary groups of Paris; and then, at the age of fifty-nine, he came
home to Maine. It was not until then that he found himself and
emerged as a significant figure.

Applying the new artistic idiom to the age-old Maine scene,
he became one of the first good American modernists. He found
that by deliberate distortion and an arbitrary use of color he
could express his deep and genuine emotional response to the
stark coastline, restless seas and brilliant skies of the land of his
birth. Although he was given only ten years to work before his
death, he—along with John Marin—must be remembered for
bringing a new attitude toward what had become almost hack-
neyed subjects.

Hartley's work was not especially appreciated during his
lifetime. He spent a large part of his final year in the tiny
coastal hamlet that I call home. Here he is remembered for his
indifference to the fact that he had almost no money, for an
almost old-maidish fussiness over the proper brewing of tea, for
his crankiness when interrupted at work and for a painting
called *Give Us This Day*. This is a large oil showing a half-dozen
sea gulls clustered around three dead fish. It is famous here not

for its artistic merit, but because it took so long to paint that the stench of the fish, ripening steadily in the heat of the sun-baked henhouse that was his studio, rendered the building unfit for any purpose whatsoever for a long time.

All of Maine, on the contrary, is extremely proud of a small-town girl who became the first woman ever to be elected to the United States Senate solely on her own merits. This admiration is shared by Republicans and Democrats alike, which is unusual in an area that takes its politics very seriously. She is, of course, Margaret Chase Smith, born in Skowhegan, onetime five-and-ten-cent-store clerk, telephone operator, bookkeeper, teacher of a one-room school, newspaperwoman, office manager and treasurer of a woolen mill.

Thus far her history is that of most attractive and intelligent Maine girls who hold one job after another, each better than the last, until they marry. Margaret Chase was married in 1930 to Clyde H. Smith, a man prominent in local and state politics. In 1936 Smith was elected to represent the Second Maine District in the Seventy-fifth Congress and re-elected in 1938. During his tenure, Mrs. Smith served as his secretary, taking care of the routine office work. Often she worked fifteen hours and answered as many as seventy-five letters a day, besides doing research on the subjects of various bills. She somehow found time to serve as treasurer of the Congressional Club, composed of the wives of Congressmen, and to receive five hundred callers a week at the Smith open house in Chevy Chase. She was a busy woman; and all the time she was working, she was learning.

Clyde Smith died of a heart attack in April of 1940, and in a special election on June 3, Mrs. Smith was chosen to occupy his seat for the remainder of the Seventy-sixth Congress. This is not an unusual gesture of respect by loyal constituents to the memory of a man who has served them well. Mrs. Smith was unusual, however, in that she was not satisfied simply to sit in her husband's place. She almost immediately began to make herself felt as a personality in her own right when she supported the Selective Service Act in opposition to most of her Republican colleagues. This certainly was not typical of a new little Representative in the presence of her elders, but it has been typical of Mrs. Smith. She votes as she sees fit. During her eight years in the House of Representatives she ran up a record of one vote in every three against the majority of her party. Nobody in Maine's Second District held it against her. Everybody there knew her personally as someone who could be trusted to do the very best she knew how. You couldn't ask more than that of anyone, they figured; so they sent her back to Washington again and again. Undoubtedly, Margaret Smith could have stayed in Congress as long as she chose. She was set for life.

In 1947 Maine's veteran United States Senator Wallace H. White decided not to run for re-election. To the dismay of her friends, Mrs. Smith announced her candidacy for his seat. In Maine, everybody is a political expert, and all the experts were for once agreed. "She's stepped out of her class," they said. "In the State o' Maine, the House is one thing and the Senate's another. The Senate is big-time. Nobody in Maine gets into the Senate without a political machine, a fat campaign fund, the right connections and the help of the Powers That Be. Margaret hasn't got any of those things, and her two opponents—Governor Horace Hildreth and former Governor Sumner Sewall—have got 'em all. They're the two biggest vote-getters in the history of the state. They've both got plenty of political savvy and plenty of money that they're willing and able to spend. Margaret's a fine girl, no doubt about that, but she can't compete against the big guns."

Margaret, however, had one big gun of her own—the kind

of personality that wins friends and commands loyalty and devotion. She was and is the sort of person with whom everyone immediately feels comfortably at home. Instinct told her that if she could only talk face to face with the people outside her own district so that they could get to know her as the home folks did, she'd be able to convince them of her fitness for the office she sought. So under appalling difficulties of transportation, through Maine blizzards and over almost impossible roads, she drove her own little car to small towns and tiny hamlets throughout the length and breadth of the state. She addressed few mass meetings. Rather she talked to a handful of people in a country schoolhouse here, to a small group in a fire station or town hall there—talked as a friend, as one of their own. In the June primaries she received more votes than her three opponents combined, and in the national elections that fall she won with the greatest total vote majority in the history of Maine politics.

She has been Maine's Lady Senator ever since, even in the years when the once rigidly Republican state has swerved from the traditional path and elected Democratic Governors and Congressmen. Maine just loves Margaret Smith. They loved it when she stood up on her two feet and denounced Senator Joseph McCarthy at a time when almost everybody else was discreetly silent, at least in public. They loved it when a radio commentator asked her what she'd do if she woke up one morning and found herself in the White House, and she replied, "I'd go straight to Mrs. Truman and apologize. Then I'd go home." Addressing the Senate on September 21, 1961, Mrs. Smith charged the Kennedy Administration with apparent lack of will to use nuclear weapons, an attitude which she claimed weakened the nation's ability to deal with the Soviet Union. Shortly afterward in a message to the British Labour Party, Premier Khrushchev called

Senator Smith "the devil in the disguise of a woman" who sur-
passed "all records of savagery." Maine really loved that description of their quiet, friendly Margaret. It did everyone good to
know that a Down East girl could get under Nikita's hide.

A great many conspicuous honors have been showered on
Mrs. Smith. Although she has never attended college, she holds
thirty-six honorary degrees. She has served as a lieutenant
colonel in the Air Force Reserve, has been chosen Woman of
the Year several times, and has three times been rated by the
Gallup Poll as one of the ten most admired women in the
world. In 1960, *Newsweek's* press gallery poll awarded her
the Most Valuable Senator rating. The Veterans of Foreign
Wars gave her their Americanism medal, and the Charm Insti-
tute designated her as The Most Charming Woman in Government.

These distinctions are both flattering and deserved, but Mrs.
Smith can claim another much harder to win than all the rest
put together. In Maine, when anybody asks, "What's Maggie's
idee on the subject?" nobody asks, "Maggie who?" In Maine,
there is only one Maggie with ideas worth listening to.

Of a very different type was another small-town Down-easter,
Mellie Dunham of Norway, in the southwestern part of the
state. Mellie Dunham was a snowshoe maker by trade, who
farmed his few acres on Crockett's Ridge, did a little hunting
and fishing in season and played his fiddle at the local square
dances. Not very much happened to him during the first
seventy-odd years of his life, except that Admiral Robert E.
Peary was wearing a pair of Dunham snowshoes when he planted
the American flag at the North Pole. The Admiral sent him a
walrus hide and narwhal horn in appreciation, and the snowshoes with Mellie Dunham's name burned into the frame may

be seen today in the Smithsonian Institution. Nobody made better snowshoes than he did, and until he was seventy-two that was his chief pride and his only claim to fame.

Then, just for the fun of it, he entered a fiddle pageant over at Lewiston, held to choose Maine's champion fiddler. He loved to play his old fiddle, sawing away like mad, stamping time with his off foot and swearing mildly under his breath. It was nothing a man would do for a living, of course, even providing he could find anyone fool enough to pay a living wage for fiddling, but it made a nice pastime. Over to Lewiston, he'd have a chance to listen to some pretty good fiddling, no doubt. He might learn a few new tricks. He came home from Lewiston the Champion Fiddler of Maine.

One morning shortly thereafter as he was looking through his mail, he remarked to his wife, Emma, "I see there's a letter from Henry here."

"Henry who?" Emma couldn't place any Henry who'd have occasion to be writing Mellie.

"Henry Ford. What other Henry is there?" Henry, it seemed, was conducting a national contest to determine who was America's greatest old-time fiddler, and he'd like Maine's champion to come out to Dearborn, all expenses paid, as a contender.

Mellie didn't see what he had to lose by going. Contest aside, it ought to be a real interesting trip. The Dunhams had never been far outside the State of Maine. So with Emma, his fiddle in its old black case and a pair of snowshoes especially made as a gift for Henry, he set forth. Norway gave him a rousing send-off. The farmers of the countryside who were still driving old Model T's or had the Model T's versatile motors hooked up to their saw rigs considered Henry Ford a national benefactor. The chance to play before the man who had made it possible for

even hard-scratching Down-easters to drive their own automobiles was a greater honor than playing before the crowned
heads of Europe. Even the Governor of the state was there, with
a personal message for Henry. Mellie took the fuss in stride. He
continued to be "just as you saw him" and "common as anybody," which is the Yankee way of saying that attention did not
go to his head and a very great compliment, in Maine.

The contest was held in the Ford dance hall in the engineering
laboratory at Dearborn. Mellie, wearing the clean khaki pants
and gray work shirt that were his fiddling clothes back home
when he played for country kitchen square dances, played as he
had always played. With his white mustache bristling and his
halo of white hair in disorder, he ripped through *"Turkey in the
Straw"* and the *"Boston Fancy,"* enjoying every minute of it.
There were thirty-eight other contestants, many of them much
younger than his seventy-two years; but after his rendition of
his own composition for the country fiddle, *"Rippling Waves,"*
everyone stood up and cheered. There was no question as to who
was the Champion Old-Time Fiddler of the United States, which
meant the Western Hemisphere and possibly the whole world.

He was paid three dollars for the performance, which was the
standard wage, and he was more than satisfied. He had had the
trip, the pleasure of talking things over with Henry, and a good
time all round. He did not anticipate what happened next, although a man more sophisticated than he certainly would have,
but he took it as it came. The Keith-Albee circuit offered him
bookings for the winter in their theaters at five hundred dollars a
week. This was a lot of money to a man who, when he left
Norway, owed ninety dollars in taxes on his farm and wasn't
sure how he was going to be able to raise it. But Mellie was not
one to sail under false colors. "I ain't no artist," he warned the

Keith agent. "I'm just an old country fiddler from Norway, Maine." That clearly understood, he accepted the new assignment.

I saw him perform in Boston that winter. The stage was set as an old New England barn, with hay mows, a rough plank floor and all the rural properties of pitchforks, oil lanterns on the walls and hay rakes in the corners. A group from the Bragiotti Dance School, dressed in some costumer's notion of what is worn at back-country Saturday night square dances, wandered about in careful aimlessness. It was all very pretty and picturesque, and very, very contrived and synthetic.

Then Mellie Dunham came on. He did not make an entrance. He just walked in, as he had into so many Oxford County barns and kitchens, shucking his coat, blowing on his hands to warm them, stripping the felt cover off his fiddle. He plucked a string here and there, listening, nodding; then he tucked his fiddle under his chin and started playing. Everything changed. This no longer seemed like a well-planned act, but like something genuine and spontaneous. It is hard to tell why. The best I can explain is that old Mellie Dunham in his honesty and simplicity took us all back to the earlier and more innocent time that is a part of our racial heritage and for which we all unconsciously suffer a deep nostalgia. But probably that's too elaborate an explanation. It may just boil down to the fact that nobody in the whole audience could help loving Mellie Dunham.

He worked hard that winter at Keith's and on a succession of night club engagements in New York. He made a record of "Rippling Waves" that sold extremely well. It looked as though people everywhere would go on paying good money to hear Mellie play his fiddle as long as he wanted to keep it up; and so very likely they would have. But he was going on seventy-three, and even in his salad days he had never been one for sky-hooting around the countryside night after night. He was getting tired. Eating outlandish foods, sleeping in strange beds, meeting new people constantly told on a man after a while. Home, he admitted, would look pretty good to him.

So he went back to Norway, and everyone agreed that his travels and success and the money he had made and the attention he had been paid hadn't altered him a whit. He was exactly as you saw him still, common as anybody. He was one of the best ambassadors that ever went out of Maine, not because of anything he said or did, but because of what he was.

Mellie Dunham has been called, both in print and out, a typical Yankee, and I suppose that he is. So were Captain Clough and Sarah Orne Jewett, whom he resembles not at all; and so were many others who seem to have little in common except the region of their birth. Lillian Nordica, who sang with the Metropolitan Opera Company for fifteen years and was acclaimed on both sides of the Atlantic, was a Down-easter. So were Cyrus Curtis and the sculptor Paul Akers, whose *Dead Pearl Diver* inspired Hawthorne to write *The Marble Faun*. So were William and Dustin Farnum, the old stage and silent screen stars, and the actress Maxine Elliot, and the singer Rudy Vallee—all Maine Yankees with the essential Down East cast of character. So was Hiram Maxim, the inventor of the automatic machine gun which revolutionized warfare and won the Maine farm boy from tiny Sangerville a knighthood.

Leon Leonwood Bean, reporting daily for work at over ninety, is a typical Yankee, too. In a ramshackle old Freeport building that has been described as a cross between grandmother's attic and a broken-down roller-coaster, he conducts a world-wide mail-order business in wilderness equipment recog-

nized as the best on earth. This enterprise started fifty years ago
with an idea for a hunting boot with a leather top and a rubber
foot and a capital of four hundred dollars. Because woodsmen
grew to like the boot "even better than their wives sometimes,"
L. L. Bean, Inc., now does about two and a half million dollars'
worth of business annually. This is at the same old original
stand, without salesmen on the road, national advertising, branch
stores, retail outlets or even an Addressograph or filing cabinets.
Mail, amounting to five thousand letters a day, is filed in empty
cardboard boxes, and 400,000 catalogues are addressed by hand
twice a year. Mr. Bean sees no sense in squandering money on a
lot of frills. " 'Tain't money that puts your business up," he says.
"It's having something that no one else has got as good as."

Nobody could be more of a Down-easter than Percival Baxter,
Maine born and bred, twice Governor of the state, five times
a member of its legislature and President of the Senate. Over the
years he has bought with his own funds nearly 200,000 acres of
wilderness around Katahdin and given it "forever to be held in
trust in its natural wild state for the benefit of the people and
as a sanctuary for the wild beasts and birds." Some Yankees
make money from a good idea, some give money away for a
good idea, and both are typical.

What then is the one characteristic that Down East Yankees
possess in common, man or woman, Republican or Democrat,
Catholic or Protestant, politician, farmer or businessman? It is
simply this: every Down-easter knows exactly who he is and
feels no compulsion to try to be somebody else. This is less
common than might be supposed. Too many people are not sure
of their own identity, and they are forever trying to be what
they think they should be. Or else for any one of several reasons
—to make more money, to climb socially, to keep the peace—

they adopt uncomfortable and ill-fitting roles. The Down-easter likes money and position and peace, too, but he likes himself better. He does what he feels like doing, no matter how odd, and because he feels like doing it, it is inevitably right for him. He hews to the line of his own individuality and lets the chips fall where they may. It is interesting how often he manages to distinguish himself simply by being, come hell or high water, his own crusty and contrary self.

Once I pointed out to a Maine Yankee during a cracker-barrel argument in a coastal general store that he and his kind were a minority. He looked at me with cool amusement. "Ay-up, I guess we be," he said complacently. "So's God, come to that. Don't seem to fret Him none either."

That's the attitude that is typical of Down-easters. It is about the only thing that is typical.

12. THE PARTICULAR FLAVOR

It is possible to write a history of a people without giving any clear picture of the people themselves. Their victories and defeats may be recorded, their progress noted, their occupations listed, statistics of their birth rate, average income, social customs, morality, incidence of crime and the nature thereof compiled, and yet the individuals themselves fail to emerge. Nothing in the mass of information conveys the true substance, the particular flavor, of their characters and personalities. Nothing tells what they are really like.

266

Perhaps this is impossible to do, just as it would be impossible to describe the flavor of olives to one who has never tasted them, or the scent of new-mown hay to one who has never filled his lungs with that haunting and delicate fragrance. Some things must be experienced to be known. Such a thing may be the character of the Maine Yankee. We may say that he is independent, taciturn, thrifty, self-sufficient and any number of other things that surely apply, but still the truth eludes us. The description is accurate enough, but limited. It is like describing an olive as a small oval drupe, esteemed as a relish and valuable as a source of oil; or hay as grass cut and dried for use as fodder. The facts are correct, but the essence is missing.

There are, however, indices to the indefinable character, and the first and most obvious are appearance and manner. All Down East Yankees do not actually look alike, of course, and yet there is a kind of family resemblance. This lies partly in the prevalent long Down East face, with its lean and angular jaw, firm mouth and level, observant eyes. It lies more in the expression on those faces. Even fat Yankees, of which there are some but not many, and jolly Yankees, of which there are even fewer, manage somehow to give the impression that behind the watchful eyes detached judgments are being made and uncompromising conclusions drawn. This is frequently a false impression, rising from the Down-easters' disinclination to expose their feelings. Ever since they first came to the Maine coast, they have necessarily been on guard against unexpected attacks from a variety of quarters, including Indians, the weather, the wrath of God, and smooth-talking, out-of-state salesmen. These centuries of defensiveness have trained the Yankee face not to lend itself to merely polite smiles, expressions of even slight concern or any surprise at all. Such might lead to commitment, and Down-easters have learned not to commit themselves readily.

The tale is told of two out-of-state duck hunters who were trying out a new bird dog. The first duck they shot fell into the water at some distance from the shore, as is usually the case. The dog unconcernedly walked across the surface of the sea and retrieved the bird, to the natural astonishment of the handlers. This was really something for the book, they told each other. This would really cause a stir from coast to coast. All they needed now was impartial witnesses to back their incredible claims. At this point two native hunters happened on the scene. The city sportsmen greeted the new arrivals cordially and offered them the services of the dog.

Shortly more ducks came over, were shot and fell well off shore. Again the dog walked out on the water and retrieved the game. No comment whatsoever was made. After this had happened a few more times, the dog's owners began to be irritated by the lack of response to an unquestionable miracle.

"What's the matter with you two?" one of them demanded. "Don't you notice anything unusual about our dog?"

The State-of-Mainers looked at him thoughtfully. "Cal'lated you might be a mite sensitive about it," the older one said finally, "but sure we do. The son of a bitch can't swim."

This ridiculous story is as true in spirit as it is false to fact. It is a very cold day when a Down-easter is caught off balance sufficiently to betray any great amount of emotion.

This same guardedness is evident in the handling of the body. Gestures are used with great economy, and gesticulations almost never. Yankees waste few motions. They cover ground fast, if necessary, but with long and deceptively leisurely strides. They are able to get a great deal of work done in a short time without ever seeming to hurry. Back of them are generations of frugality, so that aversion to squandering anything, including time, energy and words, is ingrained. They make their heads save not only their heels, but their hands, backs and tongues as well. A really bone-lazy Down-easter is uncommon. Nobody can afford to be lazy, for one thing; for another, the climate truly is bracing and conducive to endeavor—or as they say locally, "We have to rustle 'round if'n we don't want to freeze to death"; and for still another, Conscience acts as a deterrent to sloth. If there is nothing that demands to be done immediately, the Down-easter feels obliged to find something to do.

As a result, he makes the most of the very rare moment when outer pressures and the still, small, inner voice agree to allow him to sit with idle hands—"to set an' mull," as he himself calls it. This is different from sitting and thinking. This is complete immobility, while dreams and notions and impressions drift across the surface of the mind. Yankees seldom fidget. Nobody can sit stiller than they, and nobody can spring more quickly and enthusiastically back to work, the normal condition.

Work is not only normal to Down-easters; it is desirable and enjoyable. In enforced idleness, they are uneasy and unhappy. A difficult task is a challenge, and the proudest thing a man can say at sundown is, "I got through a slew of work today." Once in a general store I overheard two local women talking about the wealthy summer person by whom one of them was employed.

"She's never got her hands dirty in her life," one of them said. "She don't know the meaning of hard work."

"Poor thing, she's to be pitied," the other replied. She was not trying to be funny, and there was no tinge of sarcasm or envy in her voice. She meant exactly what she said. In her view, one who had never dirtied her hands at hard work had been deprived and was a legitimate object of pity. Down East, much can be forgiven an individual if only it can be said of him, "He's a good worker." That this is the highest possible commendation throws some light on the Yankee character.

Another index to the Yankee type is his speech. A careless and indolent people speak vaguely and sloppily, running on and on without coming to the point. Pretentious societies are given to overelaborate expression, full of euphemisms and circumlocutions. The Down East Yankee is busy, thrifty and practical, and he uses a language as direct, graphic and economical as he himself is. Rather surprisingly, it reveals also a streak of imagination and poetry of which he might not be suspected and which he goes to some trouble to conceal in his actions. His words give him away. He speaks of "Indian summer," the warm, lovely, hazy spell that often comes in November; and of "squaw winter," unseasonably raw, cold weather in August, when it's thick o' fog. To him, a hidden mooring is a "dark harbor," a warm, pearly wind from a certain quarter is a "smoky so'wester," and the predawn flush along the horizon is an "easterly glin." Instead of saying he was up early, he says he "pried up the sun"; and he goes to bed " 'fore it's dark under the table." He does not try to adapt to new conditions; he "gets his feet braced for them."

Especially do proper names reveal a hunger for the purely ornamental and pretty. One would expect a practical, no-nonsense Down-easter to call a son or daughter John or Mary, Henry or Jane; and so some of them do. But there are as many Corydons, Dallases, Geldons, Persias and Ivorys; Alluras, Florises, Leonices, Virgilias and Felixenas. I know a Bonny Lassie, whose parents had given up hope of having a little girl to cherish when she came along; and a Maple and a Fern, whose mother loved all growing things, especially the brilliant autumn tree and the delicate woodland plant. In Maine, poetic names are the gold, frankincense and myrrh offered as gifts to infants of parents who cannot provide silver spoons, and they are also fulfillment of the deep-rooted need for beauty and color in a land that is so often cold and bleak, and lives that hold little of luxury and riches.

Even dogs have fancy names—Harvard, Horace, Athena, Allouetta. At least once within the memory of men not long dead, these dogs have been listed in the census, thereby putting poetry to practical political use, a typical Yankee ploy. This occurred when a scattered settlement was petitioning for a post office, heretofore refused on grounds of insufficient population. The out-of-state postal inspectors saw no reason to doubt the authenticity of Homer Tobin or Gideon Mariner on a list that contained much less plausible but legitimate names. By the time the deception was discovered, the post office had been established. It is still in operation.

Place names in Maine, unlike the names of people, are apt to be literal. Jonesport was settled by Joneses, Winter Harbor is a good, ice-free, protected winter harbor, and Screw Augur Falls looks as though the chasm through which the water leaps had been bored by a screw augur. West Bay is the westerly arm of Gouldsboro Bay, and the pond that empties into it is West Bay Pond. The brook connecting the two is West Bay Pond Brook. In the interests of brevity and convenience, however, those following the road along the brookside usually say simply that they are going Up the Guzzle, a guzzle being, in Maine, a gulch containing running water. The hamlet of Pretty Marsh is near a pretty marsh, Skunk's Misery is a dismal place where even a skunk would be miserable, Bailey's Mistake is a deceptively lovely little harbor with a treacherous bottom in which Bailey made the mistake of anchoring, and Middle Dam is the middle one of three dams, the others being Upper and Lower Dams.

Bangor is an exception to this descriptive naming, through a misunderstanding. It was known as Kenduskeag Plantation until 1787, when it became Sunbury. In the early 1790's, when Sunbury had grown large enough for incorporation as a town, the Reverend Seth Noble was sent to Boston to file the formal petition. As the clerk was filling out the necessary papers, Mr. Noble absent-mindedly hummed a hymn. The clerk asked the name of the community, and Mr. Noble thought he meant the name of the tune, which was "Bangor." It was a rather happy error, so it was allowed to stand. Following this example, the town of China was also named for a hymn.

Usually, though, the reason for the name of a place is obvious. There are thirteen Sheep Islands, fifteen Bar Islands, and I don't know how many Hog Islands and Thrumcaps along the Maine coast. The Sheep and Hogs are islands formerly used as summer pasturage for sheep and pigs, where they could feed safely with little care. The Bar Islands are either little more than bars or are connected to the mainland at low tide by exposed sand bars. A thrumcap was a little wool cap that weavers used to fashion from the thrums, or tag ends of the warp, long ago; and any small island presenting the same peaked, shaggy appearance was so named. Ragged Arse, charted as Ragged Island, is a corruption of the Indian Racketash by the early English with their Anglo-Saxon delight in the earthy word. Junk of Pork looks like a chunk of salt pork, Ironbound Island looks ironbound, Jo Leighton Ground is a shoal discovered by Jo Leighton, Old Maid's Landing was long owned by a spinster, and Beaverlily Pond was formed when beavers dammed a brook, and contains lilies. A fanciful name may be given a child for poesy's sake, with little danger of confusion resulting. But when it comes to naming places, exact identification is important to a Yankee. He has no time to waste chasing around looking for something called Primrose Heights, when it is obviously Blueberry Hill.

The talk of the Down-easter is based on the Elizabethan English spoken by the earliest settlers and still spoken in almost pure form on Beals Island, up until a few years ago. At that time a bridge was built across to the island from Jonesport. The islanders, who had always kept themselves pretty much to themselves, thus came into closer and more frequent contact with the mainland. The bridge was there, so they used it. Inevitably, their speech is affected, although it is still sometimes incomprehensible to off-islanders. Beals Island is an extreme case, but all over Maine men ask, "Be ye a-comin' along o' me?"—not ungrammatically, but as Shakespeare, Mother Goose or their own great-great-grandfathers might have asked. They speak of flocks of birds a-gangin' out to sea, too; and a work coat, whether it be the faded denim of a truck driver, a cattleman's plaid mackinaw or the trimly tailored uniform jacket of a game warden, is more often than not a frock.

There are Biblical overtones to the speech as well; not direct quotations, although these abound, but allusions to long-forgotten texts that were common verbal currency in the early days of intense piety. The language of Christians everywhere is, of course, full of Scriptural references, but they occur more frequently Down East than in many other places. An overseasoned chowder is "as salt as Lot's wife"; of a stranger it is said, "I don't know him from Adam's off ox"; a loud voice can be heard "from Dan to Beersheba"; and a usually silent person who suddenly speaks his mind is compared to Balaam's ass. These expressions are a part of the lingual heritage.

Most of the typical Yankee talk, however, stems from the

occupations in which the people have been involved for over three centuries—seafaring and fishing, farming and lumbering. This is true of the body of the American speechway throughout the country. Many common expressions originated along this coast, to be carried westward in the several Yankee exoduses, heirlooms more durable than the material contents of a whole train of covered wagons. Prairie people who have never been aboard a ship or even seen the sea speak of learning or "knowing the ropes," of coming to "the bitter end," of being taken aback or "on their beam ends," of "riding high" and of "going on the rocks," of spilling the wind from a pompous person's sails.

To learn the ropes—the intricate network of a sailing ship's rigging—is one of the first tasks set an apprentice seaman. When he knows them, he is considered experienced enough for practical purposes. The last few feet of cable on a windlass bitt is known as the bitt, or bitter, end. When all but that has been paid out, the situation is critical. A ship is taken aback when a sudden gust presses the canvas against the mast and causes confusion and dismay. When a vessel careens so far under a gale that her deck beams are almost vertical, she is on her beam ends, or in a precarious position. If she puts to sea with no cargo or ballast, she does indeed ride too high out of the water and may be driven by unfavorable winds onto the rocks. These are all common coinage on the American exchange.

There are other expressions used on the Maine coast that have not infiltrated the language proper to any great extent. "Oil up" is one. This means to put on wet weather gear—oilskin coats, pants, hats and aprons used at sea. "Wind her in" is another. Properly this is an order to wind in the line on a windlass, but it is commonly used by mothers in urging their offspring to eat their suppers. A gunk-hole is the coastal equivalent of a one-horse town, a small harbor village. In early days, when all the settlements were on the coast and transportation was chiefly by water, horses were not common, because they were not necessary. The important livestock was cows, and towns were graded in all seriousness by the number of cows owned within their borders. Bath, for example, was known in the 1660's as a twenty-cow parish. The use has carried over, so that in Maine a crossroads hamlet may be called a one-cow town. On the coast, if a person brags at length, someone is very apt to suggest, "We'd better call the cooper. He'll bust if we don't hoop him." This is a reference to the old days before steel drums, when a very large percent of merchandise was transported in wooden barrels bound with withes or metal hoops. The cooper, or barrel-maker, was a busy and important personage in every town and aboard every ship.

Sardiners frequently moor an empty dory near a weir to indicate that they intend to come back and take fish there. This is called "holding turn." So when a coastal doctor, let us say, goes on a vacation and leaves a substitute in his place, the new man is said to be holding turn for the old. In the lumbering country, he would be "tending out." During a log drive, men are stationed at intervals to see that no jams occur, a proceeding called tending out. A boy obliged to be out of town on dance night often commissions a trusted friend to tend out or hold turn with his official girl, to keep the young lady happy (within reasonable limits) while discouraging rivals. In the lumbering country, too, an unexpected guest might be greeted with "Well, look what the cat dragged in!" or equally often by "Will you look what come down on the rear!" When a log drive is over, a crew collects timber stranded along the banks of the stream, and all sorts of interesting debris is uncovered, including by implication the guest.

Everybody knows what cabin fever is—a general feeling of

confinement and boredom that demands some relief and outlet. In the Maine uplands it is called the "down-river cant." Toward the end of a long winter, men who have spent months in the lumber camps are assailed with a craving for the bright lights and barrooms of the nearest city, which always lies somewhere down the river. They always have good reasons for wanting to

go to town. They've got to see the dentist, or they need new glasses. The boss listens, sighs and lets them go. There's no stopping a man with the down-river cant, so he might as well save his breath.

One of the most economical ways of getting one's point across is by the use of tried and true aphorisms. This saves not only words, but mental effort as well. Yankees are greatly enamored of proverbs and axioms and use them constantly, but often with a difference. Instead of saying, "All signs fail in dry weather," they say, "When 't looks like rain and don't, 'twun't." First come is first served, occasionally; but oftener "The wheel that squeaks the loudest gets the grease." Still waters run deep; or less elegantly, "The still pig gets the swill." Sometimes the shoe is on the other foot; and sometimes "It makes a difference whose ox is gored" or "whose cat's tail is caught in the door." Flattery will get you nowhere; or "Fine talk butters no parsnips."

Housewives have their own vocabulary. They "bake off" their bread, "redd up" their guest rooms, and give their living rooms "a lick and a promise." This is in contrast with "a good turning out," which is an old-fashioned housecleaning, than which nothing is more thorough. Mattresses are taken outdoors and sunned, rugs are spread on the ground and beaten within an inch of their lives, curtains and blankets are washed, windows, floors and paint, including ceilings, are scrubbed bone-white. The old-fashioned spring cleaning, outmoded elsewhere in this day of vacuum cleaners and ashless oil heat, still obtains in Maine. Even houses that don't need it get it. Tradition and Conscience see to that.

Sometimes an interim turning out takes place, as when an acquaintance of mine suspected that she was sickening of some obscure and probably fatal disease. The idea of her friends and neighbors poking around on the day of the funeral, running fingers along the tops of door frames and making remarks about her standards of housekeeping, was too much for her to entertain. She decided on a good turning out before she took to her deathbed. By the time everything was in spotless order, with bureau drawers tidy, every last stitch of her husband's clothing mended and pressed, all the glory holes and hoorah's nests weeded out, the inside of the cupboard under the sink painted and the chimney flue cleaned, she felt fine. She had, she said, worked the collywobbles out of her system. She'd never heard of occupational therapy, but that's what she meant.

Hoorah's nests and glory holes are the odd corners and closets and drawers where articles holding promise of possible future use, even though that use is not immediately evident, collect, seemingly through some motive power of their own. Down East this litter is called cultch, which means material not worth much, but still too good to throw out. That covers a lot, since Yankees are loath to discard anything at all. Even one widowed glove, a pan with a hole as big as an apple in it, six inches of twine or the rollers out of an old clothes wringer might come in handy sometime. One summer, with the help of a neighbor, I cleaned out the garage of a house I had rented, to make room for my own cultch. We came across a strange object made of wood, leather and copper, which my assistant regarded thoughtfully. "Now that's a good thing," he said.

"Good for what?" I asked. I honestly couldn't imagine the intended use for the contraption, and I was asking for information.

"Ain't got the least idee. Could be—wal, I dunno. But it's a good *thing*."

I had no room or time for things that were good only in the abstract, so I placed it on the trash pile. Later I discovered it on a bench in my neighbor's woodshed, where it has now been reposing for at least four years. And will continue to repose indefinitely on the very slim chance that sometime it might turn out to be just exactly what somebody is looking for.

Down East, words are weighed before they are spoken, and then they are weighed again after they have been heard, until every possible meaning or suggestion has been considered. There is a story about two men who met a third on the road and were greeted by a level-toned "Mornin'." After a lapse of several minutes of deep thought, one of the two inquired of the other, "Now what in tarnation do you s'pose he meant by that?" This really could happen in Maine, where a simple greeting very often conveys by inflection or lack of inflection any number of

meanings, from deep reproach, to dire threat, to sincere con-
gratulation. Laconicism has been developed almost to an art form.

One reason for this is that standing around talking is a waste
of time that might better be employed otherwise. It's enough to
make oneself clearly understood and to conform with decent
civility. The chief reason, though, is that Down-easters endorse
wholeheartedly the premise that what you don't say can't be
held against you. In the early days, when paper was scarce and
literacy rare, a man's word was his bond, and this attitude has
carried over to a surprising extent. Words have great weight, so
they are used sparingly.

This parsimony, however, is not practiced when it comes in
conflict with financial interests. Down-easters are no fools, and
early in the invasion of the tourists they discovered that their
speechway was a business asset. Since then, they have been polishing up their quaintness until it shines as bright as brass. I have
a friend who during the summer conducts an antique business in
his barn. He is a native, but he is also a Yale graduate and an
ex-officer of the Navy, and he can converse fluently, informedly,
interestingly and grammatically on a great many subjects. One
day I asked the price of a piece of cranberry glass he had in his
stock. It was fifteen dollars, which I thought and said was more
than it was worth.

"No, not really," he told me. "It's an extremely good piece."
He held it to the light so that I could admire the color and
tapped it lightly so I could hear the tone. Then he told me
where he had found it and was embarking on the history and
method of manufacture when a station wagon full of tourists
drove into the yard. "Stick around," he said, "while I try to out-
half-wit them."

The glass was the first item to come under consideration.

"Wal, thar, now," said my friend. "I dunno. Seems to me *she*—" he jerked his thumb toward the house—"claims that's wuth fifteen dollars. She's the brains of this go-round, not me. Me, I don't know beans about it. Wouldn't give two cents fer it, myself. No sirree! Feel kind of guilty even mentionin' fifteen dollars, but 'twould be as much as my life is wuth to let you have it fer less. You know women. She's got this idee in her head that this here hunk of glass is valuable. I s'pose it's all in how you look at it. Now some folks might say, jest because it's over a hundred years old and come from some historic house and has a purty color—" he held it to the light—"and rings sort of musical-like—" he flicked it with a fingernail—" 'twas wuth the money. I ain't sayin' 'tis, y'understand, but some folks might. . . ." He went on and on, getting more bucolic and quaintly philosophical with every word he said, until he managed to make the sale.

After the customers had gone, I said, "You ought to be ashamed of yourself."

"I'm not," he told me honestly. "Not a bit. The piece was worth the price, whether you agree or not. Nobody was cheated. I'm in the business of selling antiques, and I use the method that I've found most effective. I may have made somewhat of a fool of myself in the process, but it's results that count, as any big sales organization will tell you."

Oddly, he had not made a fool of himself. Down-easters seldom do They almost always know exactly what they are about and why. They are not impulsive, and those who do not know them therefore get the impression that they are cold and calculating. Newcomers to the area frequently complain about a lack of friendliness on the part of the natives. "I've lived here almost a year, and everybody *still* calls me Mrs. Smith." Everybody will continue to call her Mrs. Smith for some time to come. A friendship is a serious matter Down East, not to be undertaken without due consideration. It is better to maintain a Mr. and Mrs. footing during a probation period than be faced with the difficult task of regaining it later, should it be necessary. Once the guarded Yankee heart lets down the bars, though, it is forever. Maine friendships are as slow-growing as rock maples, and as durable.

Down East, praise has to be earned. Getting a complimentary word out of anyone is, in the local idiom, as hard as pulling hen's teeth. People are as quick with criticism as they are slow with commendation. This is generally attributed to a crabbed and carping disposition, although the true cause is entirely different. Part of it is the Yankee distrust of flattery and fulsomeness, considered to be inevitably a cover for ulterior motive. Rather than be suspected of disingenuity, the Down-easter doles out his compliments with a sparing hand. Even where no plot for gain could possibly be imagined, still he is niggardly. A beautiful view is "real pretty," and a lovely day "not bad, considerin'." It is literally true that Yankees are unable to pour out extravagant appreciation. The words actually stick in their throats.

Another cause is the impossible Yankee dream of perfection. Experience and his better sense tell him that it cannot be attained on earth, but Conscience goads him incessantly to the attempt. So he automatically seeks the flaws in any article, person or situation. Instead of telling a friend that her new dress is pretty and becoming, a woman points out that the hemline sags just a mite in the back. The minister, though a saint on earth, ought to put a smidgen more of hell-fire into his sermons. It's a nice day, but we could do with a little rain. This fault-finding is both annoying and discouraging to those who are unaccustomed to it. To the Down-easter it is neither derogatory, destructive nor mean-spirited in intent, but only a sensible means of bringing about improvement. It's inconceivable to him that anybody could be satisfied with less than the best, as he himself is not.

The old Puritanical beliefs enter into it, too; the convictions that man is born to sorrow as the sparks fly upward, that pleasure is sinful, that happiness is a snare and a delusion. To display satisfaction or joy is to ask for trouble. A jealous God will be quick to find means of reminding the lighthearted that this earth is a vale of tears. So a tender and luscious cake is described as "passable," and an enormous catch of fish as "fair," to avoid the appearance of the pride that goeth before a fall. One never admits to excellent health, but answers inquiries with "Able to get 'round" or "Middlin'," or even by complaints of some obscure ailment. If you say that someone has gained a little weight and looks very well indeed, you will be told that the added pounds are an unnatural bloat, and that the brightness of eye and pinkness of cheek are unhealthy signs. This is not a bid for sympathy. It is just a form of insurance.

Puritanism is reflected in the Yankee attitude toward food, too. Typical Down East fare is substantial, nourishing and good, but it is not fancy. Eating is a necessity. Enjoyment of eating borders dangerously on gluttony, one of the seven deadly sins. Man does not live by—and certainly should not live for—bread alone. It is sinful to waste time and thought on gourmet dishes. Oddly, the quick and convenient packaged and frozen foods, which should appeal because they save time and effort, have had a hard time establishing a foothold in the area. For years after they were standard stock elsewhere, it was impossible to buy them in the little general stores of my neighborhood. I was told, " 'Round here we don't hold with that packaged stuff. No body to it. Womenfolk here stir up their own batches. That way, they know what they're eating."

This prejudice rises partly from inborn suspicion of all things outlandish and partly a typical clinging to tradition; but chiefly, I think, it is based on the feeling that the new products are too easy—sinfully easy. They are a trap of Satan, who is undoubtedly planning mischief for the hands made idle by their time-saving use.

Much of the food consists of what are known as good keep-warms and warm-ups. Many of the occupations of the country make the establishing of a fixed meal time impossible. A woman is never sure exactly when her husband will be in from the sea, or the back wood lot, or from dickering for a new transmission for his truck. So she prepares dishes that will not be ruined by waiting—hearty stews and chowders, baked beans and brown bread, pot roasts, fish cakes and creamed codfish, pies, suet puddings and doughnuts. Leftovers are seldom thrown away. They are saved and heated up for breakfast. Down-easters really do eat pie and baked beans in the morning, and any other odds and ends left over from last night's supper.

They also avail themselves, as a duty, of foodstuffs that can be had for the taking—fish, shellfish, wild game, dandelion, dock, fiddlehead and goose-grass greens, and all kinds of pie timber, as it is called, meaning a variety of wild berries. Living off the country does more than save money and satisfy some atavistic urge. It salves the Conscience. To walk about the countryside simply for pleasure on a lovely day would be self-indulgence, and visions of tasks undone at home would rise up to haunt the walker. Staying outdoors in the sun and fresh air all afternoon to pick berries is something else again. It is a useful chore justified by tangible results and some discomfort in the form of scratched hands and a lame back. This discomfort is important to Conscience, which is to the Down-easter as real and painful as an inflamed sciatic nerve and requires equally delicate treatment.

One facet of the Yankee character seems wildly inconsistent with his generally restrained, frugal and austere nature. He loves cats. Dogs and other animals are kept and accorded good, though matter-of-fact, care; but cats! Maine has more pampered cats than any other place in the world with the possible exceptions of the royal palaces of Siam and the ancient temples of Egypt. These cats are not expected to earn their keep by catching rats and mice. They are house pets, coddled and cosseted until they have lost most of the hunting instinct and have become true parasites. Men and women who would never spoil their children or indulge themselves spoil and indulge the cat outrageously. Cats, who are both intelligent and obsessively self-interested, quickly take advantage of this weakness. They learn that they don't have to drink skim milk and eat fish trimmings. A family can be trained by a smart cat to provide whipping cream and calves' liver three times a day. Can be, and frequently is.

In Maine, a doctor is called for a member of the family only after all home remedies have failed, time seems not to be doing its healing work, and the patient is plainly headed for death's door. This is not entirely, nor even chiefly, because of the expense involved. In Maine one avoids at all costs the charge of being spleeny, which means giving in to oneself, pampering oneself, exhibiting what elsewhere would be called hypochondria. If the cat seems slightly off his feed, however, he is rushed at once to the veterinarian. Very often the most comfortable chair in a house is by common consent the cat's chair, and if he wishes to occupy it, an unwitting visitor who may be sitting in it is asked politely, but with no apologies, to move. More than once I have seen people leave social gatherings early, because the cat would be getting lonely. I thought at first that this must be a joke or a very thin excuse. It was neither, but a good sound reason that everyone understood and accepted. These are not isolated instances involving some lonely and warped spinster and her tabby, but a strikingly uniform pattern among normal, well-adjusted, sensible adults of both sexes.

Some of the cats of Maine are admittedly unusual. There are a great many tailless Manx, blue-gray Persians with copper eyes, Maltese and Angoras, descendants of pets brought home as rarities by seafarers of olden days. A cat almost unique to Maine, because it does not acclimatize easily to other places, is the coon cat. This is a gentle, beautiful and rather delicate breed with very soft, long, frosty-gray hair and dainty ringlike markings. They are often said to be the result of cross-breeding between wild coons and common domesticated cats, just as the Manx is said to be half-cat and half-rabbit. Both claims are, of course, biological impossibilities. Actually, the coon cat is descended from a cat brought home from China by Captain Samuel Clough of Edgecomb, and crossed with the common house cat. They are greatly prized in Maine.

So are the little three-colored money-cats, mottled black, white and orange. The name might well come from the bright coin spotting of their coats, but it doesn't, according to local lore. A three-colored cat is always a female. So much is fact. Years ago, or so the story goes, a thousand dollars was offered to anyone who could find a male cat of three colors. To date, none has been located, and the identity of the man who made the offer has been lost in the mists of time, if he ever existed. There is disagreement over whether he was an eccentric summer millionaire or a biology professor working on an experiment in genetics. I myself suspect that the whole tale is apocryphal. However, the name remains, and the money-cats have come to be regarded as bringers of good luck.

It is a little hard to reconcile this weakness for cats with the hard-headed, undemonstrative Yankee temperament. These cats serve no useful purpose, and they are expensive to maintain. Often a man pays more for a can of high-grade salmon for the cat than for stew beef for himself. Superficially, at least, cats would seem to represent all that the Down-easter deplores. They are voluptuous, luxury-loving, sybaritic, vain and demanding. Yet an empathy exists. Possibly in cats the Yankee recognizes an independence, competence and self-esteem even greater than his own, and admires and respects them accordingly.

Yankees do not laugh aloud very much. They somehow distrust laughter. "Laugh before breakfast, weep before supper," they say and believe. Laughter invites punishment for forgetting that life is real and earnest. This does not mean that they are seldom amused, only that they seldom show it. They do their laughing inside, with only a gleam in the eye and a quirk of the lips as outward indication. Yankee humor glints and glistens like the water of a trout brook dancing through a thicket, and is as difficult to capture. The peculiarly American phenomenon of the stock story ("Heard the one about the traveling salesman?") is almost nonexistent Down East. Prefabricated humor does not strike the native as being very funny, even if he had the time to sit around swapping foolish yarns. He is more apt to be tickled by the do-it-yourself variety, by the quick retort, the ludicrous situation, the turning-of-tables that come about naturally in the course of daily living. Professional comedians break their hearts trying to move Down East audiences to mirth, but once accepted as such, a joke is very durable.

For example, years ago there was on a Bangor radio station a daily sports program of the usual kind that gives scores, discusses sports personalities and events, and occasionally features as guest some outstanding figure of the sports world. It was conducted by a young announcer with a glib and entertaining style. He was not particularly noted, however, for his reliability, and this flaw led to his dismissal with a week's notice. He took this with apparent good grace, and all through the final week his conduct was exemplary.

For his last program, he had invited a football star from the University of Maine to go on the air with him. "It is a pleasure to have with us this evening," he began, "a young man of outstanding character and ability," and he went on at length lauding to the skies his guest's accomplishments, appearance and personality. At last, in a voice trembling with emotion, he asked rhetorically, "And who is this paragon of all the virtues, this brightest jewel in Maine's crown of sportsmen?" He paused dramatically, while the air waves hummed with anticipation. Then he concluded in a friendly conversational tone, "Well, I'll be damned if I'll tell you."

For a long time after that, it was possible simply by saying in any conceivable context, "Well, I'll be damned if I'll tell you," to get what passes as a hearty laugh from any Down-easter who had heard or heard about this tricky revenge. Down East, anything worth laughing at once is worth laughing at almost indefinitely. The hard part is getting the initial laugh.

If it is difficult to make Down-easters laugh, it is almost impossible to make them accept anything resembling charity. Since earliest days, when paupers were auctioned off annually to the lowest bidder, through the period when the indigent were taken care of in poor farms at public expense, "going on the town" has been regarded as a disgrace. In modern times, when the whole principle and philosophy of state and Federal relief has changed, and when acceptance of such relief in no way reflects on the recipient, Down-easters view it askance. They don't, they say, want to be beholden. They'll scrape along. During the depression of the thirties, relief workers approached a hard-pressed citizen of Louds Island with offers of aid, and he flew into a towering rage. "Thunderation," he shouted, "what's all the towse about? We ain't never had prosperity, so how in tarnation can we have a depression?" That's the general Maine attitude— that the state has always been poor, which is no disgrace in itself; and if it ever stops being poor, it will be through its own efforts, and not through handouts that somehow diminish a man.

Or a woman. After one of the hurricanes, Red Cross workers moved into a section of Maine that had been declared a disaster area by well-meaning outsiders. Among others, they called on an eighty-year-old woman of my acquaintance, upon whose house a tree had fallen. They found her up on a ladder, her skirts tucked up, cutting away the debris and inspecting the damage, which proved to be a hole in the roof. She didn't need any help, she said, sawing away vigorously. She could manage fine. The only thing was, cedar shingles were hard-come-by right now, so if the Red Cross happened to know where she could lay hands on a bundle, she'd take it kindly if they'd pass word along to her. The workers said they'd provide the shingles and put them on, but she said no, no call for that. She'd pay for them, and she'd put them on herself. When the day come she couldn't hammer a few shingles on her own roof, she'd know 'twas time to give up the ghost. She managed to complicate the Red Cross bookkeeping and voucher system considerably by her insistence, but she kept her own moral accounts straight. She was not beholden.

Down-easters are not easy to know and sometimes they are not easy to like. They seem deliberately to build barriers against understanding and affection, to take a perverse delight in being odd and difficult and out of step with the rest of the world. This perversity is neither whimsical nor a childish bid for attention. It is, in Down East eyes, a duty. "Everything's movin' so fast nowadays," they'll tell you, "no knowin' where we'll all end up. We ain't agin Progress, but we like to know where we're progressin' *to*. Till we find out, someone's got to drag their feet, and the way things are, looks like it's up to us."

So they vote Republican in a year when forty-six of the then forty-eight states went Democratic, enforce Blue Laws long since laughed off the books in almost every part of the nation, and refuse to dip into approved government pork barrels. When the Last Trump sounds, there they will doubtless be, swept along with the throng, but dragging their feet up to the very threshold of the Pearly Gates.

BIBLIOGRAPHY

There are scores of books on Maine or various aspects of its history, and a fine collection of periodicals in the State Library in Augusta. To list all of the books and clippings that have contributed material to this informal treatment of Maine, past and present, would be tedious for the reader and presumptuous of the author. However, the following partial list of books should be included.

Burrage, Henry S., *Beginnings of Colonial Maine*, Portland, 1914.

Coffin, Robert P. T., *Kennebec: Cradle of Americans*, New York, 1937.

Collins, Charles W., *The Acadians of Madawaska, Maine*, Boston, 1902.

Dale, Thomas N., *The Granites of Maine*, Washington, D.C., 1907.

Day, C. P., and W. E. Meyer, *The Port of Portland and Its Hinterland*, Portland, 1923.

Dow, Edward F., *A Portrait of the Millennial Church of Shakers*, Orono, 1931.

Elkins, L. Whitney, *The Story of Maine*, Bangor, 1924.

Hatch, Louis Clinton, *Maine: A History*, New York, 1928.

Helm, MacKinley, *John Marin*, Boston, 1948.

Loomis, Charles D., *Port Towns of Penobscot Bay* (monograph), St. Paul, 1922.

MacDonald, William, *The Government of Maine: Its History and Administration*, New York, 1902.

Maine Historical Society, *Documentary History of Maine*, Portland, 1919-1931.

Maunson, Gorham, *Penobscot: Down East Paradise*, Philadelphia, 1959.

Pressey, Henry A., *Water Powers of the State of Maine*, Washington, D.C., 1902.

Roberts, Kenneth, *Trending into Maine*, New York, 1944.

Rowe, William H., *Shipbuilding Days in Casco Bay*, Yarmouth, 1929.

Smith, W. B., *The Lost Red Paint People of Maine*, Bangor, 1930.

Spencer, Wilbur D., *Pioneers on Maine Rivers*, Portland, 1930.

Starbird, Charles M., *The Indians of the Androscoggin Valley*, Lewiston, 1928.

Sterling, Robert T., *Lighthouses of the Maine Coast*, Brattleboro, 1935.

Thomas, William Widgery, Jr., *The Story of New Sweden in the Woods of Maine*, Portland, 1896.

Varney, George J., *A Brief History of Maine*, Portland, 1888.

Verrill, A. Hyatt, *Romantic and Historic Maine*, New York, 1937.

Wasson, George S., *Sailing Days on the Penobscot*, New York, 1949.

Wilder, E. F., *Maine and Its Role in American Art*, Viking, 1963.

Wilkins, Austin H., *Forests of Maine*, Augusta, 1932.

Williamson, William D., *History of the State of Maine*, Bangor, 1887.

INDEX

Abenakis Indians. *See under* Indians
Acadia-in-Maine, 51 ff, 124
  plans by English to capture, 77 ff
  See also French and Indian Wars
Acadia National Park, 169 ff
Adams, George, 229 ff
  and Jaffa Pilgrimage, 146, 230-33
Agriculture and farming, 6
  and apples, 148, 186
  and blueberries, 190-91, 200-1
  and cotton trading, 148
  early, 13, 101, 107, 185 ff
  modern, 164, 185 ff, 200
  and potatoes, 186-89
Aix-la-Chapelle, Treaty of, 85, 92
Akers, Benjamin Paul, 213, 263
Alden, John, 48-49
Alexander, Sir William, 124
Alfred, 226
Allan, John, 119-20
Allegiance (ship), 120
Allen Island, 32
America (ship), 121
American Cancer Society, 177
American Revolution. *See* Revolution, American
Ames, Adelbert, 159
Andover, 159, 175-76
Andros, Sir Edmund, 61, 68
Androscoggin (ship), 147-48
Androscoggin River, 40, 159, 196
Annapolis. *See* Port Royal
Appledore, 61
Archangel (ship), 31
Archer (boat), 157-58
Argalls, Samuel, 39, 43, 94
Arnold, Benedict, 50, 111 ff
  and invasion of Quebec, 112 ff
Aroostook, 154, 187 ff
Aroostook Railroad, 179
Aroostook River, 150, 162

Aroostook War, 154
Arrowsic, 58, 71
Arts and crafts. *See under* Maine
Arundel (novel), 252
Arundel, Earl of, 31
Atahualpa (ship), 128
Atlantic Monthly, 249
Atomic Energy Commission, 177
Augusta, 48 ff
Austrian Succession, War of the. *See* War of the Austrian Succession

Bagaduce, as name for Castine, 117-18
Bahia de Casco. *See* Casco Bay
Bahia Profundo. *See* Bay of Fundy
Bailey's Mistake, 146, 271
Baker, John, 151-52, 154
Bangor, 40, 138, 166, 182
Bangor Railroad, 179
Bar Harbor, 146, 165-66, 168, 180, 182
  and fire of 1947, 169
Bar Islands, 272
Barrel, Sally Sayward, 251-52
Bath, 155
  masting at, 103
  shipbuilding at, 99
Battle of Bunker Hill, 112
Baxter, Percival, 264
Bay of Fundy, 26, 40, 74, 124, 150
Beach, Moses S., 231-32
Beals Island, 92, 273
Bean, Leon Leonwood, 210, 263
Beaverlily Pond, 272
Belfast-Moosehead Lake Municipal Railroad, 179
Bellamy, Samuel, 89-91
Bellows, George, 254
Bell Telephone Company, 176
Bénévent, Prince de. *See* Talleyrand-Périgord, Charles Maurice de

ABOUT THE AUTHOR

Louise Dickinson Rich is a native of Massachusetts (Huntington and Bridgewater), but many years ago adopted Maine as her true love. She writes: "I have lived all my life in New England, and travel outside the area has done nothing to convince me that I'd prefer living elsewhere. I moved to the Rangeley Lake region of Maine almost thirty years ago, when I married. The course of my love affair with the State of Maine has moved smoothly ever since."

Mrs. Rich has written widely on Maine, covering everything from her experiences in the wilderness (*We Took to The Woods*), to her knowledge of the coast (*The Peninsula, The Coast of Maine*), to her observations of nature (*The Natural World of Louise Dickinson Rich*). Her writing has appeared in the *Saturday Evening Post, Atlantic Monthly, Reader's Digest, Woman's Home Companion*, and many other magazines.

Mrs. Rich now feels she has found the ideal location in her adopted state. "A one-hundred-and-fifty-year-old Cape Cod cottage in Prospect Harbor, on the Gouldsboro Peninsula. The sea lies before me, and behind, beyond the lawn, the garden and the apple orchard, rise the woods. I hope never to be obliged to go anywhere else."